EXTENDING WORD 2000 FOR WINDOWS

CAROL MCKENZIE & PAT BRYDEN

Learn to pass second level exams

- RSA Text Processing Stage II Part 1
- RSA Word Processing Stage II Part 2
- RSA Mailmerge Stage II Part 2

Heinemann Educational Publishers,
Halley Court, Jordan Hill, Oxford OX2 8EJ
A division of Reed Educational & Professional Publishing Ltd

Heinemann is a registered trademark of Reed Educational & Professional Publishing Limited

OXFORD MELBOURNE AUCKLAND JOHANNESBURG BLANTYRE GABORONE IBADAN
PORTSMOUTH NH (USA) CHICAGO

First published 2000
2004 2003 2002
10 9 8 7 6 5 4 3

A catalogue record for this book is available from the British Library on request.

ISBN 0 435 45432 3

Cover designed by Sarah Garbett

Pages designed by Paul Davies and Associates

Typeset by TechType, Abingdon, Oxon

Printed and bound in Great Britain by Thomson Litho Ltd, East Kilbride, Scotland

Screen shots reprinted with permission from Microsoft Corporation

Acknowledgements

We would like to thank our respective families for their encouragement and support while writing this book.

Carol McKenzie and Pat Bryden

Tel: 01865 888058 www.heinemann.co.uk

CONTENTS

OCR/RSA TEXT PROCESSING SCHEMES

The Royal Society of Arts (RSA) Examinations Board has merged and been renamed Oxford, Cambridge and RSA Examinations (OCR). Qualifications formerly certificated by RSA are now awarded through OCR. For the purposes of this series of textbooks, the acronyms OCR/RSA will be used for brevity and clarity.

The suite of Text Processing schemes offered by OCR/RSA covers Stages I, II and III. The overall aim of these modular awards is to meet the business document production requirements of the discerning employer and to give candidates the opportunity to demonstrate competence in text processing skills to the level demanded for NVQ Administration. Specific mapping of performance criteria, range, and knowledge and understanding is given in the OCR/RSA scheme documents. An example of the mapping of the OCR/RSA Stage II Text Processing Part 1 to NVQ Administration Level 2 is given below:

Element	Performance Criteria						Range		Knowledge and Understanding		
7.2	1	2	3	4	5	8	1	2	1	2	4

Stage I indicates the candidate has sufficient knowledge or skill to begin employment, although further study would be beneficial.

Stage II shows a sound understanding of, and competence in, the subject and a recommendation for employment. It also suggests that someone who holds such a certificate may well benefit from advanced studies.

Stage III indicates an all-round knowledge and understanding of the subject and, in the practical skills, a very high degree of proficiency.

At each stage, there is a *Part 1* examination which assesses the core skills at that stage. A selection of *Part 2* examinations assesses skills in more specific applications such as word processing, typewriting and audio-transcription.

There is a Text Processing Diploma at Stages II and III; this has been designed to recognise all-round achievement in text processing. The following modules which contribute to the Stage II Diploma are covered in this book:

- Stage II Text Processing Part 1
- Stage II Word Processing Part 2
- Stage II Mail Merge Part 2

The Diploma is awarded to candidates who demonstrate competence in Text Processing *Part I* and three *Part 2* examinations, at the same stage. Additional modules include specialist applications of text processing, for example:

- in a foreign language
- using specialist terminology
- typewriting
- shorthand transcription, and
- audio-transcription.

ABOUT THIS BOOK

This book has been written as a continuation text to *Introducing Word 2000 for Windows* by the same authors. It has been designed as a progressive course and is suitable for use in the classroom, in an open-learning workshop or as a private study aid.

This book has been produced to assist people who wish to gain intermediate level accreditation through the OCR/RSA's Text Processing Schemes, using the Microsoft Word 2000 software package. It is anticipated that users will be familiar with the QWERTY keyboard and have basic competence in using computer hardware.

Units 1–5 are designed for students preparing to take intermediate examinations such as OCR/RSA Stage II Text Processing Part 1. These units are also suitable for the revision of text processing skills, without taking an examination.

Units 6–11 are designed for students preparing to take intermediate examinations such as OCR/RSA Word Processing Stage II Part 2. These units are also suitable for beginners who wish to learn how to prepare multi-page documents, tables and letters from standard phrases without taking an examination.

Units 12–15 are designed for students preparing to take the OCR/RSA Mail Merge Stage II Part 2 examination. These units are also suitable for students who wish to extend their knowledge and skills to include preparation and merging of a database and standard letter without taking an examination.

A brief outline of the examination and examination practice for each stage of learning is included in Units 5, 11 and 15.

Format of the book

Printout checks for all exercises are given at the back of the book. These should be used for checking by both students and teachers/trainers.

The Progress Review Checklist allows a record of progress through the exercises and to note the number of errors made. If completed at the end of each working session, this checklist can be referred to quickly in order to locate the unit to be worked on next.

When completing the exercises, command boxes for Word 2000 functions are given when appropriate. The commands explain keyboard, mouse and menu operation, and instruction is given on how to carry out the required function.

The Glossary provides a comprehensive, alphabetically-listed quick reference for all the Word 2000 commands introduced in the book. The commands are shown for keyboard, mouse and menu users. Shortcut (keyboard) keys are included and students may prefer to use these methods as they become more familiar with the program.

All exercise material is to be completed in Times New Roman size 12 unless indicated otherwise.

Working through a unit

1  When you see this symbol, read all the information before you begin. You may also need to refer back to this information as you carry out the exercises.

2  When you see this symbol, carry out the exercises, following the numbered steps, e.g. 1.1, 1.2.

3 Use Word 2000's spelling and grammar tool to check all your documents. You must also proofread the document carefully yourself – the spelling tool does not find every error.

4 Use the Print Preview facility to check your document and to ensure it is in the correct position on the page when printed. If it is, save your work on to your floppy disk (usually in A Drive) or into an appropriate directory. Then print your work.

5 Compare your document with the printout checks at the back of the book. (If you are using this book in class, your tutor may also wish to check your work.) Correct any errors which you find in your work and print the documents again if required.

6 Complete your Progress Review Checklist. Then exit from Word 2000 or begin work on the next unit (as appropriate).

Do not delete files from your disk – you may need them later!

INTRODUCTION TO WORD 2000

Microsoft Windows is a graphical user interface, which allows the user to communicate with the computer. The graphical nature of the messages on screen makes Windows a user-friendly operating system. Microsoft Word 2000 is a software package used for text processing which operates within the Windows environment.

The **mouse** is used to move a pointer to any required location on screen. The mouse has two buttons: *left* and *right*. As you move the mouse across the desk, an electronic sensor picks up the movement of the ball and moves the **mouse pointer** across the screen in the same direction:

- You use the mouse to *point* to the item you want on screen.
- You then *click* the mouse button (usually the left one) to highlight or *select* an option on screen (quickly pressing and releasing the button).
- Sometimes you *double-click* a mouse button to perform an action (quickly pressing and releasing the button twice).
- You may also use a *dragging* action, for instance, selecting text, by holding down the mouse button, moving the mouse and then releasing the button.
- If you are not sure of the function of an icon on one of the tool bars, just point to it with the mouse and wait for a second – a **Tool Tip** describing the function of the icon will appear to help you (Figure 1).

Figure 1 Tool Tip

Figure 1 shows the Tool Tip which is displayed when you point to the **Save** button and, in brackets, the short cut key(s) to operate this function. Short cut keys allow you to use the keyboard, instead of the mouse, to give commands to Word 2000: in this instance you would hold down the **Ctrl** key and press **S** instead of pointing to the **Save** button and clicking the left mouse button.

If you would like the Tool Tips in your document window to display shortcut keys, follow the procedure given at the end of this Introduction on page xii.

When you start the Word 2000 program, the **Document window** should be displayed on screen.

The blue bar across the top of the screen is the **Title Bar**, showing the current document name and the name of the application being used.

The **Menu Bar** (Figure 2) gives a list of **menu names** describing commands which can be selected by using the mouse or the keyboard.

File Edit View Insert Format Tools Table Window Help

Figure 2 Menu Bar

A **drop-down submenu** then gives a further range of options within the menu (in Figure 3, the **View** menu has been selected).

You may have noticed that, when a drop-down menu appears at first in Word 2000, it has a restricted range of options (in fact, those options used most recently). After a few seconds, the drop-down menu expands to include all available options. If you would prefer to see the full drop-down menu immediately and at all times, follow the procedure given at the end of this Introduction on page xii.

As you will see, some of the menu choices have one character underlined (eg **Ruler**). Selection can be carried out using the keyboard, eg pressing **R** in the example on the next page would remove the ruler line from the screen. The ruler returns if you press **R** again – this is known as a 'toggle' switch. *(A tick against a menu choice indicates the option is currently in operation. When the tick is removed, the facility is 'switched off'.)*

Selection can also be made by using the mouse. Clicking the left mouse button on **Ruler** in the example in Figure 3 would remove the ruler line from the screen.

Some menu choices are followed by a **keyboard shortcut**, eg:

Find...	**Ctrl + F**
Replace...	**Ctrl + H**
Go To...	**Ctrl + G**

Holding down the **Ctrl** key and then pressing the letter shown will activate the command. An **ellipsis** (three dots . . .) after a menu choice (eg **Zoom ...**) indicates you will be asked to give more information before the command can be executed.

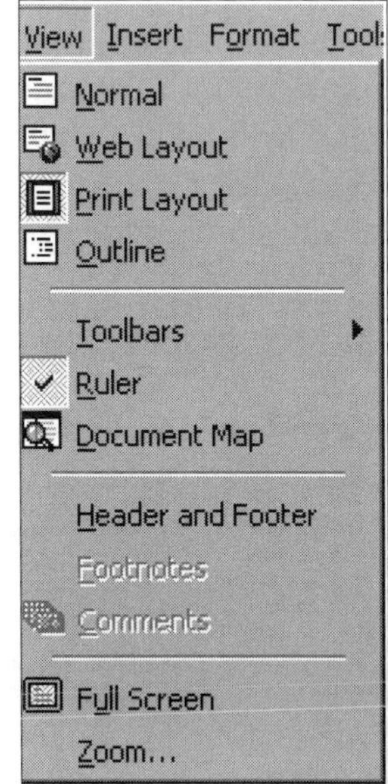

Figure 3 View menu

When Word 2000 needs to give or receive more information a **dialogue box** is displayed on screen. You can move through the dialogue box using the Tab key or you can move the mouse pointer to the box required and click the left button. Word 2000 asks you to respond by presenting information, options or questions in different ways by using boxes and buttons. The dialogue box in Figure 4 gives an example of the different types of boxes and buttons you will meet.

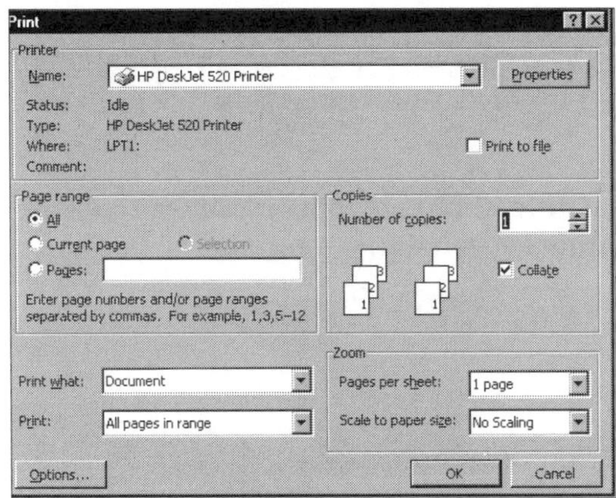

Figure 4 Print dialogue box

Clicking on OK confirms the information in the boxes.

You can close a dialogue box without giving a command by clicking on Cancel or on the icon at the top right of the dialogue box ✕.

You can minimise a document window by clicking on minimise icon. This reduces the window to a small bar at the bottom of the window.

To restore the window to its full size, click on the Word 2000 WORDINTRODUCTION button on the Task Bar at the bottom of the screen. The name of your document will also be shown on this button.

When Word 2000 is carrying out a function, it may ask you to wait. The icon for this is the hourglass. Wait until the hourglass has disappeared from the screen before proceeding with the next step.

The **Standard Tool Bar** is displayed on screen whilst you are working on a Word 2000 document (Figure 5).

Figure 5 Standard Tool Bar

This consists of a range of **icons** or **buttons**, each representing a different function related to creating and editing documents. You select a function by pointing to the icon with the mouse pointer and clicking the left mouse button. For example, clicking on the **Print** icon would activate the printer to print a copy of the current document.

The use of these icons is explained more fully throughout the book.

You may notice that the Standard Tool Bar on your screen appears to contain more items than the one illustrated in Figure 5. In fact, the Standard Tool Bar may be sharing a row on screen with the Formatting Tool Bar. All the features of the Formatting Tool Bar are not therefore visible. It is recommended you change this display now by performing the following procedure:

To display Standard and Formatting Tool Bars on separate rows:

Select: **View**, **Toolbars** from the menu
Select: **Customize**, **Options**
Click to remove the ✓ in the **Standard and formatting toolbars share one row** box
Click: **Close**

The Formatting Tool Bar is also displayed on screen in a Word 2000 document (Figure 6).

Figure 6 Formatting Tool Bar on a Word 2000 document screen

This consists of a range of icons, each representing a different formatting option. You select a function by clicking on the icon.

The function activated by each icon is shown in a **Tool Tip**, which appears when the mouse pointer is positioned on the icon (see the example of the **Save** icon Tool Tip shown in Figure 1). When an icon button is shown as having been pressed in (in which case it appears in a lighter colour – see the bold icon to the right), this indicates the function is currently in operation, ie any text keyed in would be formatted in **bold**.

The **Status Bar** at the bottom of the screen displays information about the document on screen, eg the page number, section number, line number, column number etc (Figure 7).

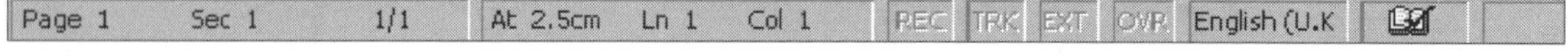

Figure 7 Status Bar

The current time is displayed in the bottom right-hand corner of the screen.

The **Scroll Bars** (Figure 8) at the right side and bottom of the screen allow text to be scrolled by the use of the mouse.

For example, clicking on the down vertical scroll arrow button will move the 'document frame' downwards so that the text moves up the screen.

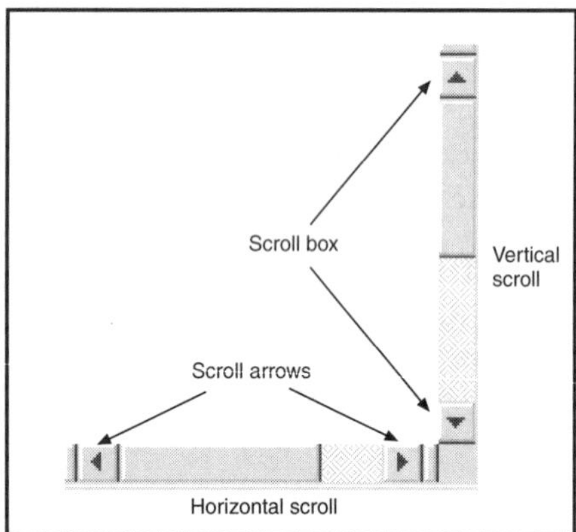

Figure 8 Scroll Bars

The horizontal scroll bar also displays buttons, at its extreme left, to select the different ways in which a document can be viewed (Figure 9).

Figure 9 View buttons

The **Task Bar** (Figure 10) at the very bottom of the screen allows you to switch between applications or tasks by clicking on the required tab.

Figure 10 Task Bar

Word 2000 offers two forms of online help to users. The **Help** command can be activated in three ways from the document screen:

- By selecting **Help** from the Menu Bar and then clicking on the **Microsoft Word Help** icon.
- By clicking on the **Microsoft Word Help** icon on the Standard Tool Bar.
- By pressing the **F1** function key on the keyboard.

Clicking the **What's This?** option on the Help drop-down menu changes the mouse pointer into a question mark so that you can click on a particular item and learn about it (Figure 11).

Figure 11 Help drop-down menu

Activating Help in any of the above ways may bring an animated character (your Office Assistant – Figure 12) on to your screen, followed by a yellow text box asking **What would you like to do?** (Figure 13).

Figure 12 Office Assistant

Figure 13 What would you like to do?

You can type in a question in your own words and then click **Search**. Office Assistant will then show you a list of topics related to your question or to the task in hand.

You may also click **Options** to access relevant dialogue boxes (Figure 14).

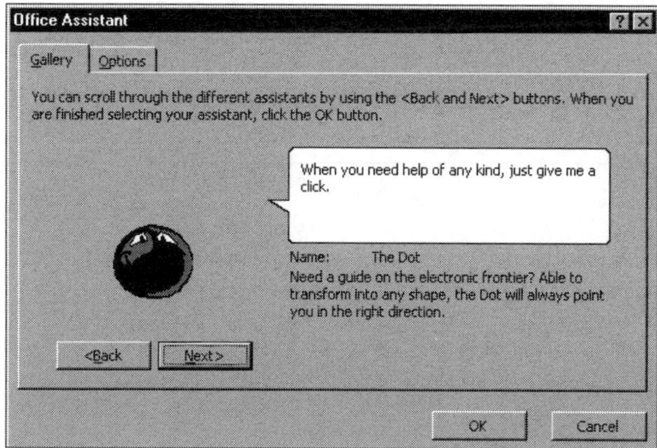

Figure 14 Office Assistant Options dialogue box

Note: Office Assistant can change its appearance – from 'The Genius', 'Rocky', 'F1' and 'The Dot', to name but a few!

If you would rather not see an Office Assistant on your screen, you can 'turn it off' by clicking the right button on the assistant and selecting **Options**, then clicking to remove the ✓ from the **Use the Office Assistant** box. When the Office Assistant is 'turned off', you can access the Microsoft Word Help dialogue box (Figure 15) by:

- Clicking the **Help** [?] button on the Standard Tool Bar
- Clicking the **Show** button and then selecting from the following options:
  - Click the **Index** tab to search for a particular topic
  - Click the **Answer Wizard** and key in your question
  - Click the **Contents** tab to see a list of topics with which you can acquire help
  - Double-click any item to obtain more information

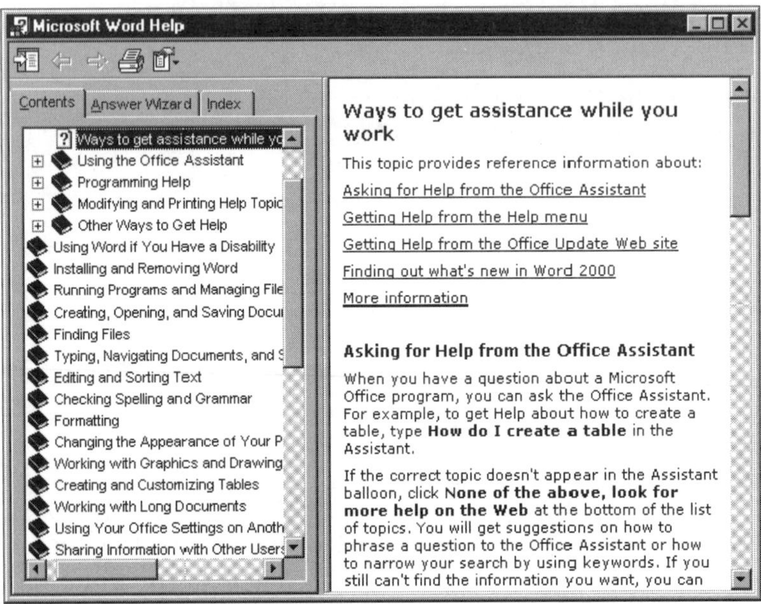

Figure 15 Help dialogue box

At this point, before you begin working through the units, you may wish to make the following changes to the way in which your document screen is set up, as mentioned earlier in this Introduction. Follow the instructions given below to make the changes.

To display shortcut keys in the tool tips:

Select: **View**, **Toolbars** from the menu
Select: **Customize**, **Options**
Click to insert a ✓ in the **Show shortcuts in screen tips** box
Click: **Close**

To display the full drop-down menu options at all times:

Select: **View**, **Toolbars** from the menu
Select: **Customize**, **Options**
Click to remove the ✓ in the **Menus show recently used commands first** box
Click: **Close**

UNIT 1 BASIC DOCUMENT LAYOUT AND APPEARANCE

By the end of Unit 1, you should have revised how to:

- **proofread text with the aid of the AutoCorrect and Spelling and Grammar tools**
- **format/emphasise text**
- **set the margin alignment and document line spacing**
- **indent text at the left and right margins**
- **change the left and right margins and typing line length of a document.**

Proofreading text

Typescript containing typographical errors

In the Stage II examinations, you will be expected to carry out more complex proofreading, text editing and formatting. Text editing may involve correcting any mistakes made in previous printouts. Watch out for uncorrected spelling errors and transposition errors. In the OCR/RSA examination, errors in the draft will be circled for you to correct. At work, however, it is often up to you to proofread for typographical errors, to decide what is wrong and to key in the text correctly. For example:

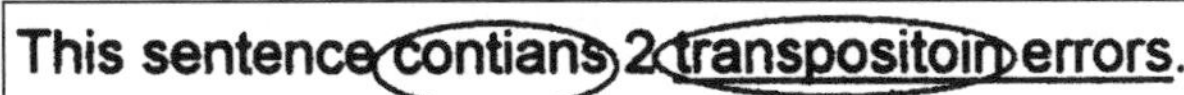
This sentence contians 2 transpositoin errors.

should be keyed in as

This sentence *contains* 2 *transposition* errors.

Typescript containing spelling errors

Remember, Word 2000 can help you with spelling because it has a built-in spelling and grammar check tool which checks as you key in for spelling and grammar errors. Word 2000 will identify a spelling error with a red wavy line and a grammatical error with a green wavy line. However, you must also proofread the text yourself, as Word 2000 will often not be able to check many proper names (eg cities, surnames etc). Also, if you have keyed in the wrong version of a word, eg *their* instead of *there*, spellcheck will not detect this as both versions are spelt correctly. In the Stage II examination you will be expected to be able to spell a list of additional words – the errors in the draft will be circled for you. For example:

This sentance contains 3 speling errers.

should be keyed in as:

This *sentence* contains 3 *spelling errors.*

Only you can tell if you have copied names of people or places correctly and if a piece of information you were asked to find is correct. You can choose to act only on those words you want to change – if Word 2000 queries a word which you know to be correct, you can ignore the prompt to change it. If you were going to use an unusual word fairly frequently that is not already in the spellcheck memory, you have an option to **Add** it to the list. Spellcheck would never stop on that word again.

You will be expected to be able to spell correctly the following words, and their derivations where marked * (eg plurals , -ed, -ing, -ment, -tion, -ly, -able, -ible):

access*	appreciate*	definite*	government*	sufficient*
accommodate*	believe*	develop*	inconvenient*	temporary*
achieve*	business*	discuss*	receipt*	through
acknowledge*	client*	expense*	receive*	
advertisement*	colleague*	experience*	recommend*	
although	committee*	financial*	responsible*	
apparent*	correspondence	foreign	separate*	

Exercise 1A

1.1 Spend a little time making sure you know how to spell all the words listed above correctly – ask someone to test you!

Spelling and Grammar check: quick method

Click: The right mouse button on top of the word with a green or red wavy line underneath it
Click: The correction you want from the list offered

Spelling and Grammar tool: to turn on/off

You can choose to check spelling and grammar automatically as you key in. However, if you find the wavy lines distracting, you can turn the facility off temporarily and then check the entire document at once after keying in.

Select: **Tools, Options** from the menu
Click: **Spelling & Grammar** tab

To turn facilities on:

Click: **Check spelling as you type**
Click: **Check grammar as you type**

To turn facilities off:

Click: **Hide spelling errors in this document**
Click: **Hide grammatical errors in this document**

Spelling and Grammar check: dialogue box method

Keyboard	Mouse
Position the cursor: At the start of the file Press: **F7**	Position the cursor: At the start of the file Select: **Tools, Spelling & Grammar** from the menu *OR* Click: The **Spelling and Grammar button**

The **Spelling and Grammar** dialogue box is displayed on screen.

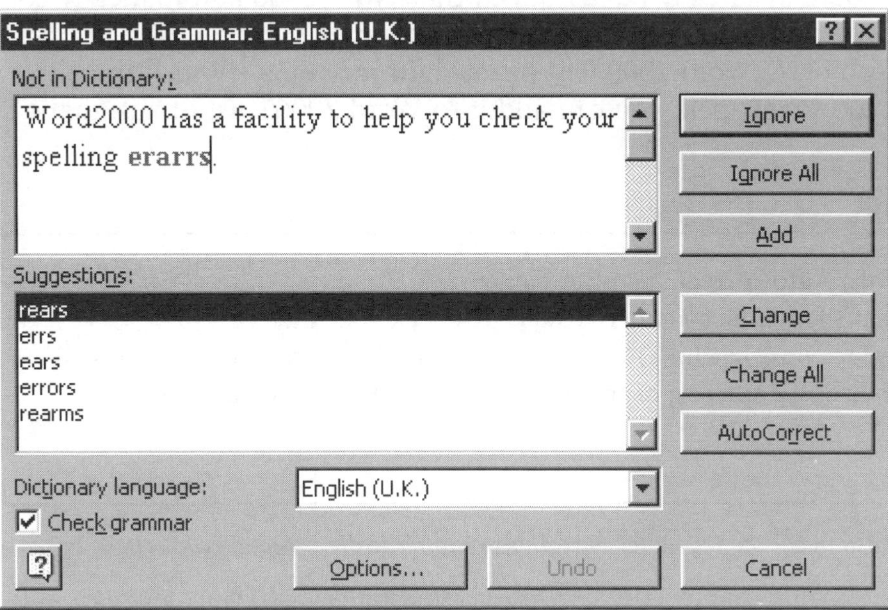

Figure 1.1 Spelling and Grammar dialogue box

- Word 2000 tells you the error in the dialogue box and tells you what type of error it is (eg not in dictionary).
- Word 2000 highlights the most obvious replacement in the **Suggestions** box and often gives a list of other likely alternatives for you to select.
- You can also edit the text yourself in the dialogue box if this is more appropriate.

Select from the spelling dialogue buttons as appropriate:

Button	Action
Ignore	Leaves the word unchanged the first time it occurs but stops on it whenever it occurs again (if you continue editing the word **Ignore** changes to **Resume**).
Ignore All	Leaves the word unchanged on every occurrence (until you restart Word 2000).
Add	Adds the word to the Dictionary.
Change	Accepts the spelling in the dialogue box or the **Suggestions** box.
Change All	Changes the first and all subsequent occurrences of the misspelt word.
AutoCorrect	Adds the misspelt word and its correction to the AutoCorrect list – ie if you ever misspell this word in the same way again as you are keying in, Word 2000 will correct it automatically for you!

Keyboard	Mouse
Press: **Esc** to finish	Select: **Cancel** to finish
Note: If you do not wish to check the spelling of the whole document, you can first select/highlight a portion of text or even one word before running spellcheck.	

AutoCorrect – automatic correction of common keying in errors

As you key in, you may already have noticed that Word 2000 automatically corrects some commonly misspelt words. For example, if you key in *'teh'* instead of *'the'* or *'adn'* instead of *'and'* or *'i'* instead of *'I'*, Word 2000 will put it right for you – try it! If there is a word that you often mistype or misspell, you can add it to Word 2000's list of automatic corrections.

AutoCorrect

- Select: **Tools, AutoCorrect** from the menu
- Check: That the **Replace Text As You Type** check box is ticked
- In the **Replace** box, key in: The word you often mistype/misspell, eg unusaul
- Key in: The correct spelling of the word in the **With** box, eg unusual
- Click: **Add**
- Click: **OK**

Word 2000 will also make the following corrections automatically if the relevant check boxes are ticked:

- Change the second capital letter to a lowercase letter if you accidentally key in two capital letters at the beginning of a word.
- Capitalise the first letter at the beginning of a sentence.
- Capitalise the first letter of the days of the week.
- Reverse accidental usage of the cAPS LOCK key.

Exercise 1B

1.2 Switch on and load Word 2000 for Windows. Insert your work disk in the disk drive, unless you are saving documents on the hard drive or network.

1.3 A good use of AutoCorrect is for replacing shortened versions of words which you find particularly difficult to spell – when you key in the shortened version, Word 2000 will automatically replace it with the correct spelling for you. Select **AutoCorrect** from the **Tools** menu. Enter the replacements (**Replace**:) of common misspellings with the correctly spelt version (**With**:) shown below:

Replace:	With:
acc	accommodate
advert	advertisement
rec	receive
sep	separate

1.4 To test your AutoCorrect entries, with a clear screen, key in the following pressing the Tab key between each word:

acc advert rec sep

If you have followed the instructions for AutoCorrect correctly, Word 2000 should automatically have converted your entries to appear on screen as:

accommodate advertisement receive separate

Note: AutoCorrect will only insert replacement entries exactly as they were entered. You would not, for instance, be able automatically to substitute the word 'accommodation' instead of 'accommodate'. 'Rec' would be reproduced as 'receive' although 'rec' could also be the abbreviation for 'receipt'. You would either have to key in the whole word correctly, or edit the AutoCorrect entry as appropriate.

1.5 Close the file without saving ready for the next exercise.

Document appearance and layout

You will also be expected to carry out more complex text formatting procedures at Stage II. This may include emphasising the text, changing the alignment of the right margin, and/or changing the line spacing. These topics were detailed in the first book of this series, but a summary is included here for easy reference.

Formatting/emphasising text

Format/emphasis	Keyboard	Mouse
Bold	Press: **Ctrl** + **B**	Click: **B** Bold button
Italics	Press: **Ctrl** + **I**	Click: *I* *I*talics button
Underline	Press: **Ctrl** + **U**	Click: U Underline button
Highlight text		Click: The **Highlight** button
Change font	Press: **Ctrl** + **Shift** + **F** Select: A font from the list	Click: The Times New Roman **Font** button Select: A font from the list
Change font size	Press: **Ctrl** + **Shift**+ **P**	Click: The 12 **Font Size** button
Next larger point size:	Press: **Ctrl** + **]**	Select: A point size from the list
Next smaller point size:	Press: **Ctrl** + **[**	
Remove emphasis (back to plain text)	Select: Text to change back: Press: **Ctrl** + **Spacebar**	Select: Text to change back: Click: The appropriate command button

To format text while keying in:

- Click: The appropriate command button (eg click on the **B** button to switch bold text on)
- Key in: The text
- Click: The appropriate command button again to switch the emphasis off

To format existing text:

- Select: The text to be changed
- Click: The appropriate command button (eg click on the **B** button to switch bold text on)

To remove emphasis from text:

- Select: The emphasised text
- Click: The appropriate command button to deselect the feature *or* Press: **Ctrl + Spacebar**

Margin alignment		
Alignment	**Keyboard**	**Mouse**
Centre text (between left/right margins)	Press: **Ctrl + E**	Click: The **Centre** button
Align to the left (ragged right margin)	Press: **Ctrl + L**	Click: The **Align Left** button
Fully justify (justified right margin)	Press: **Ctrl + J**	Click: The **Justify** button
Align to the right (ragged left margin)	Press: **Ctrl + R**	Click: The **Align Right** button

Line spacing		
Format/emphasis	**Keyboard**	**Mouse**
Single line spacing	Press: **Ctrl + 1**	Select: **Paragraph** from the **Format** menu
Double line spacing	Press: **Ctrl + 2**	Select: **Indents and Spacing, Line Spacing**
Add or delete a line space	Press: **Ctrl + 0** again to remove line space	Select: The appropriate line spacing from the drop-down menu

Exercise 1C

1.6 Starting with a clear screen, key in the document below. For the purpose of this exercise, key in all the misspelt words – those with a dotted line underneath – exactly as shown so that you can practise using Word 2000's spellcheck facility. Notice, however, that as you key in, sometimes Word 2000 will automatically correct misspelt words for you! Use a justified right margin, Times New Roman, font size 12 for the main text and apply text formatting where indicated.

DIGITAL RADIO

Centre, bold and highlight Font: Arial, fontsize: 14

This sentence only in italics

The portable radio has definately come a long way since the advent of its early ancestor, the wireless. Once a popular youth culture of the 50's, known as the ghettoblaster in the 80's, the radio of the 90's now accomodates new acheivements in digital technology. With the develloppment of paper thin transistor cards, portable radios are smaller and lighter than ever before. Sometimes the weight of the batteries can be more than that of the radio itself.

Digital technology also offers enhanced sound quality and clearer reseption with radios retuning themselves to receive a station when listeners are on the move. Graphics and other display information, such as phone numbers, are being advertised on the more sophisticated and expensiv models.

This paragraph only in double line spacing

It is easy to apreciate the benefits of replacing the old manual tuning dial thrugh the more accurate digital display. As with digital televeision, compressed signals enable each waveband to carry more information than the old analoge systems.

Digital radio allows listeners more opportunities to experiance many more radio stations.

Another breakthro' has been the windup radio. Cranking a handle for a few seconds powers an internal generator inside the radio, eliminating the need for electricity or battery power. The wind up radio is particularly useful for radio access in remote foreign parts where electricity or battery power is unavailable or when it is simply inconveniant.

Underline the last sentence

Centre this paragraph and use a larger font size

1.7 Use Word 2000's spelling and grammar tool to check your work, and proofread it yourself carefully.

1.8 Save and print your document, using the filename **EX1C**. Check your printout with the printout check at the back of the book. If you find any errors, correct them and print again if necessary.

Change the document line length

You may need to change the format of a document by changing the document line length for the whole of a document or for certain sections only. You can do this by increasing or decreasing the margins, or using the indent facility.

If you are asked to leave a specified amount of horizontal space at any point in a task, you may choose to use either the indent function or alter the margin settings as appropriate.

You should not confuse indenting text with setting left and right margins:

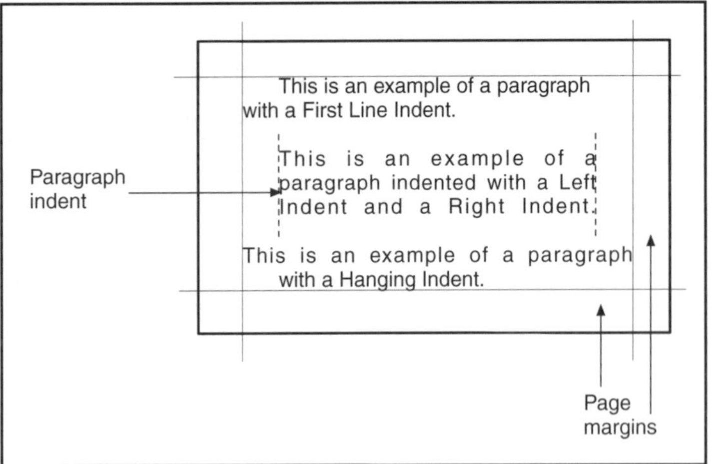

Figure 1.2 Paragraph indent

- Margins set the overall width of the main text and the amount of space between the main text and the edges of the page.
- Indenting moves the text in or out from the margins.

When you operate the indent feature, the cursor moves to the first pre-set tab stop (usually defaulted to 1.27 cm from the left margin). As you carry on keying in, the text will 'wrap around' the indent point until you operate the command to go back to the original left margin.

You can choose to indent the text from both the left margin and right margins or from the left margin only. It is often more convenient to use the indent function to indent a single paragraph, rather than changing the margins.

Change margin settings

Mouse/menu

Select: **Page Setup** from the **File** menu
Click: The **Margins** tab

The **Page Setup** dialogue box is displayed on screen.

Figure 1.3 Page Setup dialogue box

Mouse/menu

Key in: **The required measurement** in the **Left** spin box
Key in: **The required measurement** in the **Right** spin box
From the **Apply to** drop-down menu: Select: The document portion for the new margin settings
Click: **OK**

Mouse/ruler

To display the ruler on the document screen:

- Select: **Ruler** from the **View** menu
- Check: That you are in Print Layout View
- Point to: The left or right margin boundary on the horizontal ruler (where the dark grey and white section of the ruler meet); when the pointer changes to a double-headed arrow: Hold down: The mouse button and drag margin boundary to required position on the ruler

To see the exact measurement on the ruler:

- Hold down: The **Alt** key as you drag the margin boundary:

Figure 1.4 Exact ruler measurement

This method also lets you view the typing line length measurement on screen:

- Hold down: The **Alt** key as you click on the left or right margin boundary or on the indent *(you will see the measurements of the margins, indents and typing line length displayed across the horizontal ruler)*

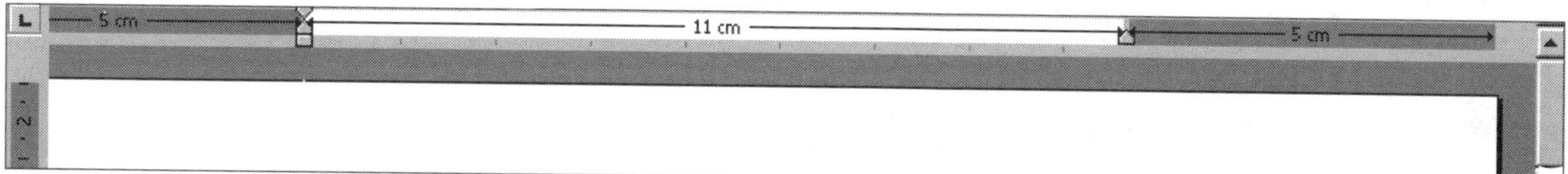

Figure 1.5 Typing line length

Indent a portion of text

Using the keyboard

Indent to the next tab stop	Press: **Ctrl** + **M**
Indent to the previous tab stop	Press: **Ctrl** + **Shift** + **M**
Indent as a hanging paragraph	Press: **Ctrl** + **T** (and press the **Tab** key)
Remove indent and return to standard margins	Press: **Ctrl** + **Q**

Using the formatting Tool Bar

Indent to the next tab stop	Click: The **Increase Indent** button
Indent to the previous tab stop	Click: The **Decrease Indent** button

Using the ruler

- To display the horizontal ruler on screen (unless it is already visible): Select: **Ruler** from the **View** menu
- Check: that you are in Print Layout View
- Select: The paragraph(s) you want to indent
- Drag: The indent markers to the required position on the horizontal ruler

To set a right indent: drag △

To set a first line indent: drag ▽

To set a left indent: drag ⌂

To set a hanging indent: drag ⌂

To set a negative indent, ie scroll into the left margin:

- Hold down: The **Shift** key
- Drag: The left first line indent marker to the required position
- As you drag the margin indent, press and hold down: The **Alt** key to see the exact measurement on the ruler

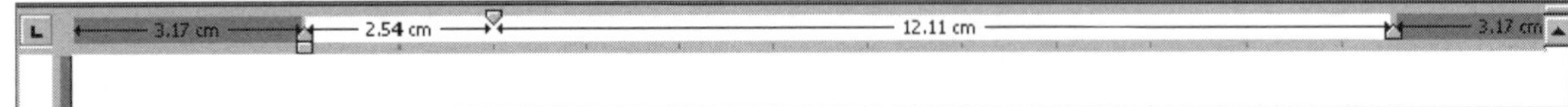

Figure 1.6 Ruler measurement

Using the menu

To display the horizontal ruler on screen (unless it is already visible):

- Select: **Ruler** from the **View** menu
- Check: That you are in **Print Layout View**
- Select: The paragraph(s) you want to indent
- Select: **Paragraph** from the **Format** menu
- Select: **Indents and Spacing**

The **Indents and Spacing** dialogue box is displayed on screen.

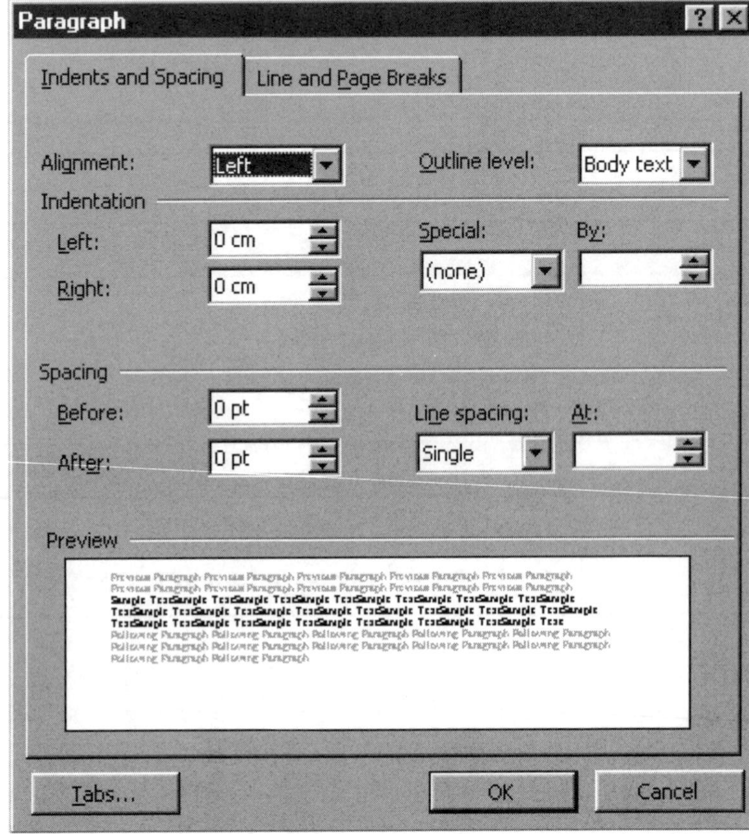

Figure 1.7 Indents and Spacing dialogue box

- Select: The paragraph alignment from the **Alignment** drop-down box
- In the **Indentation** boxes: Select or key in: The left and right indent measurements required
- Select: **First Line** or **Hanging** indents (or none) from the list in the Special drop-down menu
- If the default measurement is not appropriate: Select: An alternative measurement for the first line or hanging indent from the **By** drop-down menu
- Click: **OK**

Change the typing line length

You may be asked to change the 'typing line length' (or typing line) of a document to a fixed number of characters. This is achieved by insetting the margins or indenting using the indent function. (It is not always possible in word processing to be completely accurate in this respect and examiners should be aware of this and be lenient in their marking of this feature.)

The width of an A4 page is 21 cm. The typing line length is the difference between the page width and the two margin measurements. For example, if the left and right margins are both set by default to 2.54 cm:

width of A4 page	=	21.00 cm
minus left margin		– 2.54 cm
minus right margin		– 2.54 cm
typing line length	**=**	**15.92 cm**

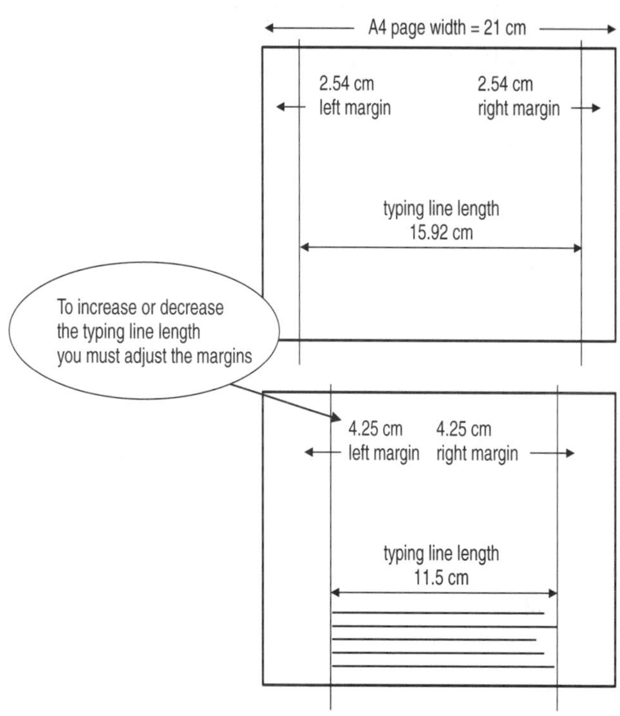

Figure 1.8 Typing line length

To increase or decrease the typing line length, you must adjust the margin settings.

Figure 1.8 shows equal left and right margins but this is not absolutely necessary. You could have a wider left margin than right margin providing the overall result is the same. As shown in Figure 1.8, if you were asked to set a typing line length of 11.5 cm you would need to increase both the left and right margins. You could either increase both margins to 4.75 cm, or you could set a left margin of 5.5 cm and a right margin of 4 cm.

To change the typing line length for the whole document:

Calculate what the new margin settings need to be in order to give the correct typing line length. Use either the Page Setup method (Mouse and menu, page 9) or the Alt key facility (Mouse and ruler, page 9) to change the margin settings before or after keying in the document. You may even wish to use a combination of the two methods, ie change the left and right margins using the Page Setup method, then check the typing line length on the horizontal ruler using the Alt key facility.

To change the typing line length for part of a document:

Follow the instructions given earlier (To indent a portion of text, page 9).

Exercise 1D

1.9 Open the document you saved as **EX1C**. Save it as **EX1D**.

- Replace the highlight from the main heading with underline, and change the font style to one of your choice.
- Remove any centring and align all text to the left with a ragged right margin.
- Use a typing line length of 13 cm.
- Indent the last paragraph by 1.27 cm at both left and right margins.
- Use single line spacing apart from the first paragraph which should be in double line spacing.
- Remove italic from the sentence beginning: **Sometimes the weight of** ...
- Add italic to the paragraph beginning: **Digital radio allows listeners**... and also change the font size to 12.

1.10 Save your document again (using the same filename). Use Word 2000's Print Preview facility to compare your document with the printout check at the back of the book. If the format is not correct, re-read the instructions and amend the format if necessary. If the format is correct, print out a copy of your document.

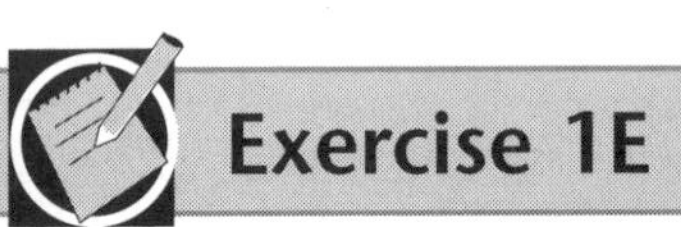

Exercise 1E

1.11 Starting with a clear screen, key in the manuscript draft below. Correct all the words that are incorrectly spelt – those that are circled. Use a justified right margin, Times New Roman and font size 12 for the main text and apply the text emphasis where indicated. Please use a document line length of 11 cm.

Centre the heading and emphasise with bold and highlight. Use Arial font size 14

TRAVEL HEALTH

This paragraph only in double line spacing

unnecessarily

Every year thousands of holidaymakers suffer ~~needlessly~~ from the effects of travelling or too much sun. Yet, many holiday illnesses are relatively easy to prevent, using a combination of common sense and adequate preparation.

Emphasise all the subheadings with bold, as shown in this example

Travel Sickness

Symptoms – nausea, dizziness, vomiting.

half

To combat air, boat or car travel sickness ensure you take medication at least an hour before setting off to give it suficient time to work. Check the instructions on the packet as some products cause drowsiness and are not reccommended for drivers.

Indent all the lines beginning with 'Symptoms' by 1.27cm at left margin and emphasise in italic, as shown in this example

Prickly Heat

Symptoms – red, itchy, spotty rash.

Altho' there is no specific remedy for this you can prevent it by keeping as cool as possible. Prickly heat is caused by sweat temporaraly clogging the skin around the sweat glands. Wear light, loose cotton clothes and apply a soothing, mildly astringent body lotion all over and an antiperspirant to vulnerable areas.

Sunburn

Symptoms – very red, painful skin, blisters can develop in bad cases.

Drink plenty of water and use lotion calamine on the skin. Prevention is better than cure so use a high factor sun cream which protects against both UVB and UVA rays which are responsable for sunburn.

Heatstroke

Symptoms – body is uncomfortably hot, faintness, nausea.

Avoid direct sunlight and drink as much water as you can. Try to stay in a place with air conditioning or access a fan, loosen clothing and seek proper attention from someone with appropriate medical experiance

Avoid tea, coffee and alcohol which cause dehydration and worsen symptoms.

1.12 Use the spelling and grammar tool to check your work, and proofread it yourself carefully.

1.13 Save and print your document, using the filename **EX1E**. Check your printout with the printout check at the back of the book. If you find any errors, correct them and print again if necessary.

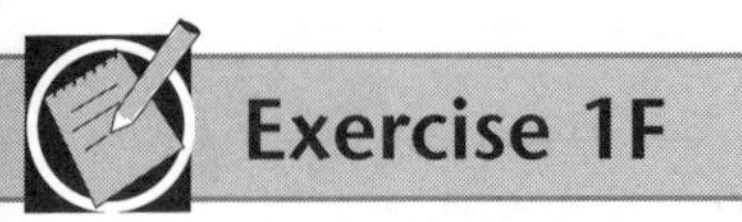

Exercise 1F

1.14 You are now going to use text emphasis to create a standard file for a business memorandum head. You will recall this memo template later in Unit 3 when practising business memo layout – the purpose of this exercise is to practise using text emphasis for effective display.

Starting a new file, key in the following text, centring both lines and using the text emphasis indicated:

OFFTEC CORPORATE SERVICES ←	Arial font size 18 bold
MEMORANDUM ←	Arial font size 22 bold

1.15 Save and print your document using the filename **Memotemp**.

1.16 Use Print Preview to check your work against the printout at the back of the book. If there are any errors, correct them before printing out a copy of your document for use in a later unit.

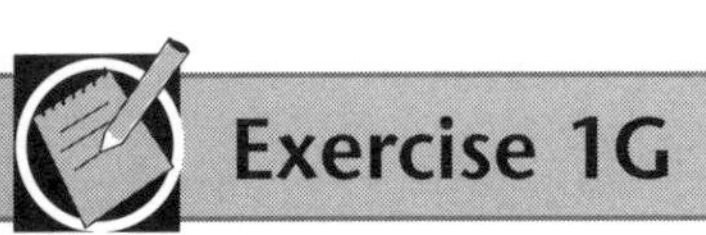

Exercise 1G

1.17 You are now going to use text emphasis to create a standard file for a business letterhead. You will recall this file later in Unit 3 when practising business letter layout – the purpose of this exercise is to practise using text emphasis for effective display.

Starting a new file, key in the following text, centring all lines and using the text emphasis indicated:

OFFTEC CORPORATE SERVICES ←	Arial font size 18 bold
197 Highbury Road WAKEFIELD WF3 2AS ←	Arial font size 14
Tel no: 01924 349211 e-mail: info@offtec.co.uk ←	Arial font size 10 italic

1.18 Save and print your document using the filename **Lettertemp**.

1.19 Use Print Preview to check your work against the printout at the back of the book. If there are any errors, correct them before printing out a copy of your document for use in a later unit.

1.20 Exit the program if you have finished working or clear your screen and continue straight on to the next unit.

UNIT 2 MULTI-PAGE DOCUMENTS

By the end of Unit 2, you should have learnt how to:

- identify and correct grammatical and punctuation errors
- expand correctly commonly used abbreviations
- amend documents in accordance with correction signs
- insert additional blocks of text into existing documents
- insert page numbering on continuation sheets
- identify and correct inconsistencies in text
- insert accented letters in international text.

Typescript containing grammatical and punctuation errors

As you are keying in text, you should make sure that what you are keying in makes sense. You should watch out for:

- errors of agreement when the noun and the verb in a sentence do not agree
- incorrect use or omission of punctuation, eg apostrophes
- incorrect use of punctuation in documents using the fully-blocked, open punctuation style
- omission of capital letters for proper nouns and at the beginning of sentences.

Examples

Errors of agreement

> The difference between the two word processing programs were demonstrated by the supervisor

should be keyed in as:

The difference between the two word processing programs was demonstrated by the supervisor

- There are *two* programs but only *one* difference.

Incorrect use of apostrophe

> Its too late now to go to the shops' as they close at 5.30 pm on Thursday's

should be keyed in as:

It's too late now to go to the shops as they close at 5.30 pm on Thursdays

- *It's* is a shortened form of It is: the apostrophe shows that the letter **i** has been omitted.
- *Shops* does not require an apostrophe after the **s** as this would indicate possession, eg the shops' awnings were brightly coloured. In this instance, shops is simply plural, ie more than one shop.

- *Thursdays* does not require an apostrophe before the **s** as this would indicate possession, eg Thursday's delivery was late. In this instance, Thursdays is plural, ie more than one Thursday.

Further information on the use of apostrophes is included in *Advancing Word 2000 for Windows*.

Incorrect use of capital letters

We found barbara's letter. it was in a pile of mail in one of the Offices.

should be keyed in as:

We found Barbara's letter. It was in a pile of mail in one of the offices.

- *Barbara* should have a capital letter as it is a name. Note the apostrophe before the **s**, indicating possession – the letter belongs to Barbara.
- *It* should have a capital **I** as it is the first letter of the first word in a sentence.
- *Offices* does not need to have a capital letter as it is not a special office.

Grammar tool 

Word 2000 will check your document for possible grammar and style errors and offer suggestions for correcting them. If you know your grammar is weak, this is a useful facility, but it still does not replace personal proofreading skills. Sometimes it can create confusion by suggesting amendments to sentences which are already satisfactory.

Remember, spelling and grammar checks are not sufficient on their own. You must check your work thoroughly too!

The Grammar check facility can be 'switched off' by selecting **Tools** from the main menu, **Options, Spelling and Grammar** and then clicking in the '**Check grammar as you type**' box and the '**Check grammar with spelling**' box to remove the ✓. Reverse the process to switch the facility on again.

Typescript containing abbreviations

Text authors often use abbreviations when writing out copy which is to be keyed in by a word processor operator. In the work situation, you would quickly get used to individual authors' 'shorthand'. The following list shows some abbreviations you can expect to come across in intermediate examinations such as OCR/RSA's Stage II Text Processing. You should key in these words in full whenever you see them, unless instructed otherwise. In the OCR/RSA examinations, open punctuation is used so there are no 'full stops' after the abbreviations shown in the following list.

a/c(s)	**account(s)**	**opp(s)**	**opportunity/ies**
approx	**approximately**	**org**	**organisation**
cat(s)	**catalogue(s)**	**poss**	**possible**
co(s)	**company/ies**	**ref(d)**	**refer(red)**
dr	**dear**	**ref(s)**	**reference(s)**
gntee(s)	**guarantee(s)**	**sec(s)**	**secretary/ies**
immed	**immediate(ly)**	**sig(s)**	**signature(s)**
info	**information**	**temp**	**temporary**
mfr(s)	**manufacturer(s)**	**yr(s)**	**year(s)**
misc	**miscellaneous**	**yr(s)**	**your(s)**
necy	**necessary**		

Some abbreviations should be kept as they are, for example:

etc	**eg**	**ie**	**NB**
PS	**plc**	**Ltd**	**& (in company names)**

Note: Word 2000's spelling check may suggest that some abbreviations such as ie and eg should have full stops, for example i.e. and e.g. In word processing, it is now common practice to omit the full stops in such instances. You can add the abbreviations without full stops to the spelling memory as follows:

- Key in the abbreviations and run spelling check.
- When the spellcheck stops on the abbreviation, click the **Add** button.
- Word 2000 will then add this to its memory and will not suggest full stops for it again.

You will also be expected to key in the following words in full:

- days of the week, eg **Wednesday, Thursday**
- months of the year, eg **February, September**
- words in addresses, eg **Grove, Drive, Crescent**
- complimentary closes, eg **Yours faithfully/sincerely**

Exercise 2A

2.1 Starting a new document, key in the following text, correcting circled spelling and grammatical errors and expanding abbreviations as you go along.

THE WAY IN PROGRAMME ← underline

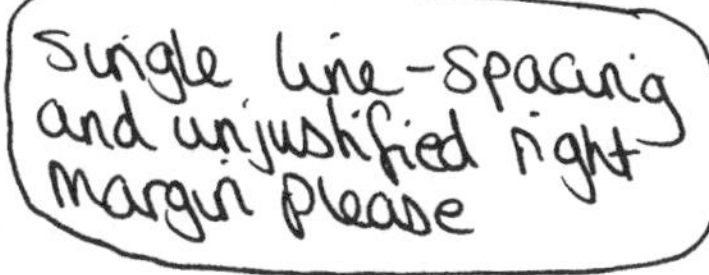

Single line-spacing
and unjustified right
margin please

INTRODUCTOIN AND INFO ← bold

The Way In Programme is designed so that learners can select a number of skills from the misc programmes listed below.

Art & Design
Brickwork
Plumbing
Woodwork
Painting and Decorating
Mathematics
English
Computers

After taking into a/c previous experiense and intrests, each learner can makes up their own individual programme , Learners can study what they want and we gntee that tutors are specially trained to meet learner needs and draw on learner strengths. The Way In Programme offer's nationally recognised qualifications and later an opp to progress onto a vocational programme. Each learner is given a personal plan immed and specific support is provided for students with learning difficulties.

Tutor support

Tutors can help with spoken and written english and with understanding and carrying out basic calculations, etc .

This work is integrated into the practical skills to enhance understanding and competence.

Computers

Many jobs' need some understanding of computers nowadays. It is poss for students to spend approx 2 hrs per week learning keybaord skills and acquiring some knowledge of the everyday use of computers necy in offices and in industry. Local orgs and mfrs may provides short work placements towards the end of the yr in Jun or Jul.

2.2 Proofread your work carefully on screen, comparing your document with the printout check at the back of the book. If you find any errors, correct them.

2.3 Save your document as **EX2A**. There is no need to print at this stage.

Typescript containing correction signs

A word processor operator often has to make amendments to documents after the text author has proofread them. You will already be familiar with basic text-correction signs. In this unit, you will learn additional correction signs. The following list shows all the correction signs you can expect to come across in intermediate examinations such as OCR/RSA's Stage II Text Processing Awards.

Correction sign	Meaning
[or //	Start a new paragraph here
	Run on – join paragraphs or sections of text
	Insert a word (or words) here. The words may be immediately above the insertion sign or circled and joined to the insertion sign by an arrow or line
	Transpose horizontally
	Transpose vertically
word	Close up – ie don't leave a space
twowords	Leave a space – ie split the words at this point
✓ word	Let it be. Key in or retain the word(s) with the dashed underline

Insert additional text into an existing document

Text authors often require additional text to be incorporated into a document while it is being prepared or after it has been printed. In the OCR/RSA Stage II Text Processing Part 1 examination, the invigilator will simulate this by issuing an extra sheet of paper to candidates between 15 and 30 minutes after the start of the examination. The sheet will contain text which is to be included in one of the examination documents.

Make sure that you insert the additional text in the correct position. There will be a hand-written note to indicate where this should be.

Exercise 2B

2.4 Retrieve the document you saved as **EX2A**, save as **EX2B** and amend the text as shown below.

Justified margins please

THE WAY IN PROGRAMME → centre

INTRODUCTION AND INFORMATION ← Make all side headings same format as this one – CAPS & bold

The Way In Programme is designed so that learners can select a number of [vocationally related] skills from the miscellaneous programmes listed below.

Art and Design
Brickwork
Plumbing
Woodwork
Painting and Decorating
~~Mathematics~~ Numeracy
~~English~~ Literacy
Computers

Health + Social Care

Hair dressing

Change to double line-spacing

After taking into account previous experience and interests, each learner can make up their own individual programme. Learners can study what they want and we guarantee that tutors are specially trained to meet learner needs and draw on learner strengths. // The Way In Programme offers nationally recognised qualifications and later an opportunity to progress onto a vocational programme. Each learner is given a personal plan immediately and specific support is provided for students with learning difficulties.

Tutor support ← CAPS and bold, no underline

Tutors can help with spoken and written English and with understanding and carrying out basic calculations, etc.

This work is integrated into the practical skills to enhance ~~understanding~~ ~~knowledge~~ and competence. ✓ Spelling, vocabulary, attention to detail, numeracy and commercial awareness are developped in a realistic manner.

Computers

Many jobs need some understanding of computers nowadays. It is possible for students to spend approximately 2 ~~hrs~~ hours per week learning keyboard skills and acquiring some knowledge of the everyday use of computers ~~necessary~~ in offices and in industry. [Local organisations and manufacturers may provide short work placements towards the end of the year in June or July.

* Insert extra paragraphs here

APPLICATION AND ENROLMENT ← bold

Details available from the Guidance Unit.

2.5 Insert the following text in the document at the point indicated. Save the document, then read the sections on pagination and page numbering and go on to step 2.6 to complete the exercise.

ADVICE & GUIDANCE ← (bold)

Our advisers give advice and offer guidance on all aspects of education and training through out the yr. Prospective students can drop in at anytime. Facilities are available for confidential interviews.

Assistance

~~Help~~ with costs (on full-time courses)

Many students ~~qualify~~ are eligible for ~~assistance~~ help with travel and childcare costs. Although it is not poss to gntee a place for everyone, the majority of students are ~~a~~ given the opp of placing (there) child or children in the College's own ~~nursery~~ crèche.

Pagination for continuation sheets

When you are keying in a long document of several pages, Word 2000 automatically inserts 'soft' page breaks for you. In 'Normal View' mode, a page break is shown by a horizontal dotted line on the screen with the words **Page Break** in the centre of the line. The printer will start a new page at this point. However, you may need to insert new page breaks yourself in a specific place – these are often called 'hard' page breaks. Page breaks should be inserted in sensible places within a document so that it is easy to read. When paginating (inserting page breaks):

- The complimentary close of a letter (Yours . . .) should never be the *only* text on the last page.
- You should not divide a word between one page and the next.
- You should not leave only the first line of a paragraph at the bottom of a page (a 'widow').
- You should not carry forward only the last line of a paragraph on to the next page (an 'orphan').

Widow/orphan control

Word 2000 allows you automatically to avoid widows and orphans. Check that Word 2000 is defaulted to do this:

- Select: **Format, Paragraph, Line and Page Breaks**
- Check that the **Widow/Orphan** box is ticked
- All other boxes should be blank.

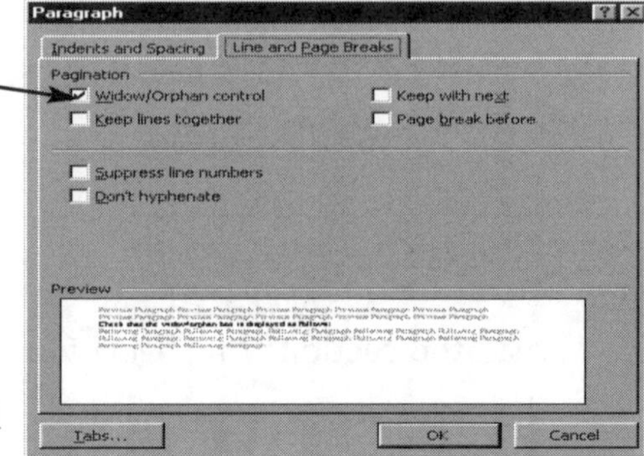

Figure 2.1 Widow/orphan control

Insert a new page break

Position the insertion pointer where you want to insert the page break:	
Keyboard	**Mouse/menu**
Press: **Ctrl** + ↵ (return)	Select: **Insert, Break, Page break, OK**

Page numbering for continuation sheets

It is customary to number the pages of a multi-page document so that readers can follow the page sequence more easily. Word 2000 has a page numbering command that allows you to set the page numbers once, so that page numbers will then appear automatically on all pages of the document.

In some instances you may not want the page number to appear on page one, eg the first page of a multi-page letter is not usually numbered. You can tell Word 2000 not to show the number on the first page where appropriate. However, in OCR/RSA examinations you will not incur a fault for numbering the first page.

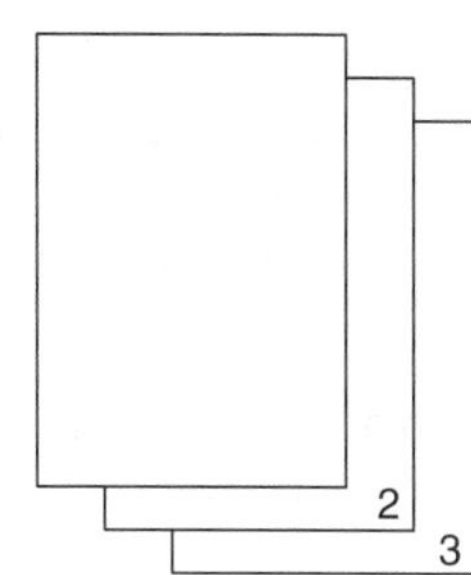

Figure 2.2 Page numbering

Insert page numbers

Keyboard	Mouse/menu
Position the cursor: At the required position Press: **Alt** + **Shift** + **P** *(the page number appears on screen)* *Note*: You have to repeat the instruction on each page so this method is not entirely satisfactory. It is better to use the menu method.	Select: **Page Numbers** from the **Insert** menu

The **Page Numbers** dialogue box is displayed on screen.

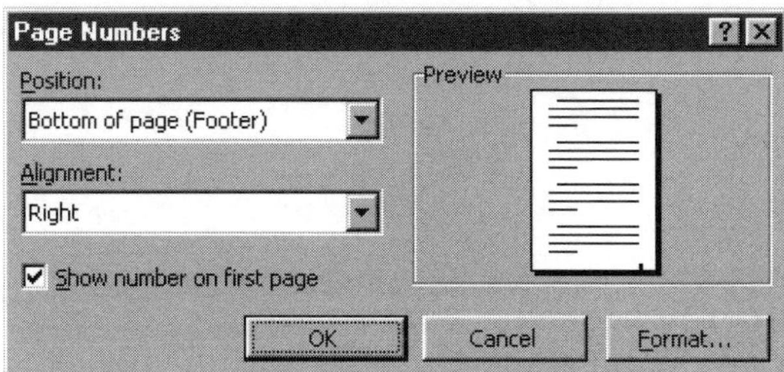

Figure 2.3 Page Numbers dialogue box

Page numbering offers a choice of:	
◎ **Position** ◎ **Alignment** ◎ **Show number on first page** ◎ The **Preview** box allows you to see the position of the page number *Note*: Page numbers only show on screen in **Print Layout View** and **Print Preview**.	
Select from the page numbers dialogue box as appropriate:	
Button	**Action**
Position	Select position on page *vertically* – **Bottom** (footer) or **Top** (header)
Alignment	Select position on page *horizontally* – **Left**, **Right** or **Centre** (**Inside** and **Outside** are used with binding margins, ie facing pages)
Show number on first page	Remove the ✓ if you don't want a number to appear on the first page (eg on a multi-page letter)
Preview	Allows you to see the position of the page number
Format	Allows a different format of page number to be selected, ie Arabic (1,2,3), Roman numerals (I,II,III/i,ii,iii) Letters (A,B,C/a,b,c)
Page numbering (under format menu)	Allows you to decide on the page numbering sequence
Note: Page numbers show on screen in Print Layout View and Print Preview. Select from the page numbers dialogue box as appropriate.	

Exercise 2B continued

2.6 Insert a page break in a sensible place in the document and insert page numbering so that both pages will show a number at the bottom centre.

2.7 Proofread your work carefully, comparing it with the printout check at the back of the book. If you find any errors, correct them. Print one copy and save your document as **EX2B**.

Consistency of presentation

Measurements, weights, times and money

You should always be consistent in the way you present information within a document. The following are examples of points you should watch out for.

Be consistent in the use of an abbreviation to represent a measurement or weight, such as mm, cm, ft, in, kg, oz, lb. For example, don't key in **30"** in one place and **30 in** somewhere else in the document. Be consistent – use either " or **in** but not a mixture of the two.

You may leave one space before the abbreviation or no spaces but you must be consistent. For example, don't key in **46kg** in one place and **46 kg** somewhere else in the document.

Stick to the 12-hour clock or the 24-hour clock when showing times. For example, don't key in **1600 hrs** in one place and **7.30 am** somewhere else in the document. Be consistent in the use of **pm, o'clock, hrs**.

When using an abbreviation for currency (eg $, £, DM, F), stick to one method of presentation. For example, don't key in **FF100** in one place and **100 French Francs** somewhere else in the document. Don't key in **£15** in one place and **£12.50** somewhere else in the document. Both amounts should show the pence (**£15.00** and **£12.50**). You should use either **£** or **p** but not both together in one amount – **£0.50p** is wrong.

Words and figures

Be consistent in the way you present numbers within a document. For example, don't key in **40 miles** in one place and **fifty-five miles** somewhere else in the document. Look through the text first and decide on words or figures. Think about these two examples.

- 1,234,650 is difficult to express in words
- 1 looks strange as the first word of a sentence.

Other possible inconsistencies

Be consistent in using the dash (–) or the hyphen (–) between words and symbols. The keyboard symbol is the same; the spacing either side of the symbol is different. A dash 'separates' words and has one space before and after. A hyphen 'joins' words and has no spaces before and after. Don't key in **4 – 6** in one place and **16-21** somewhere else in the document. The word **to** can also be used instead of a dash: **3 to 4 weeks' time, Tuesday to Thursday**. However, don't key in **4 to 6** in one place and **16-21** somewhere else in the document. Don't key in **Friday – Sunday** in one place and **Monday to Wednesday** somewhere else in the document.

Take care in the use of initial capitals for words – it is not necessary for words which are not proper nouns ('names') to have a capital letter unless they start a sentence. The words **personnel** and **organisations** do not need to have capital letters in the following sentence:

We sent invitations to the Personnel departments in all local Organisations.

It should be keyed in as:

We sent invitations to the personnel departments in all local organisations.

Be consistent in the presentation of percentages. For example, don't key in **50%** in one place and **50 per cent** somewhere else in the document.

When keying in words which can be spelt in two different ways, make sure all occurrences match. For example, don't key in **organise** in one place and **organize** somewhere else in the document.

Be consistent in the amount of space you leave after punctuation. For example, don't leave **1 space** after a full stop in one place and **2 spaces** after a full stop somewhere else in the document. Don't mix open and full punctuation styles in business letters – see Unit 3 (p 32).

Be consistent in the amount of line space between separate parts of a document, eg between paragraphs and after headings. It is normal practice to leave at least one clear line. It is not always necessary, however, to leave a clear line space between items which are listed or numbered.

You should standardise the layout of any document which you are producing. For example, don't mix paragraph styles (eg keep them all blocked to the left or all indented) and make all headings the same style (eg all in capitals or all in lower case and underlined).

Insert a non-breaking space between words

Word processors have a feature called 'wraparound' which simply means that a new line of text is commenced at an appropriate point on the typing line at a space between words. Most of the time, the results of this are acceptable. However, there are occasions when it is better not to have a line break between two words or symbols.

Example

It was decided that the group would meet in the Conference Room every Wednesday at 10.30 am. These meetings should prepare the group for the Managers' Meeting which is held at 1.30 pm on the same day.

This sentence would be more legible if am and pm were not separated from the numbers denoting the time:

It was decided that the group would meet in the Conference Room every Wednesday at 10.30 am. These meetings should prepare the group for the Managers' Meeting which is held at 1.30 pm on the same day.

To insert a non-breaking space between two words:

Key in: The first word (do *not* key in a space after it)
Press: **Ctrl + shift + spacebar**
Key in: The second word

Insert a non-breaking hyphen

A similar method can be used to insert a non-breaking hyphen between two words which are intended to be joined in this way.

Example

Many posts were advertised in the Staff Newsletter and then later in the press. Many part-time positions were filled very quickly but it was noted by the Personnel Unit that only 30-40 per cent of the full-time positions attracted sufficient applicants.

This sentence would be more legible if part-time and 30–40 were not separated:

Many posts were advertised in the Staff Newsletter and then later in the press. Many part-time positions were filled very quickly but it was noted by the Personnel Unit that only 30-40 per cent of the full-time positions attracted sufficient applicants.

To insert a non-breaking hyphen between two words:

Key in: The first word
Press: **Ctrl + shift + hyphen**
Key in: The second word

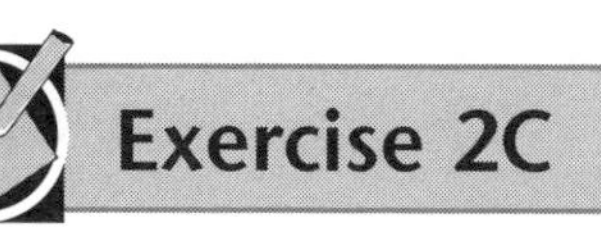

Exercise 2C

2.8 Key in the following document, ensuring consistency of presentation throughout.

SPECIAL OFFERS ON NEW PRODUCTS ← centre and bold

Autumn Season ← change to CAPS

In response to the feedback our sales men have recieved from customers, we are proud to announce the following new products. These will be available from 1 Aug and a 10% reduction on prices will be offered thro to the end of Nov.

Haze nut dessert in 125 g square pots; packs of 4, six packs per box. A popular new flavour to add to the range; £6 per box, RRP £1.49.

Peach and mango yoghurt in 150g round pots; packs of six, 6 packs per box. An exotic addition to your Bonavitale yoghurt range; £8.00 per box, RRP £1.75.

Organic chocolate dessert in 125g square pots; packs of four, 6 packs per box. An old favourite brought up to date; £7.10 per box, RRP £1.69.

Geisha soy sauce in 100 ml bottles; 4 packs per box, packs of 6. A delicious new version of an old Japanese speciality; £11 per box, RRP £0.65p.

Decaffeinated Ceylon tea in 40 bag cartons; packs of 24, twenty-four packs ~~in 1~~ per box. A refreshing drink for your health-conscious customers; £18.73 per box; RRP £1.

* Insert extra paragraphs here later

How to order ← change to CAPS

Simply complete order forms and forward in the usual way.

Please note: VAT at 17.5 per cent to be added to all items. ← change to CAPS

2.9 Proofread your work carefully. If you find any errors, correct them.

2.10 Save your document as **EX2C** and print one copy. Compare your work with the printout check at the back of the book and correct any errors.

Add characters not available on the keyboard

You may be required to reproduce symbols such as:

- fractions, eg $^1/_4$ $1^1/_2$ $6^3/_4$
- accented letters, eg à é ñ ä

Fractions

Word 2000 automatically creates common fractions such as $^1/_4$, $^1/_2$, $^3/_4$ as you key in the numbers with the oblique stroke (solidus) between them: for example if you key in 1/4 Word 2000 will convert this to $^1/_4$. Some other fractions such as 1/3 and 2/5 are not automatically converted in this way but are available by using the Insert Symbol function and selecting a font style which contains the fraction you require.

Accented letters

You can insert accented letters by using the Insert Symbol function and selecting a font style which contains the accented letter you require.

Insert Symbol function

- Select: **Insert** from the File menu
- Select: **Symbol** from the drop-down menu
- Select: The **Symbols** tab on the dialogue box
- Select: (normal text) in the **Font** box

The Symbol dialogue box is displayed on screen.

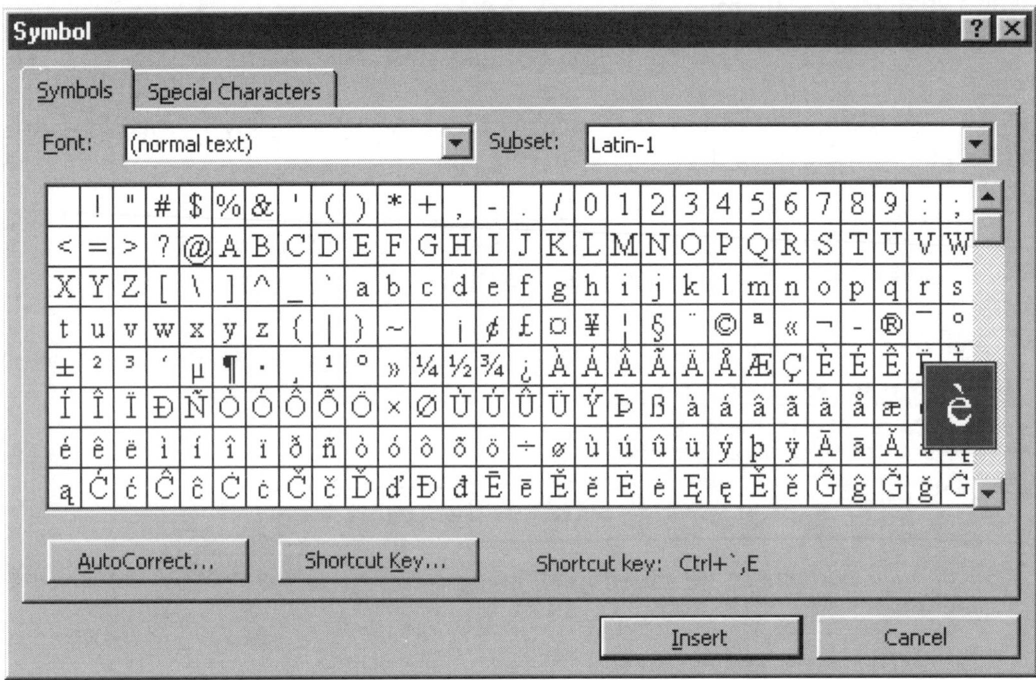

Figure 2.4 Symbol dialogue box

In Figure 2.4, the lower case letter **è** with a grave accent has been selected by clicking on the character. This allows you to check that you have chosen the correct character.

Note: Also displayed are the shortcut (combination) keys you could use to reproduce the same character.

- Click: **Insert** to select this character and insert it into the text
- Click: **Close** to return to the document

Shortcut keys

You can also apply accents to text in other languages using the **combination keys** function (ie pressing two or more keys simultaneously).

Figure 2.5 shows the combination keys to be used to reproduce accented letters. (This table can be found in the **Help** menu index under **Insert an international character by using a shortcut key**.)

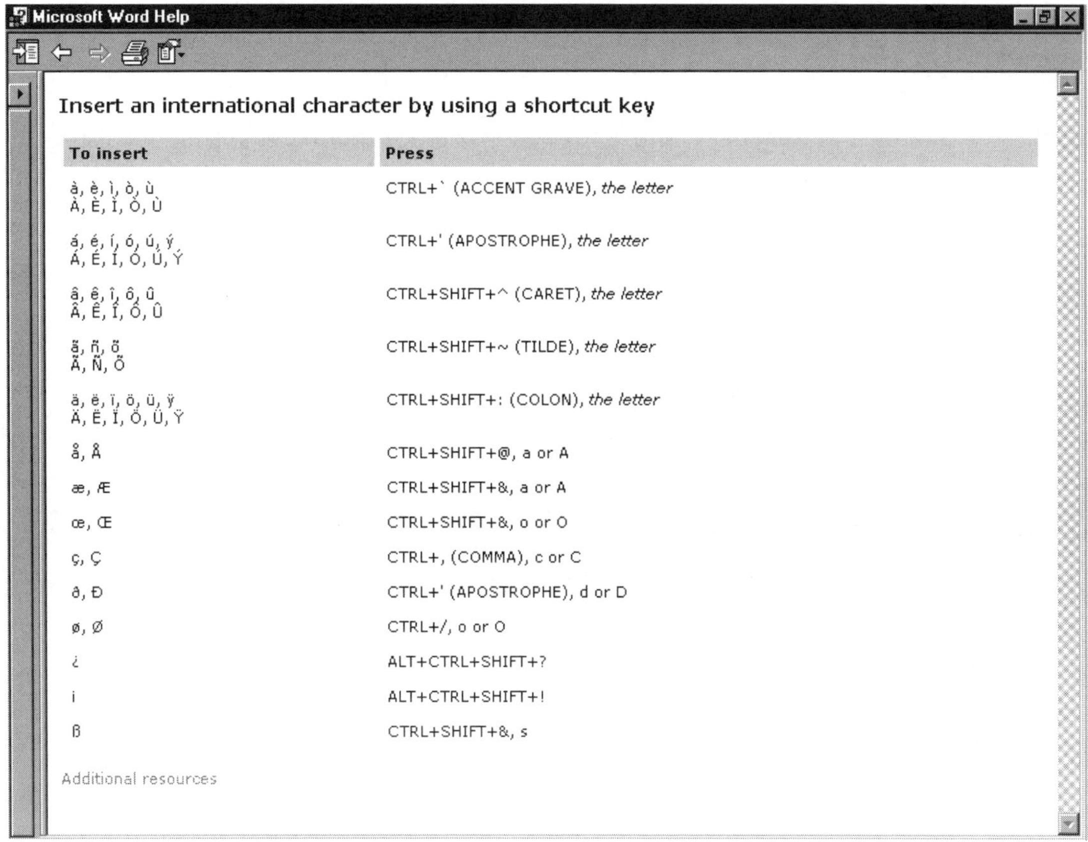

Microsoft Word Help

Insert an international character by using a shortcut key

To insert	Press
à, è, ì, ò, ù À, È, Ì, Ò, Ù	CTRL+` (ACCENT GRAVE), *the letter*
á, é, í, ó, ú, ý Á, É, Í, Ó, Ú, Ý	CTRL+' (APOSTROPHE), *the letter*
â, ê, î, ô, û Â, Ê, Î, Ô, Û	CTRL+SHIFT+^ (CARET), *the letter*
ã, ñ, õ Ã, Ñ, Õ	CTRL+SHIFT+~ (TILDE), *the letter*
ä, ë, ï, ö, ü, ÿ Ä, Ë, Ï, Ö, Ü, Ÿ	CTRL+SHIFT+: (COLON), *the letter*
å, Å	CTRL+SHIFT+@, a or A
æ, Æ	CTRL+SHIFT+&, a or A
œ, Œ	CTRL+SHIFT+&, o or O
ç, Ç	CTRL+, (COMMA), c or C
ð, Đ	CTRL+' (APOSTROPHE), d or D
ø, Ø	CTRL+/, o or O
¿	ALT+CTRL+SHIFT+?
¡	ALT+CTRL+SHIFT+!
ß	CTRL+SHIFT+&, s

Additional resources

Figure 2.5 International characters table

For example, when keying in the word fricassée, to produce the é:

- Press: **Ctrl** + **' (apostrophe)**
- Press: **e**

To insert an accent with an upper case letter:

- Press: The key combination
- Press: **Shift** + the letter

For example, when keying in the word NOËL, to produce the Ë:

- Press: **Ctrl** + **Shift** + **: (colon)**
- Press: **Shift** + **E**

Other symbols

Note: You will find many other useful symbols such as ticks, fractions, arrows etc by investigating the different fonts in the Symbol dialogue box.

Some examples are: 8 § © ♈ ℞ ⅖ œ̃ 🗗 ✓ ♥ ❀ Σ ➔ E

Experiment with these when you have some spare time. However, remember to confine the use of some of the more unusual symbols to your own work – do not use them in examinations!

Exercise 2D

2.11 Starting with a clear screen, key in the following memorandum, ensuring consistency of presentation throughout.

MEMORANDUM ← (bold and larger font size)

To: Paul Brillow, Administration Unit
From: √Training Unit (Michèle Dupré,)
Ref: TU/MD/0097/WP
Date:

Training Programmes for new software ← (CAPS)

Further to our ~~earlier~~ discussion three days ago, I am writing to confirm the √times, (dates,) venue and ~~topics~~ subjects (✓) for training.

At each session, there will be (sufficiant) space for 6 employees in the IT Training Room (D10) and not four as I stated earlier.

Please let me have names / (and unit details) of (employes) allocated to each 1¼ - 1½ hour session when you have drawn up a rota.

(Use 3-column display for this section)

Tuesday 4 Oct	1300 hrs	~~D10~~	Mail Merge
Wed 19 Oct	1.00 pm	~~D10~~	Templates
Tues 11 Oct	1330 hrs	~~D10~~	Tables
Wednesday 26 Oct	1.30 hrs	~~D10~~	Symbols
Tues 1 Nov	1330 hrs	~~D10~~	International (correspondance)

Detailed training schemes are attached. [During training / (needs) analysis, more than 95% of operators identified the last two topics on the [list / above] as unfamiliar to them. In addition, 86 per cent said that they would use black pen or, worse still, ignore them, when faced with symbols such as Ö, ç, ¥ and ¢ (to be reproduced)!

Encs

(Sort into Chronological order. Ensure corresponding details are also rearranged)

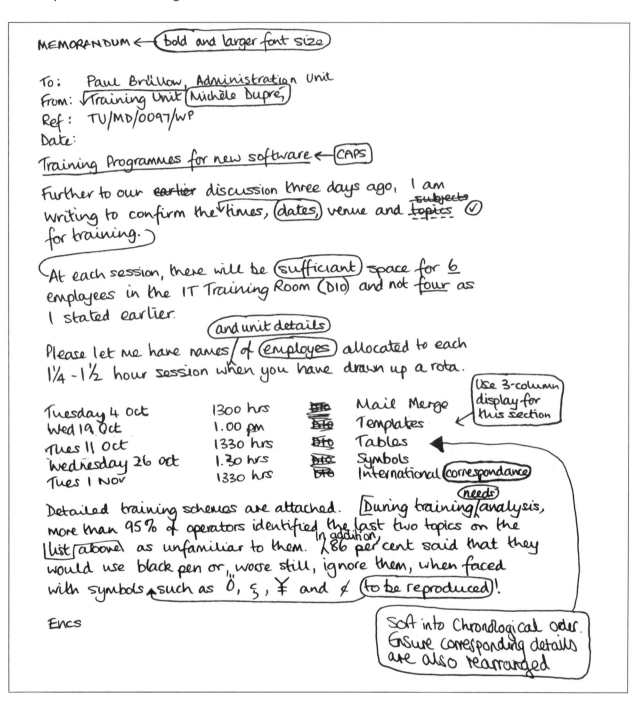

2.12 Proofread your work carefully. If you find any errors, correct them.

2.13 Save your document as **EX2D** and print one copy. Compare your work with the printout check at the back of the book, checking particularly that the accented letters have been correctly reproduced.

Exercise 2E

2.14 Retrieve the document **EX2C**. Save as **EX2E** and add the following text at the point which was indicated in the copy at step 2.8 (p 27). Ensure consistency of presentation with the remainder of the document.

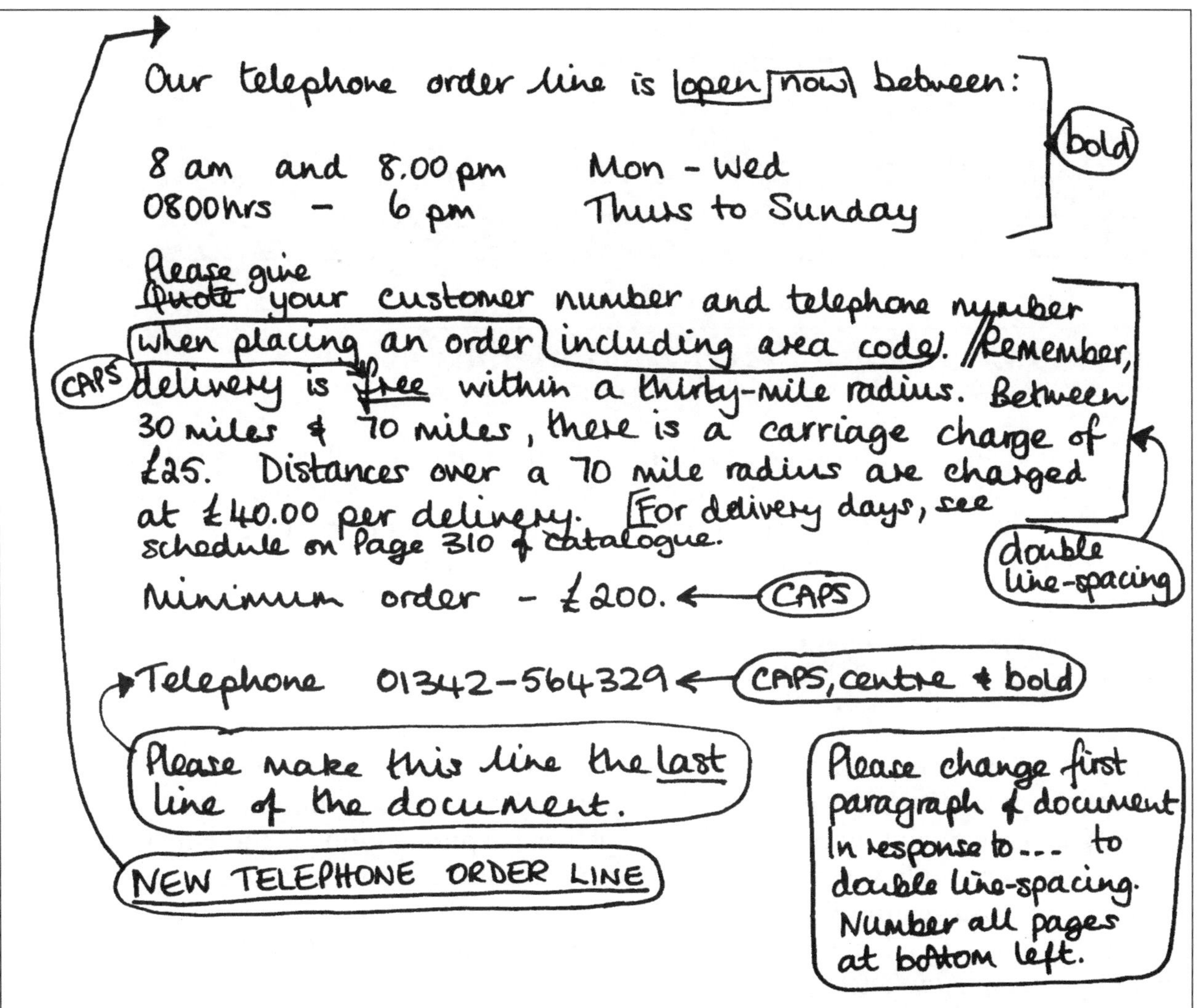

Our telephone order line is open now between:

8 am and 8.00 pm Mon - Wed
0800hrs - 6 pm Thurs to Sunday

bold

Please give Quote your customer number and telephone number when placing an order including area code. Remember, delivery is free within a thirty-mile radius. Between 30 miles & 70 miles, there is a carriage charge of £25. Distances over a 70 mile radius are charged at £40.00 per delivery. For delivery days, see schedule on Page 310 of catalogue.

double line-spacing

CAPS

Minimum order - £200. CAPS

Telephone 01342-564329 CAPS, centre & bold

Please make this line the last line of the document.

NEW TELEPHONE ORDER LINE

Please change first paragraph of document In response to ... to double line-spacing. Number all pages at bottom left.

2.15 Proofread your work carefully. If you find any errors, correct them.

2.16 Re-save your document and print one copy. Compare your work with the printout check at the back of the book.

2.17 Exit the program if you have finished working or continue straight on to the next unit.

UNIT 3 PRODUCING BUSINESS DOCUMENTS

By the end of Unit 3, you should have learnt how to:

- **produce a business letter and a memorandum on preprinted forms and templates using open punctuation and fully blocked style and with special marks and enclosure marks**
- **confirm facts by locating information from another document and including it where indicated.**

Note: Although Word 2000 has an in-built **Letter Wizard** facility, it is not entirely suitable for OCR/RSA examination purposes.

Business documents – letters and memos

In the OCR/RSA Text Processing Stage II Part 1 examination you will be expected to produce a business letter and a memorandum either by printing on to a preprinted form, or by using a template file. You will have already learnt most of the requirements at Stage I, but some details are repeated here as a reminder and for ease of reference.

Business letter layout

A business letter is written on behalf of an organisation and is printed or typed on the organisation's own letterhead. An attractive letterhead gives a good impression of the organisation and contains all relevant details such as telephone number and e-mail address. Only the name and address of the addressee (recipient of the letter) have to be typed because the sender's details are already printed on the letterhead. The company's letterhead may be stored as a template file (blueprint) on your computer – you can recall it whenever you need to complete a company letter.

Use preprinted forms or templates

In the Stage II examination you will be asked to print business documents using either a preprinted form or a template file stored on the computer. Both methods are described here to enable you to choose the one you feel most comfortable with or which is accessible to you.

Using a preprinted form

In Word 2000 the top margin is usually set by default to 2.54 cm. When printing on a preprinted form, the top margin on the first page only should be increased to accommodate the printed heading. (Second and subsequent pages are usually printed on plain paper.) You may need to measure the depth of the preprinted heading on the form you intend to use, and experiment to find the top margin measurement required. Make sure you know how to insert headed paper into the paper feed tray of your printer so that the document is printed in the correct position.

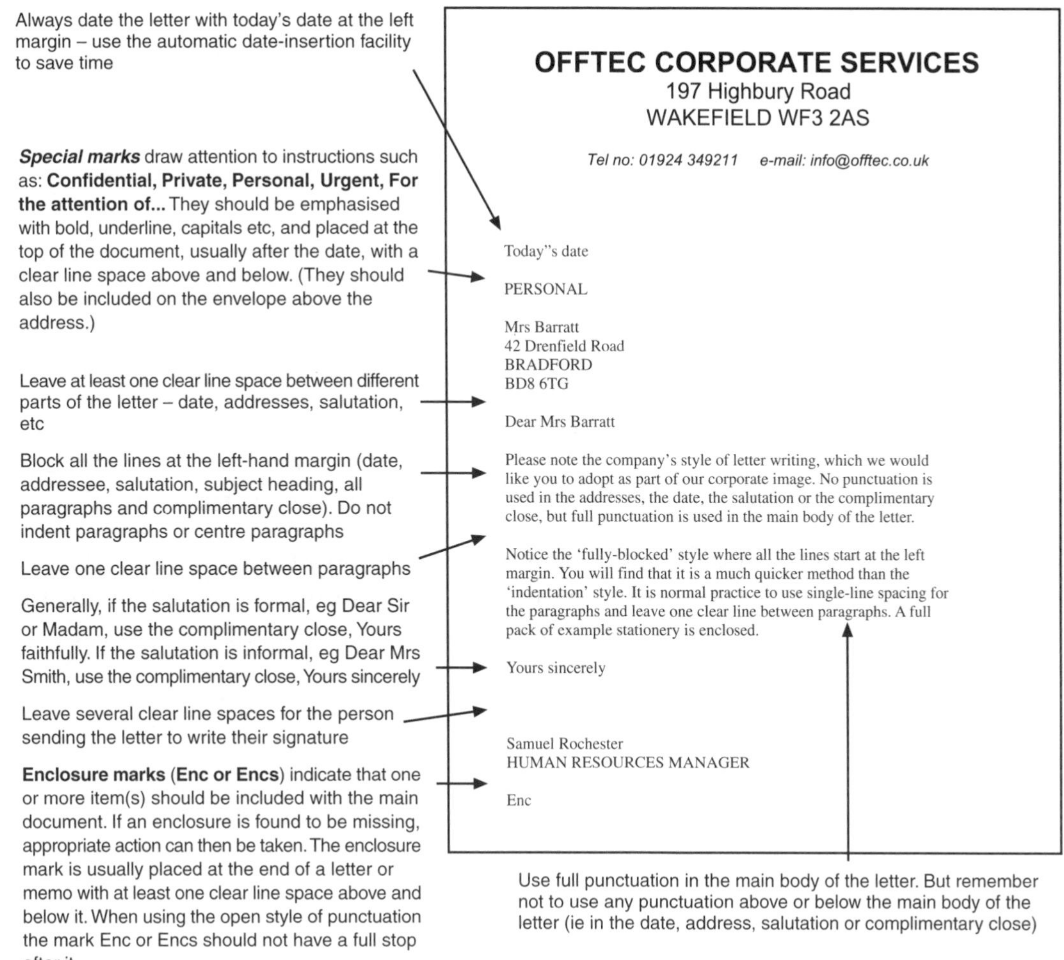
OFFTEC CORPORATE SERVICES
197 Highbury Road
WAKEFIELD WF3 2AS

Tel no: 01924 349211 e-mail: info@offtec.co.uk

Today''s date

PERSONAL

Mrs Barratt
42 Drenfield Road
BRADFORD
BD8 6TG

Dear Mrs Barratt

Please note the company's style of letter writing, which we would like you to adopt as part of our corporate image. No punctuation is used in the addresses, the date, the salutation or the complimentary close, but full punctuation is used in the main body of the letter.

Notice the 'fully-blocked' style where all the lines start at the left margin. You will find that it is a much quicker method than the 'indentation' style. It is normal practice to use single-line spacing for the paragraphs and leave one clear line between paragraphs. A full pack of example stationery is enclosed.

Yours sincerely

Samuel Rochester
HUMAN RESOURCES MANAGER

Enc

Always date the letter with today's date at the left margin – use the automatic date-insertion facility to save time
Special marks draw attention to instructions such as: **Confidential, Private, Personal, Urgent, For the attention of...** They should be emphasised with bold, underline, capitals etc, and placed at the top of the document, usually after the date, with a clear line space above and below. (They should also be included on the envelope above the address.)
Leave at least one clear line space between different parts of the letter – date, addresses, salutation, etc
Block all the lines at the left-hand margin (date, addressee, salutation, subject heading, all paragraphs and complimentary close). Do not indent paragraphs or centre paragraphs
Leave one clear line space between paragraphs
Generally, if the salutation is formal, eg Dear Sir or Madam, use the complimentary close, Yours faithfully. If the salutation is informal, eg Dear Mrs Smith, use the complimentary close, Yours sincerely
Leave several clear line spaces for the person sending the letter to write their signature
Enclosure marks (**Enc or Encs**) indicate that one or more item(s) should be included with the main document. If an enclosure is found to be missing, appropriate action can then be taken. The enclosure mark is usually placed at the end of a letter or memo with at least one clear line space above and below it. When using the open style of punctuation the mark Enc or Encs should not have a full stop after it
Use full punctuation in the main body of the letter. But remember not to use any punctuation above or below the main body of the letter (ie in the date, address, salutation or complimentary close)

To alter the top margin to leave space for a pre-printed form heading:

One-page documents

- Select: **File**, **Page Setup**, **Margins** (from the menu)
- In the **Top** box: Notice: the default top margin is normally set at 2.54 cm

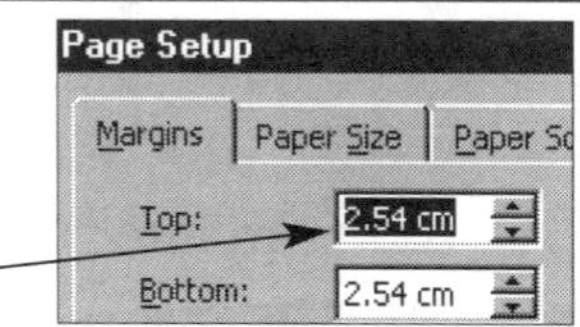

Figure 3.1 Page Setup dialogue box – default settings

- To replace this with the extra measurement needed, either select or overtype with the required measurement to leave sufficient space for the depth of the preprinted heading plus one or more clear line spaces
- Select: **Whole Document** from the **Apply to** box
- Click: **OK**

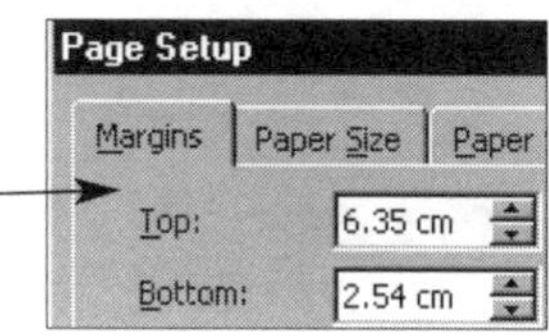

Figure 3.2 Page Setup dialogue box – extra measurements

Multi-page documents

- Repeat: The above procedure for the page on which you want to leave space – usually page 1
- Then, to revert to a normal top margin for all subsequent pages:
- Position the cursor: At the bottom of the page which carries the extra heading space
- Select: **File**, **Page Setup**, **Margins**
- In the **Top** box: Select or key in: 2.54 cm – or an alternative standard top margin measurement
- Select: **This point forward** from the **Apply to** box
- Click: **OK**

Note: This ensures that the increased top margin measurement is only set for the page with the preprinted heading on it – all other pages in the document follow standard top margin settings. It is often better to carry out this procedure after keying in the document but before inserting page breaks.

Using a template file

Templates are often used in business to give a consistent look to the company's documents. A template is a blueprint for specific text, graphics and formatting which will always appear in a document. Memos are a good example of template use as they contain the company name, standard headings, a date field, and place holders to indicate where you type the text.

Note: Word 2000 does have a set of templates that you can use as they are or adapt. However, these require saving in a different format. For the purposes of this book and the elementary examination requirements, therefore, you will save your template files in the normal way.

After retrieving your original template file, and before keying in additional details, you should always ensure that you give the second document a different filename. This means that you will not 'overwrite' your template file and you will then be able to retrieve and use the template blueprint over and over again.

To create a template:

- Key in: Only those details you want to re-appear every time you open the template file
- Save: The file in the normal way as a Word 2000 document using a relevant filename, eg **letterhead** or **memohead**

To open/retrieve a template for use:

- Select: **Open** from the **File** menu and open/retrieve your template file in the normal way
- Select: **Save As** from the **File** menu
- Enter: A different filename for your second document so that you don't overwrite your template blueprint
- Add: The rest of the information to the template. For example, if you have retrieved a memohead, key in the rest of the details for the memo. Resave your document to include the added text

Exercise 3A

3.1 To complete **Exercise 3A**, you will need to open **Lettertemp**, the letterhead template file you saved in Unit 1. The **Offtec Corporate Services** letterhead should now appear on the screen ready for you to complete with the rest of the details. Before keying in anything, select the **Save As** command from the **File** menu (so that you don't overwrite your letter template file) and save the file as **EX3A**.

3.2 Key in the rest of the letter from the manuscript copy below.

Note: Before keying in any additional details, you may need to re-set the font to Times New Roman, font size 12. You may also need to alter the margin alignment and remove italic format.

Our ref LB/tw

Mark the letter: URGENT

Mr Raymond Burns
Burns Installation Ltd
37 Ellerdale Cres
NORWICH
NR3 2PS

Dr Mr Burns

Thank you for yr ~~fax~~ e-mail (recieved) yesterday, which has been passed to me by a (coleague). // I am pleased to enclose a cat detailing our wide range of consultancy services.

As you are aware, we are a looking forward co and all our consultants (is) trained to the highest standards. Our experts can provide you with a number of (buisiness) solutions, all of which can be ~~specially~~ tailored to meet yr needs & available resources.

Also enclosed is an info pack about ~~of~~ our org. The pack includes testimonials from some of our satisfied (customer) who have used our services in the past and are happy to (reccomend) them to other mfrs.

We would be pleased to discuss yr requirments (in more detail) with you and can arrange for a preliminary consultation should you wish to ~~discuss~~ ~~explore~~ ✓ opps further. This would place you under no obligation.

(put this sentence in bold)

I look forward to hearing from you shortly.

Yrs scly
Linda Braithwaite
Senior Consultant

3.3 Resave your document and print one copy. Check your printout with the key at the back of the book. If you find any errors, retrieve the document and correct them.

Note: If spellcheck stops on the enclosure mark, **Enc** or **Encs**, and prompts you to add a full stop, you can simply **Add** the open punctuation version to spellcheck's memory so that it does not query it again.

Exercise 3B

3.4 If you cannot access the printer, complete Exercise 3B in the same way you completed Exercise 3A, using the template file. Otherwise, open **Lettertemp**, the file you saved in Unit 1. Print out a copy. Measure the depth of the preprinted letter heading from the top of the page to the bottom of the heading text and allow for 2 or 3 clear line spaces after it. In total, this should be approximately 6.35 cm. You are going to print Exercise 3B directly on to this preprinted form in step 3.6.

3.5 Close the file **Lettertemp**. Starting a new file, key in the following letter, using the line spacing shown.

Mark the letter: PERSONAL

Our ref MG/ZA

Mrs Ruth Ayre
Bramwell Lodge Park
Nelson Rd
LEICESTER
LE22 4RS

Dr Mrs Ayre

I have recently recieved a cat in which you have placed an advert offering special discounts for cos wishing to take advantage of week end breaks at yr Park. [We are hoping to ~~sent~~ approx 12 sales consultants for a two-night ~~stay~~ team-building event and are looking for ~~a~~ suitable acomodation.

I would aprecaite it if you could ~~send~~ forward some additional info about the misc ~~facilit~~ facilities and resources that you can ~~provide~~ offer to ~~bus~~ buisness ~~groups~~ cleints.

As (finanshial) arrangements are not immed (aparent) from the brochure, could you also advise on the discount [available and whether we could pay by a/c.

Please address all further (correspondance) to my sec, Janet Patel, whose card is enclosed.

Yrs scly

Mahsood Dabhad
Personnel Manager

3.6 Following the instructions given previously, alter the top margin so that the body of the document does not 'overprint' on top of the preprinted letter heading. Remember, you will probably need to enter a setting of approximately 6.35 cm for the top margin in order to allow for several clear line spaces after the letter heading text.

3.7 Save your document using filename **EX3B**.

3.8 Insert the preprinted letterhead form (ie the document **Lettertemp** which you printed out at step 3.4) correctly into your printer. Print the document **EX3B** directly on to the preprinted letterhead. Check your printout with the key at the back of the book. If you find any errors, retrieve the document and correct them.

Memorandum

A memorandum is a document sent 'internally' to convey information to people who work in the same organisation.

At the top of the document, it is customary to enter the name of the person **From** whom the document is being sent and that of the person **To** whom it is being sent, as well as a **Reference**, the **Date** of sending and usually a **Subject Heading**. There is no complimentary close in a memorandum.

You should always insert the date, even if there are no specific instructions to do so – this will be expected of you in the OCR/RSA examination. Some people like to sign or initial their memos but this is not absolutely necessary.

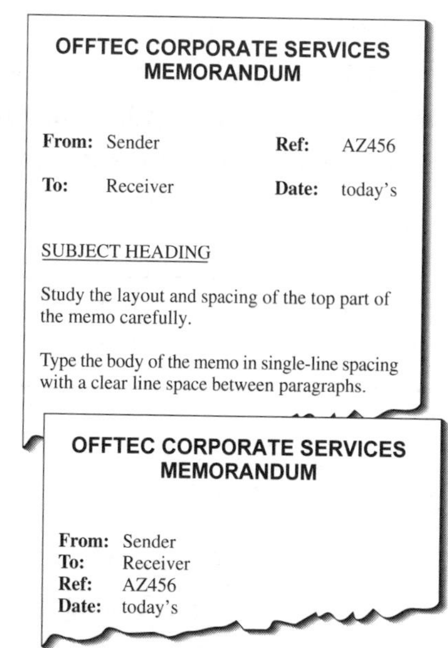
OFFTEC CORPORATE SERVICES
MEMORANDUM

From: Sender **Ref:** AZ456
To: Receiver **Date:** today's

SUBJECT HEADING

Study the layout and spacing of the top part of the memo carefully.

Type the body of the memo in single-line spacing with a clear line space between paragraphs.

OFFTEC CORPORATE SERVICES
MEMORANDUM

From: Sender
To: Receiver
Ref: AZ456
Date: today's

Figure 3.3 Memorandum layout

Organisations have different ways of aligning and setting out the items on the memo. Two acceptable versions are shown in Figure 3.3.

Confirming facts

As part of the examination, you will be asked to insert additional information into a document. (At work you would be expected to consult paper files, computer databases etc.) Take notice of the text you are keying in so that you will be able to select the correct piece of information to make your document accurate.

Automatic date insertion

Word 2000 will insert the current date in letters and memoranda, as follows:

Keyboard	Mouse/menu
Press: **Alt + Shift + D**	Position the pointer: In the correct place for date to be inserted Select: **Insert** from the menu bar Select: **Date and Time**

The **Date and Time** dialogue box is displayed on screen.

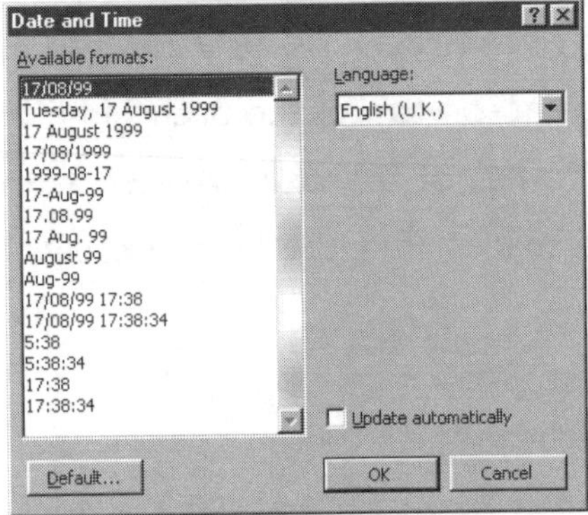

Figure 3.4 The Date and Time dialogue box

- Word 2000 displays a selection of available date formats
- In the UK the third style is usually adopted for letters and memos, ie 17 August 2000
- Click: On the date style that you want to insert
- Check: That the **Update automatically** box does not have a tick in it – if it does, Word 2000 would automatically update the date or time whenever you print the document – *(in some instances, this would be useful)*
- Click: **OK**

Note: To save making changes when using the keyboard shortcut (**Alt + Shift + D**) you can select the date style as the default style by clicking on **Default** instead of **OK**.

Exercise 3C

3.9 To complete the memo, you will need to open **Memotemp**, the memo template file you saved in Unit 1. The **Offtec Corporate Services** memo template should now appear on the screen ready for you to complete with the rest of the details. So that you don't overwrite your memo template file, select **Save As** from the **File** menu and save the file as **EX3C**.

3.10 Key in the rest of the memo from the manuscript copy for Exercise 3C.

Note: Before keying in any additional details, you will need to re-set the font to Times New Roman, font size 12. You may also need to alter the margin alignment.

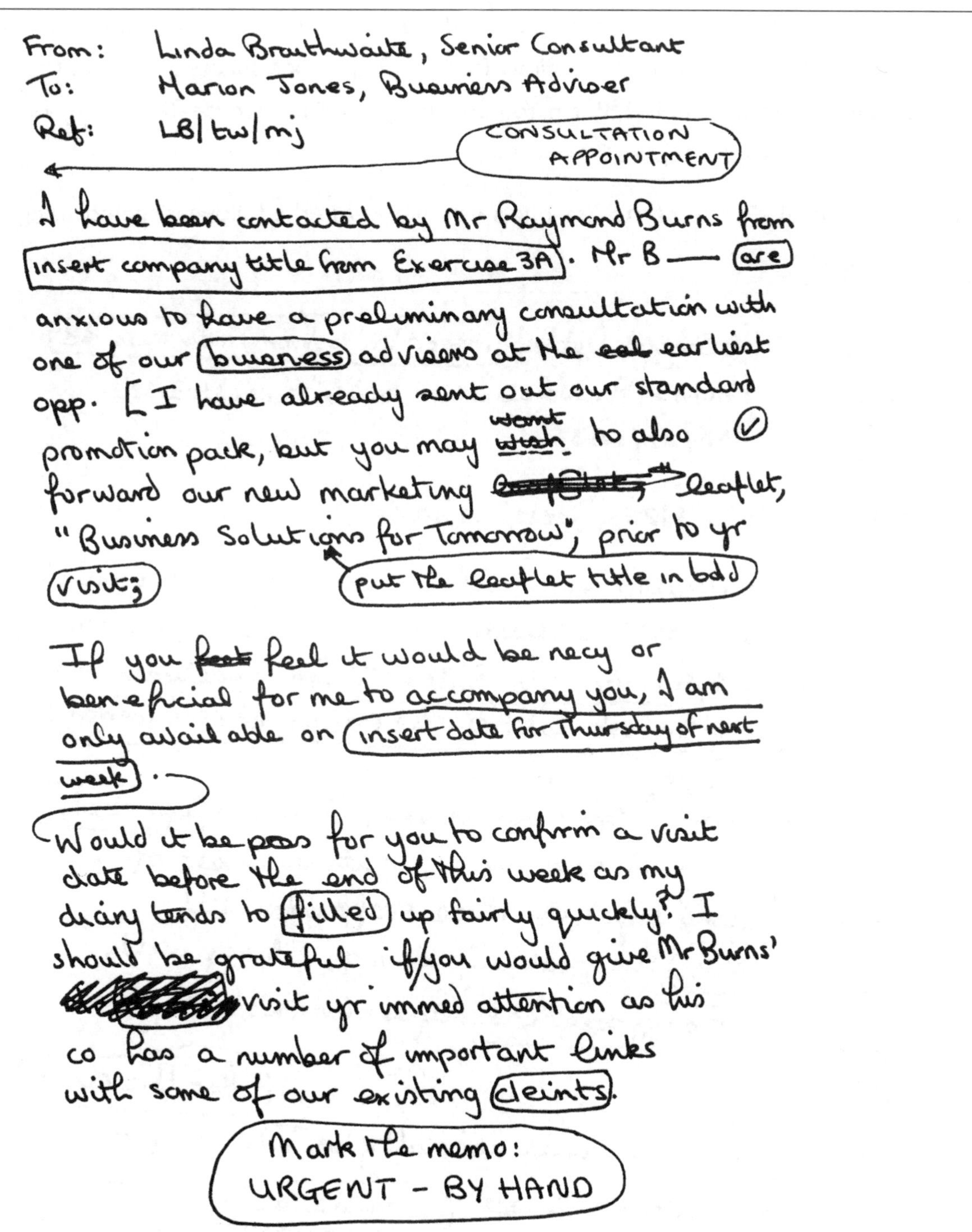

From: Linda Braithwaite, Senior Consultant
To: Marion Jones, Business Adviser
Ref: LB/tw/mj

CONSULTATION APPOINTMENT

I have been contacted by Mr Raymond Burns from (insert company title from Exercise 3A). Mr B— (are) anxious to have a preliminary consultation with one of our (busness) advisers at the ~~eal~~ earliest opp. [I have already sent out our standard promotion pack, but you may ~~wish~~ want to also ✓ forward our new marketing ~~booklet~~ leaflet, "Business Solutions for Tomorrow", prior to yr (visit;)

(put the leaflet title in bold)

If you ~~feet~~ feel it would be necy or beneficial for me to accompany you, I am only available on (insert date for Thursday of next week).

Would it be poss for you to confirm a visit date before the end of this week as my diary tends to (filled) up fairly quickly? I should be grateful if you would give Mr Burns' visit yr immed attention as his co has a number of important links with some of our existing (cleints).

(Mark the memo: URGENT – BY HAND)

3.11 Resave your newly completed memo and print one copy. Check your printout with the key at the back of the book. If you find any errors, retrieve the document and correct them.

Exercise 3D

3.12 If you cannot access the printer complete Exercise 3D using the template file, as you did for Exercise 3C. Otherwise, open **Memotemp**, the file you saved in Unit 1. Print out a copy. Measure the depth of the preprinted memo heading from the top of the page to the bottom of the heading text and allow for 2 or 3 clear line spaces after it. In total, this should be approximately 6.35 cm. You are going to print Exercise 3D directly on to this preprinted form in step 3.16.

3.13 Close the file **Memotemp**. Starting a new file, key in the following memo, using the line spacing as shown.

From: Mahsood Dabhad (insert title from exercise 3B)
To: Linda Braithwaite, Senior Consultant
Ref: MD/ZA/LB3

SALES TEAM WEEK END AWAY

I have contacted ~~several~~ 3 poss venues which would be appropriate for the team-building weekend event you are hoping to hold for the Sales Team, ~~week to~~ commencing (insert date of 3rd Friday of next month).

In order that I can ~~confirm~~ book places, I would (apreciate) it if you could supply me with a list of names (and sigs) of those staff who will (definately) be participating, along with any ~~diet any~~ special requirements they may (had).

(Acommodation) will normally be two staff to a room, altho' I ~~see~~ (acnowledge) that it may be necy for some staff to have (there) own (seperate) room. (the) Staff Development (Comitte) (have) agreed that all (expences) (for the event) will be paid for by the co, apart from drinks &

snacks from the bar. [Please let me know if you would like me to select a venue on yr behalf or if you would prefer to look at the brochures yourself first.

emphasise this sentence only in italic

3.14 Following the instructions given previously, alter the top margin so that the body of the document does not 'overprint' on top of the preprinted memo heading. Remember, you will probably need to enter a setting of approximately 6.35 cm for the top margin in order to allow for several clear line spaces after the letter heading text.

3.15 Save your document using filename **EX3D**.

3.16 Insert the preprinted memohead form (ie the document **Memotemp** which you printed out at step 3.14) correctly into your printer. Print the document **EX3D** directly on to the preprinted memohead form. Check your printout with the key at the back of the book. If you find any errors, retrieve the document and correct them.

3.17 Exit the program if you have finished working or continue straight on to the next unit.

UNIT 4 CONSOLIDATION 1

By the end of Unit 4, you will have revised and practised all the techniques and skills needed for the OCR/RSA Stage II Text Processing Part 1 Award.

Look at your Progress Review Checklist and at your completed exercises to remind yourself of what you have learnt so far and to identify any weaknesses. Then complete the following exercises as revision.

Exercise 4A

4.1 Retrieve your letterhead template file and save the document using the filename **EX4A**. Key in the following text. Use either a ragged or justified right margin.

4.2 Resave your document using the same filename **EX4A** and print one copy.

Mark the letter: For the attention of Mr Will Fry, General Manager

Our ref: NB/RTS
Your ref: WF/227

Peterson Tools Ltd
Mount View Business Park
Mount View Rd
HUDDERSFIELD
HD7 2BS

Dr Sirs

Thank you for yr recent correspondance concerning the photocopying machine we supplied to you earlier this month and which has since develloped a number of faults.

who has confirmed that the goods are not repairable

We have now obtained a full report from the mfr's own engineer. We understand that the engineer supplied you with a temp replacement machine to service yr immed requirements until we had the opp to make you an offers. Under the terms of yr gntee we are able to offer you a brand new replacement or, alternatively, we will credit yr a/c with the ~~full~~ total amount paid. I am ~~advised~~ told by our Stock ✓ Department that we could deliver & install a new copier in approx ~~two~~ 2 (weeks) time. If this is ~~alright~~ acceptable I would (aprecaite) it if you could add yr sig to the enclosed form & return it in the envelope provided. As a gesture of good will we are prepared to offer you a 2½% discount off the price of the (goods') to compensate for the (inconveneince) caused.

I look forward (shortly) to hearing from you.

Yrs scly

Nasreen Begum
Customer Care Manager

emphasise this sentence in bold

Exercise 4B

4.3 Retrieve your memorandum template file and save the document using the filename **EX4B**. Key in the following text. Use either a ragged or justified right margin.

From: (insert name from Ex4A), Customer Care Manager
To: Jim Gannon, Finance Officer
Ref: NB/RTS/JG17

CUSTOMER DISCOUNT

We have arranged to give Peterson Tools Ltd a discount of (insert the percentage amount from Ex4A) against the ~~price~~ cost of a new ~~replacement~~ photo copier, which they have ordered from us today as a replacement ~~against against~~ for ~~one~~ which was faulty.

(a previous machine bought from us earlier this month)

The ~~next~~ order number (are): RB200031ZX. ← (this sentence in bold)

Please can you credit their a/c with the amount appropriate and confirm, in writing, their new balance to ~~the~~ their General Manager, Mr W — F —. [I have arranged for the ✓ new ~~copier~~ goods to be delivered to their (premises') on (insert date of Friday of next week). I would (aprecaite) it if the ~~paper~~ necy documentation could (been) processed immed to avoid any further complaint from this customer.

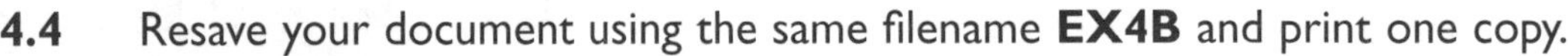

4.4 Resave your document using the same filename **EX4B** and print one copy.

Exercise 4C

4.5 Key in the following document using single line spacing except where indicated and following all the amendments shown. Use a justified right margin and number the pages at the bottom right.

4.6 Save your document using the filename **EX4C** and print a copy.

FAMILY LIFE ← (bold and centre)

The family has been ~~described~~ ref'd to as a kinship group, ie, a group of persons directly linked by kin connections, the ~~older people~~ adult members of which assume (responsability) for caring for children. Kinship (connection's) are based on blood, marriage or adoption. ← (keep this section only in double line spacing)

Types of Family

A recent study revealed that approx one quarter of households in the United Kingdom consists of a married couple and their dependent children. The traditional 'nuclear' family is where a husband and wife live with their children in the same house hold. ~~Sometimes~~ Often this is described as the [packet][cereal] family. ✓

The 'extended' family is where two or more generations either live together in the same household or see each other on a regular basis, eg daily. There has been a significant rise in the number of '1-parent' families . Over 22% of families with children is headed by a lone parent – nearly three times the proportion in 1971. This increase is beleived to be linked to the rise in the divorce rate and also in the number of births outside marriage (34% of babies are born to unmarried mothers, compared with 8% in 1971).

Their is also a rise in then number of 'reconstituted' families (step-families). divorce can lead to a new family being formed as one or both partners bring children from their past relationships into the new family.

Many of todays' families are subject to change and fluidity. Family members grow older, move in and out of different households through death, birth, divorce, marriage, or simply personal choice. Some people now advocate that family life has to be viewed more as a process, or a set of practices changing, rather than a permanent structure of relatively fixed roles and expectations.

Another example of the way in which family structures are becoming more diverse is the 'same-sex' family. This would be where, for instance, a woman leaves her husband and takes her children to live with another woman.

The Symmetrical Family

In 1975 the idea of the 'symmetrical' family was fashioned as Young and Wilmott put forward the view that relationships between husbands and wives had become far more balanced and egalitarian than in the past., with household chores and child care being increasingly shared.

It is apparent from earlier studies of working class families that marriage roles were highly segregated. Young and Wilmott's studies showed that seventy-two per cent of husbands regularly helped with the housework and that domestic labour was no longer a solely female preserve.

However, Ann Oakley in the 'Sociology of Housework', 1974, found no evidence to support this view. Her studies revealed that of the families she researched, only 15% of men had a high level of participation in housework. This has been supported by the further research of Jonathan Gershuny which shows that, altho' it is possible that there has been a moderate shift towards a 'symmetrical' pattern, the main burden of domestic work definately continues to be carried by the woman.

Additional text for Exercise 4C

Operator: this is the extra section for Exercise 4C

The Family in Society

(Altho') it is argued by some that the needs of pre-industrial society were met by the immobile extended family, historical research on family life in 17th century England by Peter Laslett, shows that the nuclear family, not the extended family, was the norm, and that considerable (mobility) geographical existed. However, a later study in 1861, found that the extended family was dominant and functioned as a 'mini-welfare state'.

From the middle of the twentieth century the extended family was 're-discovered' in working class communities such as Bethnal Green and Hull. The term 'dispersed extended family' was introduced to emphasise how families keep in touch with relatives through visits and the telephone.

Operator: replace the underline on all subheadings with bold and italic

UNIT 5 EXAMINATION PRACTICE 1

By the end of Unit 5, you will have completed a mock examination for the OCR/RSA Stage II Text Processing Part 1 Award.

OCR/RSA Stage II Text Processing Part 1

This examination assesses your ability to produce, from handwritten and typewritten draft, a letter, a memorandum and a report or article. The award demonstrates that you have acquired intermediate level skills in word processing (or typewriting).

The examination lasts for $1^1/_4$ hours and you have to complete three documents. Printing is done outside this time.

Examinations are carried out in registered centres and are marked by OCR/RSA examiners. The centre will give you instructions regarding stationery.

Letters must be produced on letterheads (either preprinted or template). Memos may be produced on preprinted forms, by keying in entry details or by use of a template. An additional piece of paper containing text to be incorporated into one of the documents will be handed to you during the examination.

Examination hints

When sitting your examination:

- you may use a manual prepared by the centre or the software manufacturer
- put your name, centre number and document number on each document
- check your work very carefully before printing – proofread, spellcheck
- assemble your printouts in the correct order at the end of the examination.

You are now ready to try a mock examination for Stage II Text Processing Part 1. Take care and good luck!

The list of assessment criteria for this mock examination is long and detailed. To be sure that you have reached the required standard to be entered for an examination, you need to work through several past papers and have these 'marked' by a tutor or assessor who is qualified and experienced in this field.

Document 1

Retrieve the letterhead template file and key in the following text. Use either a ragged or justified right margin. Save the document as **EX5A** and print one copy.

Our ref: JA:JP:dtv32

Mr Jordan Parry
264 Mayview St
SKIPTON
BD25 1TN

please mark the letter:
PERSONAL

Dr Mr Parry

I am writing with regard to yr recent job application for the post of Sales Adviser (Temp) with our co. I am pleased to advise you that you have been short-listed for the post and the panel would like to invite you to attend for an interview on (insert date of first Wednesday of next month) at 2.30 pm.

If this time is (unconveiniant), please let me know as soon as poss.

It will be necy for you to bring your qualification certificates with you for verification purposes. The interview will last for approx 30-45 minutes. You will also be asked to give a short presentation of 5 to 10 minutes summarising yr previous (experaince) & outlining yr plans for ~~extending~~ (develloping) the post. In the meantime, I shall contact yr referees to obtain their written refs. // (please) report to the main reception at 1415. A map showing the location of the co is enclosed.

Yrs scly

Jennifer Allwood
Personnel Assistant

during which you will be given an opp to ask questions about the org and (discus) various aspects of the post

operator:
emphasise the sentence about the short presentation in bold

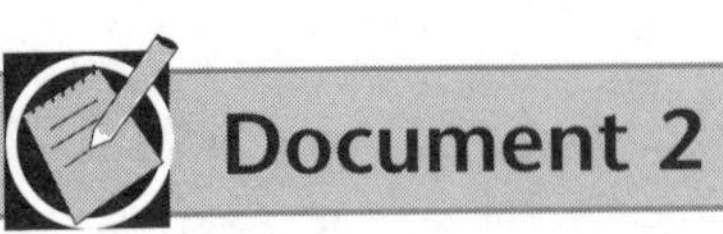

Document 2

Retrieve the memorandum template file and key in the following text. Use either a ragged or justified right margin. Save the document as **EX5B**, and print one copy.

From: Jennifer Allwood, P____ A____
To: Marion Jones, (insert title from Exercise 3c)
Ref: JA: MJ: dtv32

TEMP SALES ADVISER: POST DTV32

The date for interviewing candidates for the above post is now set for (insert date from Exercise 5A).

We will be interviewing a total of three applicants between 1.30 pm - 4.30 pm and I beleive you will be chairing the panel. I am enclosing the applications and CVs of each candidate for you to ~~look~~ check over and bring to the interview with you. [I also propose to hold a seperate pre-interview meeting next week to ~~do~~ discuss methods of scorings, agree the interview questions to be asked and to

Please can you e-mail me with the days and times are you available.

We also need to confirm finanshal arrangements for the post, as I understand from Payroll that their have been recent changes to the Sales Teams rates of commission and ~~also to the teams~~ claimable expences.

Document 3

Key in the following document using single line spacing except where indicated and following all the amendments shown. Use a justified right margin. Save the document using the filename **EX5C** and print one copy.

PAINTING WITH SPECIAL EFFECTS ← bold and centre

There are a number of different painting techniques, which can be applied to enhance the interior design of a room by giving a special effect. To create a soft, subtle effect, stick with colours from the same colour family. For a more dramatic effect, experiment with strong, contrasting colours. You can use ordinary paint, rather than a special effect paint, but remember that these will not be semi-transparent and will ~~do~~ dry much more quickly. Before applying any of the special effects refd to below, you will first need to apply a background colour using ordinary ~~emulsion~~ emulsion paint.

(This paragraph only in double line spacing)

RAG ROLLING

A natural sponge is the best type of sponge for this te4chnique.Use the appropriate size for the surface to be sponged, ie a large sponge for walls and a smaller sponge for corners, woodwork or furniture. be careful not to overload the sponge with paint – wipe of any excess first and practise on a piece of spare card. Dip the frilly side of your dampened sponge into the paint and on to your surface dab the sponge at different angles to obtain a random, freckle-like print. Try not to concentrate on isolated areas which will appear patchy, but rather to obtain an over all effect across the surface as a whole.

If you are using several colours, allow suficeint time for the first colour to dry thoroughly before applying the next. If you make a mistake, leave to dry, before re-applying the background paint or simply wipe over and re-sponge.

SPONGING

(then ~~xxxx~~ immed paint an adjacent block,)

Different rag rolling effects can be obtained by using a chamois, an old lace curtain, or even a 'scrunched up' plastic bag. Using a brush or roller, apply the paint evenly over a small section of the surface area. Then, while the paint is still wet, dampen your bunched ragging tool and roll it roughly across the surface to 'rag off' the paint in a random pattern. If you are covering a large areas rag one block, using a roller or brush to blend the two areas together before ragging the join;

Stand back from your work every now and again to make sure that you are blending the blocks together so that their are no obvious separate patches or marks where the wet edges have dried.

(Operator: insert the additional text here)

(number the pages)

DRAGGING

Apply the paint evenly in strips of approx 60 cm width. Then, dip a clean dragging brush into the paint, wipe excess on to a rag, then drag the brush (using the flat side) downwards thro' the paint.

After each stroke, it is advisable to wipe the brush with a rag to avoid a build up of paint. If the brush becomes clogged, dry on a rag, rinse it through quickly, and continue.

This is quite a difficult technique to apply to very ~~large~~ big areas, such as walls, and is best applied to smaller areas such as doors, window frames, cupboards, etc. When dragging wood, always ensure you drag in the same direction as the natural grain. When dragging a panelled door, drag each individual panel before doing the surrounding areas.

COLOUR WASHING

Use a special colourwash brush or a very soft, large decorating brush. Dip the brush into the paint, remove any excess, and apply to the surface in a haphazard criss-cross manner, at different angles. For the first coat, you should deliberately miss some patches. When the first coat are dry, apply a second coat of paint (either using the same colour or an alternative) in the same manner, going over the patches you missed earlier, to give a soft build up of colour. You can experiment with thinning the paint to acheive a more gradual colour build up and translucent effect – try 2 parts paint to one part water. Its best to work systematically across the surface and complete a whole wall at a time to create a soft, clouding effect. Stand back from your work every now and again to make sure that there are no obvious patches or marks where the wet edges have dried.

If the paint starts to ~~crack~~ dry and spreading it becomes difficult it may be necy to either moisten the brush with water or dampen the walls with a wet roller.

Additional text for Document 3

Keep re-bunching your ragging tool and apply the rag at different angles to obtain a random effect. If the rag becomes clogged, rinse it thro' quickly, squeeze out any excess water, & continue.

UNIT 6 ADVANCED MULTI-PAGE DOCUMENTS

By the end of Unit 6, you should have revised previously-learnt text processing skills such as:

- **changing the typing line length**
- **indenting text**
- **insetting margins**
- **rearranging text**
- **finding and replacing text.**

You should also have learnt how to:

- **insert headers and footers to appear on each page of a multi-page document**
- **allocate space within a document**
- **sort items, paragraphs or lists of information into a specific order.**

Changing the typing line length, indenting text and insetting margins

Please refer to Unit 1 of this book to refresh your memory on the methods for carrying out the above operations.

Exercise 6A

6.1 Open the document you saved as **EX2B** Save as **EX6A** and make the following amendments:

- Change the typing line length for the whole document to 13 cm.

Note: In OCR/RSA examinations, it is not necessary for left and right margins to be equal although this does give a balanced appearance to a document. It is acceptable to change the typing line by changing only the left or right margin. However, in practice, you will be governed by the use of the document, eg whether it is to be inserted into a binder, house style, author's preference etc.

- Change the right margin format for the whole document to ragged (unjustified).
- Change the paragraph commencing **After taking into account . . .** to single line spacing.
- Indent the whole section headed **ADVICE AND GUIDANCE** by 4 cm at the right to allow for the later insertion of a graphic.
- Indent the left and right margins of the paragraph headed **TUTOR SUPPORT** by 3 cm.

6.2 Using the Print Preview facility, check the format of the document carefully comparing it with the printout check at the back of the book. If you find any discrepancies, correct them. Resave your work and print one copy.

Rearrange text in a document

One of the most useful facilities of word processing is the ability to rearrange text on the screen and then print out when all the changes have been made. The first draft is then sent to the author of the text who marks up the printout to show what changes are needed. The word processor operator can recall the document from disk, edit the text and then print out the final copy.

Look back at Unit 2 to refresh your memory on correction signs.

Rearrangement of a document involves selecting, moving and copying blocks of text. Rearrangement of a document may involve the deletion of blocks of text, with or without replacement text being inserted. Rearrangement of a document frequently involves moving blocks of text from one position to another.

Rearrangement of a document can involve copying text, ie reproducing a block of text in another position within the document.

Note: Take care when following instructions – don't confuse **move** and **copy**.

Read the following sections to learn quick and efficient methods of selecting, deleting, moving and copying text.

Select text

When you want to change a block of text in some way, it is necessary first of all to shade or highlight the particular section of text. In Word 2000, this is called **selecting** text. The selected text shows in reverse – white letters on a black background, eg **selected text**.

To select	Keyboard	Mouse
One character (or more)	Press: **Shift** + → *or* **Shift** + ← (repeat until all required text is selected	Click and drag: The mouse pointer across the text
One word	Position the pointer: At the beginning of the word Press: **Shift** + **Ctrl** + → *or* Position the pointer: At the end of the word Press: **Shift** + **Ctrl** + ←	Double-click: The word
To the end of the line	Press: **Shift** + **End**	Click and drag: The mouse pointer right or down
To the beginning of the line	Press: **Shift** + **Home**	Click and drag: The mouse pointer left or up

To select	Keyboard	Mouse
A full line	Position the pointer: At the beginning of the line and press: **Shift + End** *or* position the pointer: At the end of the line and press: **Shift + Home**	Position the pointer: In the left margin (selection border) next to the required line and click
A paragraph	—	Position the pointer: In the selection border and double-click *or* Position the pointer: Within the paragraph and triple-click
The whole document	Press: **Ctrl + A**	Position the pointer: In the selection border and triple-click
Any block of text	—	Position the pointer: At the beginning of the text Hold down: The **Shift** key Position the pointer: At the end of the text and click
To remove selection:		
Click: In any white space within the document screen		

Delete a block of text

To delete larger portions of text, select the block of text you wish to delete and then operate the commands for deletion:	
Keyboard	**Mouse**
Select: The text to be deleted (as previously described in 'Selecting text') Press: **Del(ete)** *or* Press: ← (**backspace/delete key**)	Select: The **Cut** button on the Standard Tool Bar, *or* Select: **Cut** on the **Edit** menu, *or* Click: The right mouse button: Select: **Cut**

Quick delete and insert text

To delete an incorrect section of text (of any size) and replace with correct text (of any size).

Select the incorrect text and key in the new text:

Select: The text to be deleted (as previously described in **Selecting Text**)
Key in: The new text (without moving the cursor)
The incorrect text which was initially selected will disappear.

Restore deleted text (undo)

You can restore text which has been deleted accidentally. It is important that the pointer is in the correct place before you begin.

<table>
<tr><td colspan="2">To restore text immediately after deleting:</td></tr>
<tr><th>Keyboard</th><th>Mouse</th></tr>
<tr><td>Press: Ctrl + Z</td><td>Select: Edit from the menu bar
Select: Undo Clear
OR
Click: The Undo button on the Standard Tool Bar</td></tr>
<tr><td colspan="2">Word 2000 allows you to 'undo' many previous actions. These can be accessed by clicking on the button to the right of the Undo button on the Standard Tool Bar.</td></tr>
</table>

Move a block of text

You can move sections of text quickly without deleting and retyping. This facility is sometimes called **Cut and Paste**. Text to be moved is 'cut' and placed on the 'clipboard', and then 'pasted' into its new position.

Keyboard	Mouse
Select: The block of text to be moved Press: **F2** Move: The pointer to the new position Press: ↵ (**return/enter**) *OR*	Select: The block of text to be moved Select: **Edit** from the menu bar Select: **Cut** (the text disappears from screen and is put on the clipboard) Move: The pointer to the new position Select: **Edit** from the menu bar Select: **Paste** (the text reappears in its new position) *OR*
Select: The block of text to be moved Press: **Ctrl** + **X** (the text disappears from the screen) Move: The pointer to the new position Press: **Ctrl** + **V** (the text reappears in its new position)	Click: The **Cut** button on the Standard Tool Bar Move: The pointer to the new position Click: The **Paste** button on the Standard Tool Bar *OR* Click: The right mouse button Select: **Cut** Move: The pointer to the new position Hold down: **Ctrl** *and* Click: The right mouse button; *or* Click: The right mouse button Select: **Paste**

Copy a block of text

Copying a block of text means that the text will remain in its original place in the document and a copy of the same text is inserted elsewhere. This facility is sometimes called **Copy and Paste** – a copy of the text to be 'copied' is placed on the 'clipboard' and then 'pasted' into its new position.

Keyboard	Mouse
Select: The block of text to be copied Press: **Ctrl + C** Move the pointer to the required position Press: **Ctrl + V**	Select: The block of text to be copied Select: **Edit** from the menu bar Select: **Copy** (the text remains on screen and a copy is put on the clipboard) Move: The pointer to the required position Select: **Edit** from the menu bar Select: **Paste** (a copy of the text appears in its required position) *OR* Click: The **Copy** button on the Standard Tool Bar Move: The pointer to the new position **Click:** The **Paste** button on the Standard Tool Bar *OR* Click: The right mouse button Select: **Copy** Move: The pointer to the new position Click: The right mouse button Select: **Paste**

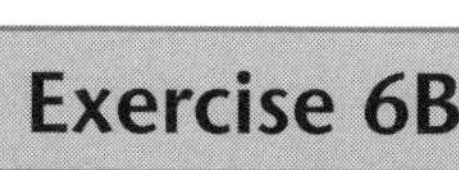

Exercise 6B

6.3 Open the document saved as **EX2E**.

6.4 Change the paragraphs in double line spacing to single line spacing.

6.5 Save as **EX6B** and then rearrange the text as shown below.

Left-align heading

SPECIAL OFFERS ON NEW PRODUCTS

AUTUMN SEASON

In response to the feedback our salesmen have received from customers, we are proud to announce the following new products. These will be available from 1 August and a 10% reduction on prices will be offered through to the end of November.

HOW TO ORDER

Simply complete order forms and forward in the ~~usual way~~. pre-paid envelope

Hazelnut dessert in 125g square pots; packs of 4, 6 packs per box. A popular new flavour to add to the range; £6.00 per box, RRP £1.49.

Peach and mango yoghurt in 150g round pots; packs of 6, 6 packs per box. An exotic addition to your Bonavitale yoghurt range; £8.00 per box, RRP £1.75.

Organic chocolate dessert in 125g square pots; packs of 4, 6 packs per box. An old favourite brought up to date; £7.10 per box, RRP £1.69.

Geisha soy sauce in 100ml bottles; packs of 6, 4 packs per box. A delicious new version of an old Japanese speciality; £11.00 per box, RRP £0.65.

Decaffeinated Ceylon tea in 40-bag cartons; packs of 24, 24 packs per box. A refreshing drink for your health-conscious customers; £18.73 per box; RRP £1.00.

NEW TELEPHONE ORDER LINE

*

Our telephone order line is now open between:

8.00 am - 8.00 pm Monday – Wednesday
8.00 am - 6.00 pm Thursday – ~~Sunday~~ Sat 10.00 am – 4 pm Sun

Please give your customer number and telephone number including area code when placing an order. Copy to end of document

DELIVERY

Remember, delivery is <u>FREE</u> within a 30-mile radius. Between 30 miles and 70 miles, there is a carriage charge of £25.00. Distances over a 70-mile radius are charged at £40.00 per delivery.

For delivery days, see schedule on Page 310 of catalogue.

MINIMUM ORDER – £200.00.

PLEASE NOTE: VAT AT 17.5% TO BE ADDED TO ALL ITEMS.

TELEPHONE 01342-564329 Copy to * and align at left margin when copied

Change position of page number to bottom centre

6.6 Using the Print Preview facility, check the format of the document carefully. Do not close the file. There is no need to print at this stage.

6.7 Add the following text to the end of the document on your screen. Insert immediately before the centred text Telephone **01342-564329**.

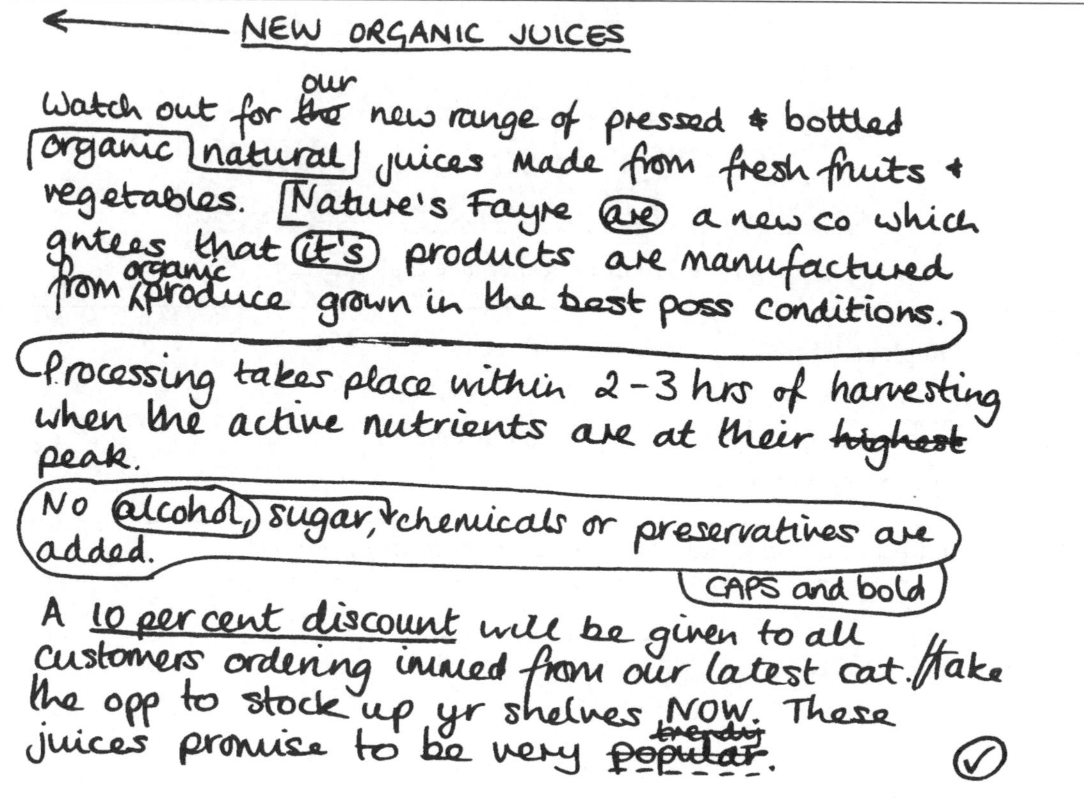

NEW ORGANIC JUICES

Watch out for ~~the~~ our new range of pressed & bottled organic natural juices made from fresh fruits & vegetables. Nature's Fayre are a new co which gntees that it's products are manufactured from organic produce grown in the best poss conditions.

Processing takes place within 2-3 hrs of harvesting when the active nutrients are at their ~~highest~~ peak.

No alcohol sugar, chemicals or preservatives are added.

CAPS and bold

A 10 per cent discount will be given to all customers ordering immed from our latest cat. Take the opp to stock up yr shelves NOW. These juices promise to be very ~~popular~~ trendy.

6.8 Proofread the additional text carefully. Do not close the file. Resave the document. There is no need to print at this stage.

Find (search) and replace

In word processing, it is possible to find automatically a given word or phrase and exchange it for another given word throughout a document.

You can use Word 2000's find and replace function in two different ways (the first method is the safer in examinations):

1 You can ask Word 2000 to stop every time it has located the 'find' word and wait for your confirmation before it 'replaces' the word (Replace). If you find an entry that you do not wish to be changed, you can skip over it and move to the next occurrence of the search (Find Next).

2 You can allow Word 2000 to go straight through the document 'finding and replacing' without stopping for confirmation from you (Replace All).

Keyboard	Mouse/menu
Press: **Ctrl + H**	Select: **Edit, Replace**

The **Find and Replace** dialogue box is displayed on screen.

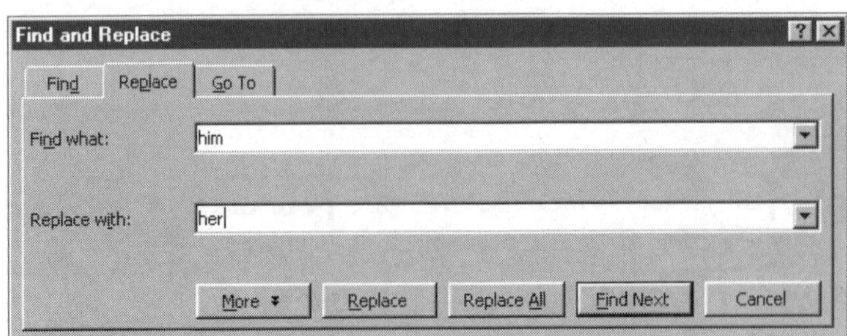

Figure 6.1 Find and Replace dialogue box

- Select: The **Replace** tab
- In the **Find what** box, key in: The text to be searched for
- In the **Replace with** box, key in: The replacement text
- Click: The **Find next** button

Select from the find and replace dialogue buttons as appropriate:

Button	Action
Find Next	Skips an entry which you do not wish to be changed and moves to the next occurrence of the search
Replace	Allows control over each replacement one at a time
Replace All	Replaces all occurrences automatically
More	Displays more advanced find and replace criteria. (**More** changes to **Less** when you select more advanced criteria.) This option includes:
Match case	Finds the exact combination of upper-case and lower-case letters
Find whole words only	Finds occurrences that are not part of a larger word (eg the word *rate* could appear in *irate*, *crate*, *desecrated*)
Format	Replaces text formatting, eg replace bold with underline
Special Search	Finds special characters such as paragraph mark, graphic etc: **All** – searches through all the document **Down** – searches from the insertion point to the end of the document **Up** – searches from the insertion point to the start of the document

Keyboard	Mouse/menu
Press: **Esc** to finish	Select: **Cancel** to finish

Find text (without replacing)

If you only want to find text (without replacing it) similar commands can be accessed through the **Find** dialogue box.

Keyboard	Mouse/menu
Press: **Ctrl+F**	Select: **Edit**, **Find** from the menu

Exercise 6B continued

6.9 Use the Find/Replace function to change **pots** to **tubs**, **organic** to **pure** throughout the document on your screen.

6.10 Check your document carefully comparing it with the printout check at the back of the book. If you find any errors, correct them. Resave your work and print one copy.

Headers and footers

A header is a piece of text in the form of a title, heading or reference which appears at the top of all pages of a multi-page document. A footer is the same kind of text appearing at the bottom of all pages. Headers and footers are printed within the top and bottom margins.

This word processing function allows you to 'set' the headers and footers by keying in the text once only. The header and footer will then appear automatically on all pages (see Figure 6.2). Headers and footers can be edited if the text or layout needs to be changed.

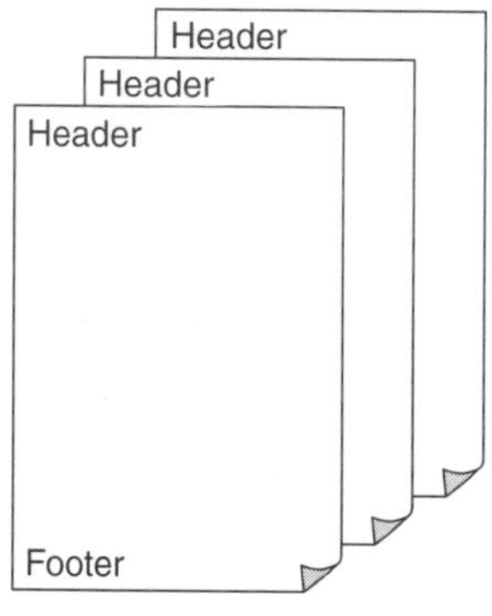

Figure 6.2

Using the header/footer function in intermediate examinations

In intermediate examinations, you will be asked to insert a header or a footer in a two- or three-page document, and also to insert page numbering. Unfortunately, Word 2000 does not allow you to omit the page number on the first page and use a header/footer because page numbering operates within the header/footer text box. Therefore, we recommend that you insert the header or footer and accept page numbering on all pages. Otherwise, you would have to key in the header twice.

Although the benefit of using a header and footer in this way may not be apparent in a two-page document, if you were producing a document with many pages, the value of the header/footer command would be clear. You should practise using headers/footers so that you are familiar with the concept and you could use them in employment.

Set the format for headers and footers

Before keying in *or* after keying in:

Mouse/menu

- Position the cursor: At the beginning of the document
- Select: **Header and Footer** from the View menu

The **Header** text box and the **Header and Footer** Tool Bar are displayed on screen.

Figure 6.3 Header text box and Header and Footer Tool Bar

To insert a text header:

- Key in: The required text in the **Header** text box
- Click: **OK**

Note: Header and Footer text can be formatted in the same way as document text – eg tab stops, text emphasis, font changes.

To insert a text footer:

- Click: The **Switch between Header and Footer** button on the Header and Footer Tool Bar
- Key in: The required text in the **Footer** text box
- Click: **OK**

The following options are available on the Header and Footer Tool Bar:

Tooltip title	Function
Insert Autotext	Inserts selected text into the header/footer, eg **Page 5 of 12, Last saved on . . .**
Insert Page Number	Adds the page number to the header/footer at the current insertion marker position
Insert Number of Pages	Inserts total number of pages in the document
Format Page Number	Allows page number format changes – eg Arabic (1,2,3), Roman (I/II/III, i/ii/iii) etc
Insert Date **Insert Time**	Automatically inserts current details from computer settings into the header or footer
Page Setup	Displays the **Page Setup** dialogue box – to allow changes to margins, layout etc

Tooltip title	Function
Show/Hide Document Text	Shows or hides the current document on screen – a toggle switch
Same as Previous Show Previous Show Next	Used when creating different headers and footers for even/odd pages
Close	Closes the Header and Footer Tool Bar and returns to the document screen
Note: Headers and footers show on the screen in Print Layout view and Print Preview only.	

Delete headers, footers and page numbering

Mouse/menu
◎ Select: **Header and Footer** from the **View** menu ◎ Select: The header text, footer text or page number using the mouse ◎ Press: ← (backspace key) or **Del(ete)** ◎ Check: The deletion using Print Preview or Print Layout View

Exercise 6C

6.11 Open the document you saved as **EX6A**. Save as **EX6C** and delete the page numbering already present. Set a header to show the following details:

Your name Exercise 6C Your OCR/RSA Centre No (if applicable)

If you have already keyed in these details at the top of Exercise 6A, delete them from the document – otherwise they will be printed twice!

6.12 Refer to the instructions on **page numbering** in Unit 2 and insert page numbers in Arabic (ie 1, 2, 3) format at the bottom left of each page.

6.13 Check that the header and page numbering is present on both pages of the document by selecting Print Layout View or by selecting File, Print Preview.

Note: If you find that headers and footers are not present in Print Preview, it may be necessary to increase the header/footer space allowance by changing the Page Setup as follows:

◎ Select: **File**, **Page Setup**
◎ Increase the measurement in the **From edge** box (Header or Footer as appropriate)

6.14 Change the line length of the document to 15 cm, but retain the indented right margin for the paragraph headed **Advice and Guidance** at 4 cm from the new right margin.

6.15 Reduce the indentation of the left and right margins of the section headed **Tutor support** from 3 cm to 2 cm.

6.16 Indent the list of skills commencing **Art and Design** by 4 cm from the left margin.

6.17 Check your document carefully comparing it with the printout check at the back of the book. If you find any errors, correct them. Save your work and print one copy.

Multi-page document – formatting requirements

In intermediate examinations, you will be expected to move around the document quickly, organise the editing of text, and make the following formatting changes to multi-page documents:

- Allocate space
- Sort (rearrange) items

Allocating space

You may be required to leave space within a document for the later insertion of a picture or diagram. In OCR/RSA examinations the measurement required is given in centimetres. The best time to insert the space is *after* all text insertion and amendments have been done but *before* pagination.

To leave a space of a given measurement in inches, mm, cm, points, use the Format, Paragraph command:

- Delete: Any space already present
- Position the cursor: Just before the first character of the text that is going to come after the space
- Select: **Format**, **Paragraph**, **Indents** and **Spacing** from the menu bar
- Key in: The required measurement (in the stated unit of measurement) in the **Before** box

Word 2000 will accept the measurement in centimetres, inches or points, and will then convert this into the unit of measurement currently in use (usually centimetres).

Organise text in a multi-page document

When a document runs into several pages and there are many changes to be made, you may sometimes get a feeling of being 'lost' – particularly if you have been distracted. The following is a suggested method of working which you might like to adopt in order to avoid this:

1. Set the headers and page numbering and view them to check that they are correct.
2. Carry out all the necessary text amendments, eg inserting or deleting of text throughout the whole document.
3. Move and copy blocks of text as requested throughout the whole document.
4. Find and replace text as requested.
5. Allocate space (using the given measurement) and indent or inset margins as requested.
6. Paginate your document as requested or as you think fit (read the instructions).
7. Use the 'Spelling and Grammar' tool to check the whole document, amending as necessary.
8. Proofread the whole document, comparing it word for word with the original.
9. Print Preview your document to make sure that it will be printed correctly.
10. Print your work.

Moving around the document – quick methods

When you are checking and proofreading a multi-page document, you need to be able to move quickly from one section to another. Practise the following quick cursor movements so that you become familiar with them and use them regularly:

To move	Keyboard
Left word by word	Press: **Ctrl** + ← (arrow key) (hold down the Ctrl key and press the ← key whilst the Ctrl key is still held down)
Right word by word	Press: **Ctrl** + →
To the end of the line	Press: **End**
To the start of the line	Press: **Home**
To the top of the paragraph	Press: **Ctrl** + ↑
To the bottom of the paragraph	Press: **Ctrl** + ↓
Up one screen	Press: **Page Up**
Down one screen	Press: **Page Down**
To the top of the document	Press: **Ctrl** + **Home**
To the bottom of the document	Press: **Ctrl** + **End**

Go To command

Keyboard	Mouse
Press: **Ctrl + G**	Select: **Edit, Go To**

The **Find and Replace** dialogue box is displayed on screen.

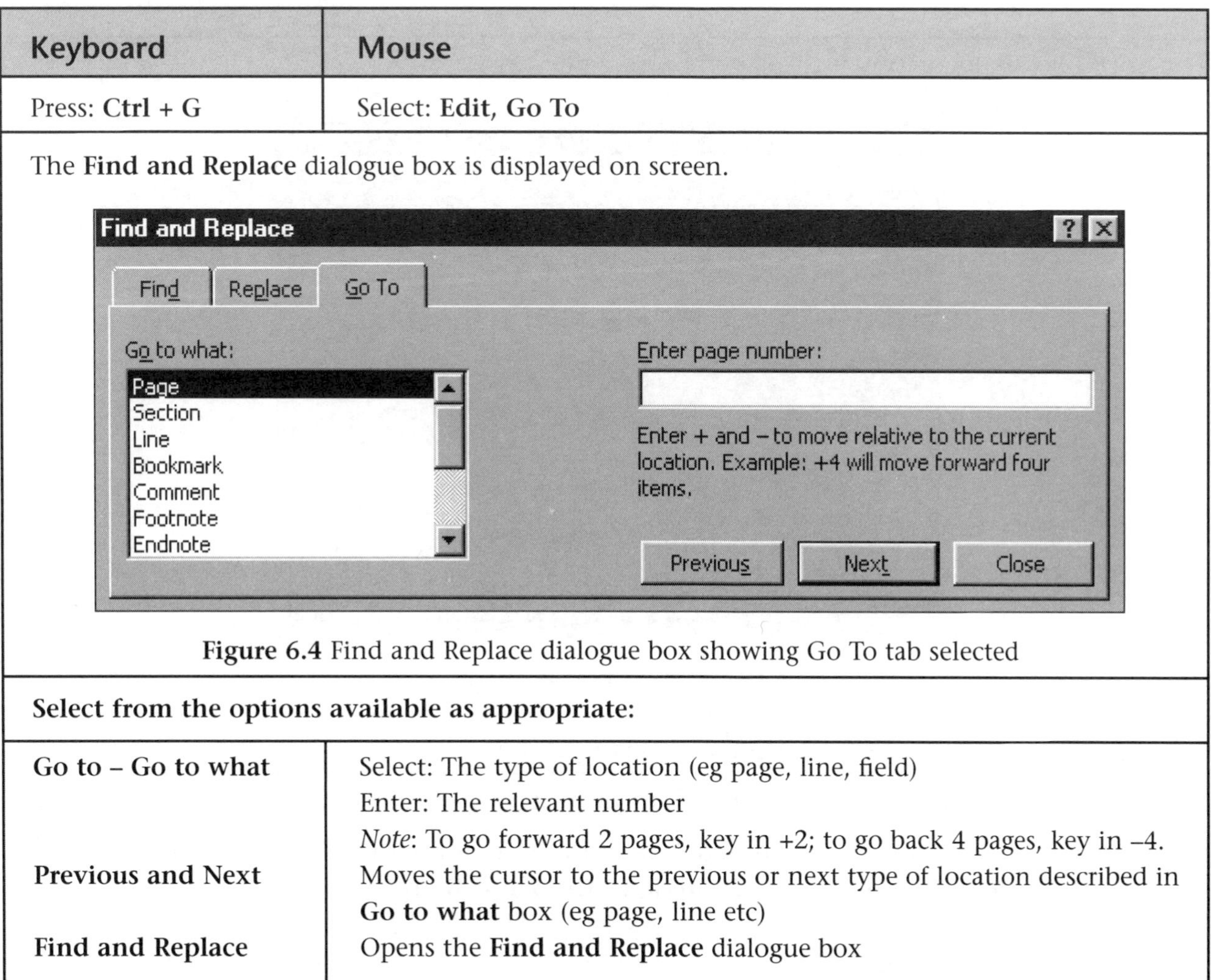

Figure 6.4 Find and Replace dialogue box showing Go To tab selected

Select from the options available as appropriate:

Go to – Go to what	Select: The type of location (eg page, line, field) Enter: The relevant number *Note*: To go forward 2 pages, key in +2; to go back 4 pages, key in –4.
Previous and Next	Moves the cursor to the previous or next type of location described in **Go to what** box (eg page, line etc)
Find and Replace	Opens the **Find and Replace** dialogue box

Sort (rearrange) items

Rearrangement of a document often includes sorting a list of items into a given order. There are several ways to do this:

- Before keying in the items, use a piece of scrap paper to note down, in advance, the order in which the entries should be keyed in.
- After keying in, use the cut and paste functions to sort/rearrange the items into the required order.
- After keying in, use Word 2000's automatic sort facility.

Word 2000 will rearrange automatically information in selected rows, lists or in a series of paragraphs. The items may be sorted alphabetically, numerically or by date, and in either ascending (A-Z) or descending (Z-A) order. It is possible to sort an entire list, or to select a section of the list. If appropriate you can sort a list before or after adding numbers to it – Word 2000 renumbers the list automatically if the order changes.

If two items start with the same character, Word 2000 takes account of subsequent characters in each item to determine the sort order. If an entire field is the same for two items, Word 2000 takes account of subsequent specified fields to determine the sort order (eg surnames and first names).

- Select: The items or text to be sorted
- Select: **Sort Text** from the **Table** menu (if the items are in a table the command name changes to Sort)

The **Sort Text** dialogue box is displayed on screen.

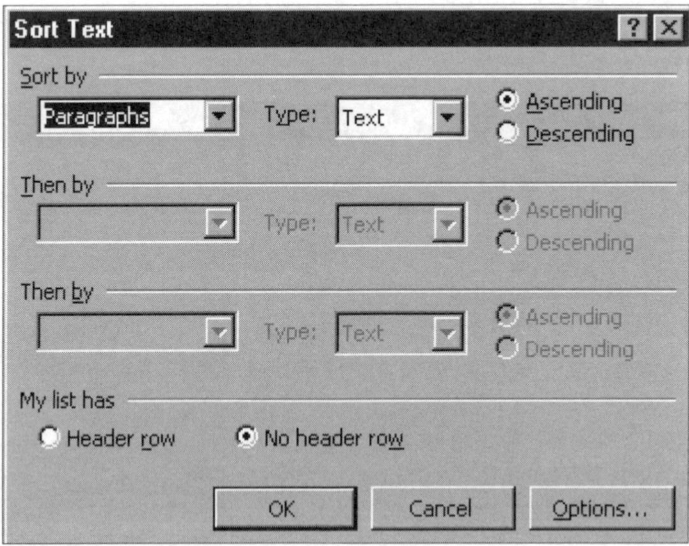

Figure 6.5 Sort Text dialogue box

Select from the sort dialogue options as appropriate:

Sort by	Select: **Paragraphs** or a **field number** – you can sort up to 3 fields or criteria
Then By	You may specify subsequent sort criteria for additional fields/columns by entering further sort criteria in the **Then By** boxes

Type	Select: The type of information to be sorted – text, numbers or dates Word 2000 will accept several different date formats (eg Jan 27 2001, 27 Jan 2001, Jan-01, 1-27-01, 1/27/01, 1-27-01)
Header Row /No Header Row	Select: The appropriate setting according to whether you wish the header row of your list to be included in the sort or not
Ascending	To sort in ascending order (eg A-Z, 1-100, 1 January 20xx – 31 December 20xx)
Descending	To sort in descending order (eg Z-A, 100-1, 31 December 20xx – 1 January 20xx)
OK	Click: **OK** to operate sort
Undo Sort	Click: The **Undo** button on the Standard Tool Bar

Exercise 6D

6.18 Open the document you saved as **EX6C** if it is not already on the screen. Save the document as **EX6D** and carry out the following amendments:

- Change the position of the header to the top right of the document.
- Change the position of the page numbering to the bottom right of the document.
- Change the alignment of the document to the fully-justified style.
- Rearrange the text as shown.

THE WAY IN PROGRAMME

INTRODUCTION AND INFORMATION

The Way In Programme is designed so that learners can select a number of vocationally related skills from the miscellaneous programmes listed below.

Art and Design
Health and Social Care
Brickwork
Plumbing
Painting and Decorating
Woodwork
Hairdressing
Numeracy
Literacy
Computers

Copy to *

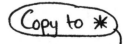

After taking into account previous experience and interests, each learner can make up their own individual programme. Learners can study what they want and we guarantee that tutors are specially trained to meet learner needs and draw on learner strengths.

**
Insert extra text here later

The Way In Programme offers nationally recognised qualifications and later an opportunity to progress onto a vocational programme. Each learner is given a personal plan immediately and specific support is provided for students with learning difficulties.

leave a space of at least 3cm here

Change to single line spacing

TUTOR SUPPORT

Tutors can help with spoken and written English and with understanding and carrying out basic calculations, etc. This work is integrated into the practical skills to enhance understanding and competence. Spelling, attention to detail, vocabulary, numeracy and commercial awareness are developed in a realistic manner.

COMPUTERS

Many jobs need some understanding of computers nowadays. It is possible for students to spend approximately 2 hours per week learning keyboard skills and acquiring some knowledge of the everyday use of computers in offices and in industry.

Local organisations and manufacturers may provide short work placements towards the end of the year in June or July.

move to **

ADVICE AND GUIDANCE

* retain indented right margin for copied paragraph here

Our advisers give advice and offer guidance on all aspects of education and training throughout the year. Prospective students can drop in at any time. Facilities are available for confidential interviews.

leave a space of 4cm at least here please

ASSISTANCE WITH COSTS

Many students on full-time courses are eligible for help with travel and child care costs. Although it is not possible to guarantee a place for everyone, the majority of students are given the opportunity of placing their child or children in the College's own nursery.

APPLICATION AND ENROLMENT

Details available from the Guidance Unit.

Exercise 6D continued

6.19 Add the text shown below, sorting the items into ascending alphabetical order and allocating space between paragraphs as requested.

Students have been ~~fortunate enough~~ (able) to gain valuable experience with the following local orgs. All of the cos listed below have indicated that they would be happy to take ~~students~~ (learners) on placements again in the future.

Woods Direct
Cross & Wilkinson Ltd
Yorkshire Elevators Plc
Sugden Electronics Ltd
Fernville House
Designs on You (Hair and Beauty)
Inn Place
Lancaster & Derby Building Society
Carey, Roy, Howard & Co

Single line-spacing for this list

Alphabetical order and indent by 4cm please

6.20 Replace the word **learners** with the word **students** throughout the document wherever it occurs.

6.21 Proofread your work carefully. Using the Print Preview facility, check the format of the document carefully comparing it with the printout check at the back of the book. If you find any errors, correct them. Resave the document and print one copy.

Exercise 6E

6.22 Open the document you saved as **EX6B**. Save it as **EX6E** and carry out the following amendments:

- Change the line length of the document to 13 cm.
- Change the alignment of the document to the fully-justified style.
- Insert a header:

Your name **Exercise 6E** **Centre No** (if appropriate)

- Insert a footer: **Autumn Catalogue** using Times New Roman font size 10, italic and centred.
- Delete the existing page numbering and insert page numbering at the top right of each page.
- Centre the main heading and increase the font size to 16.
- Embolden all the underlined headings.
- Change the word **dessert** to **mousse** wherever it occurs.
- Leave a space of at least 5 cm above the heading **NEW PURE JUICES**.

6.23 Using the Print Preview facility, check the format of the document carefully comparing it with the printout check at the back of the book, If you find any errors, correct them. Resave the document and print one copy.

6.24 Exit the program if you have finished working or continue straight on to the next unit.

UNIT 7 TABLES

By the end of Unit 7, you should have learnt how to:

- **complete a table with sub-divided columns and multi-line headings**
- **rearrange/sort items in the table into a specified order.**

Tables

Data is often presented in columns within letters, memos and reports to convey information quickly and clearly. Tabulated columns of information are also used for separate tables and accounts. Word 2000 offers several different methods for producing a table layout, including the **Insert Table** and **Tables and Borders** facilities which allow you to organise information on a page using a grid. You should practise using both methods and choose the one you feel most comfortable with, although you can actually use a combination of both if you wish. Some of the benefits of Word 2000's Table facilities are that it is easy to:

- position tables anywhere you want on the page
- move or 'drag' the table to a different position on the page
- edit the lines, fills, borders, and cell colours
- add rows and columns
- merge and split cells to display sub-divided columns and multi-line headings
- re-size either the entire table or the individual table cells
- control the alignment of text and/or objects within the table cells
- sort cell contents into a particular order, eg alphabetical
- wrap text around the table
- position several tables side by side
- insert a table within a table
- rearrange items in the table in a specified order.

In the Stage II Word Processing Part 2 examination you will be asked to key in a table with a number of columns containing a large amount of data, and which may include sub-divided or multi-line column headings. You will also be asked to sort the data into a particular order. Instructions on the different methods of producing a table were included in the first book of this series but are repeated in this unit for ease of reference.

If the table is quite large, you may also need to give consideration to making it fit on the page/paper size being used by reducing the left and right margins to 1.27 cm or reducing the font size. It is best to do this before the table is inserted. Although extra rows can be added quite easily, adding extra columns can create difficulties.

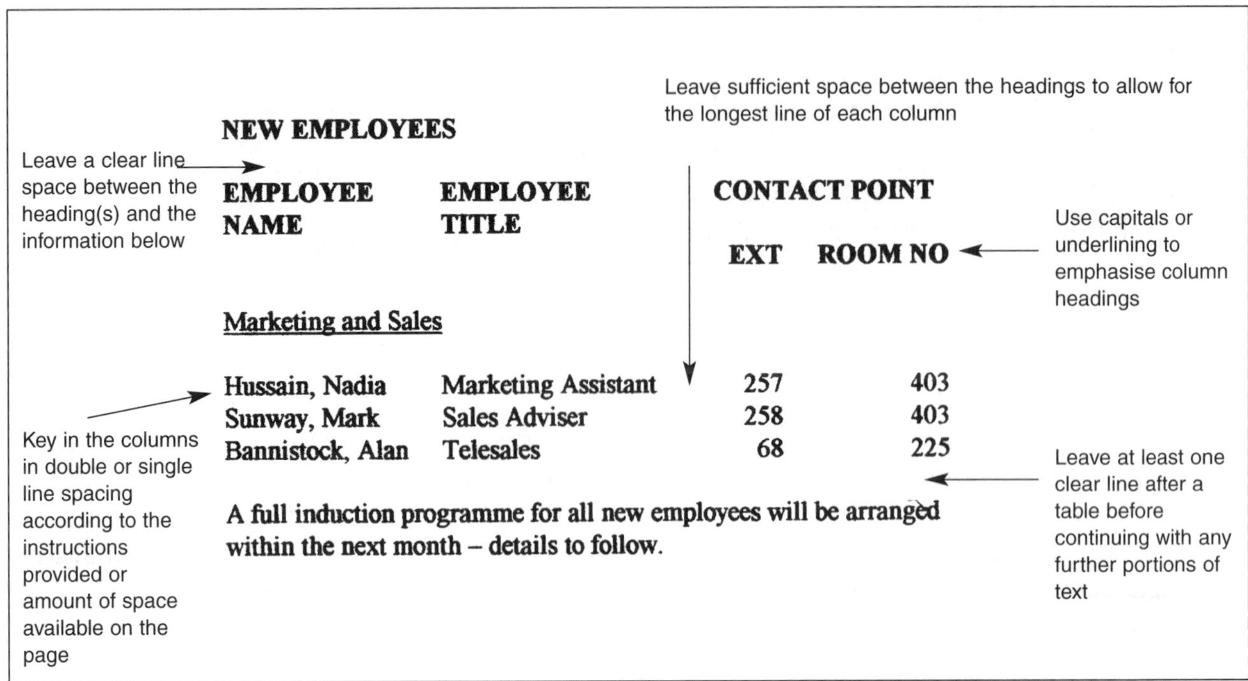

Note: In the examination you will be asked to move a section of the table, such as a column, to a different place. If the table has sub-divided and/or multi-line column headings it is often more difficult to change the layout afterwards. It is suggested that you plan out the table layout on a piece of scrap paper beforehand. Spending a few minutes at the planning stage may save you a lot more time and frustration later!

Insert Table facility

Mouse/tool bar method

- Position: The cursor where you want the table to be placed
- Click: The Insert Table button on the Standard Tool Bar (a drop-down grid of rows and column cells appears on screen)
- Select: The number of rows and columns required by moving the mouse pointer across the grid until the bottom of the grid displays the correct layout (eg 4 × 4 table). The grid will increase in size as you drag the mouse. Release the mouse button.

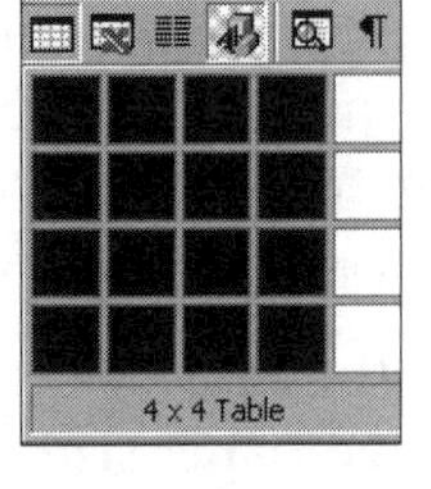

Figure 7.1 Insert Table drop-down grid

Menu method

- Position: The insertion point where you want the table to be placed
- Select: **Insert Table** from the **Table** menu.

  The Insert Table dialogue box appears on screen.

  After making your selections, click: **OK**.

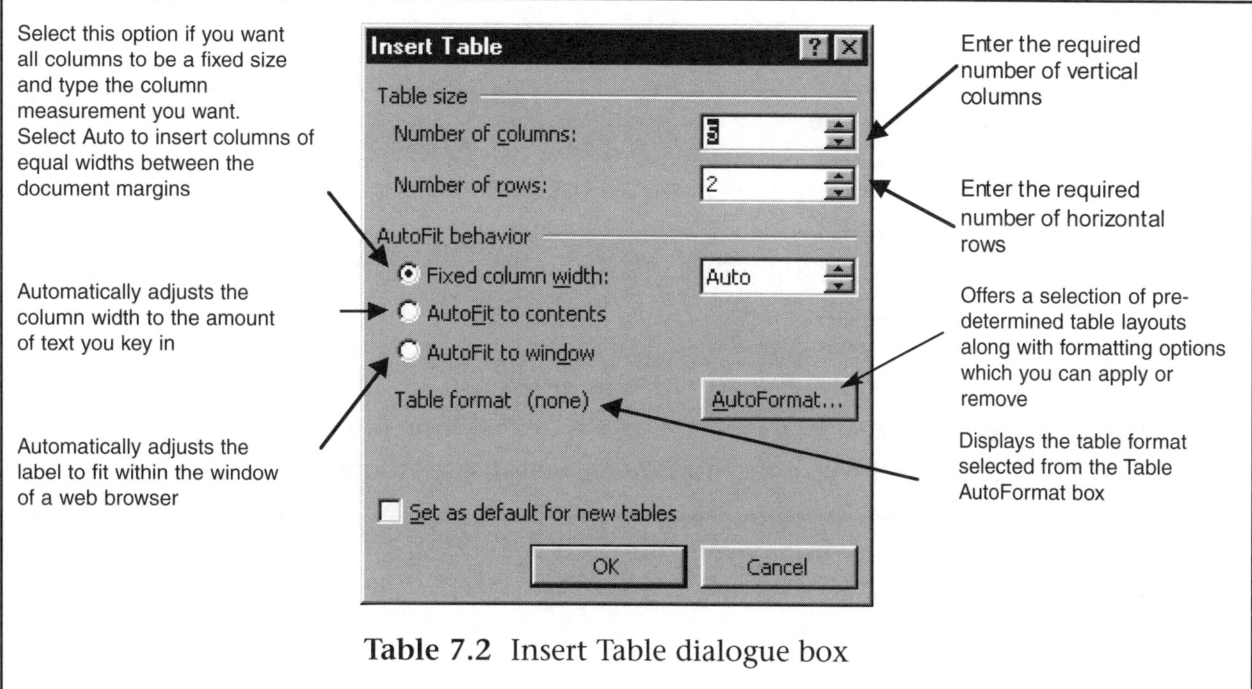
Select this option if you want all columns to be a fixed size and type the column measurement you want. Select Auto to insert columns of equal widths between the document margins
Automatically adjusts the column width to the amount of text you key in
Automatically adjusts the label to fit within the window of a web browser
Insert Table
Table size
Number of columns:
3
Number of rows:
2
AutoFit behavior
Fixed column width:
Auto
AutoFit to contents
AutoFit to window
Table format (none)
AutoFormat...
Set as default for new tables
OK
Cancel
Enter the required number of vertical columns
Enter the required number of horizontal rows
Offers a selection of pre-determined table layouts along with formatting options which you can apply or remove
Displays the table format selected from the Table AutoFormat box

Table 7.2 Insert Table dialogue box

Tables and Borders facility

Mouse/tool bar method

- Position: The insertion point where you want the table to be placed
- Click: The **Tables and Borders** button on the Standard Tool Bar

The **Tables and Borders** Tool Bar appears on screen.

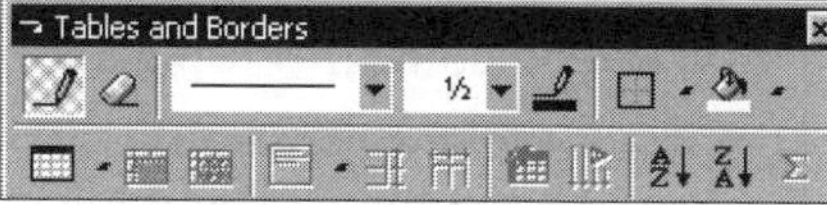
Tables and Borders
½

Figure 7.3 Tables and Borders Tool Bar

Use the **Draw Table** tool like a pen to draw your table layout directly on to the screen.

Click and drag: To draw the table outline and the cell divisions inside the table.

You can edit the table later to make individual cells any height and width you want.

Use the **Eraser** tool to remove any cell, row or column partition that you don't want, or to merge two adjacent cells vertically or horizontally.

Use the **Border** tool to set the table's ruled lines. Select: The entire table or the individual cells to which you wish to apply a border, or no border. To choose no lines on the table, click on the **Border** tool, then select the **No Border** button from the drop-down menu.

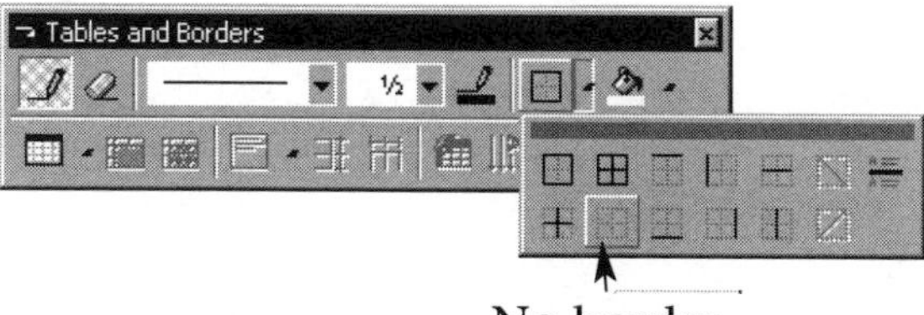
Tables and Borders
½
No border

Figure 7.4 Border styles drop-down box

Moving around

Keyboard	
Arrow keys	You can move around the table using the appropriate arrow keys
Tab	Moves right one cell (or inserts a new row when pressed in the last table cell)
Shift + **Tab**	Moves left one cell
Ctrl + **Tab**	Moves to next tab stop in the cell
Alt + **Home** or **End**	Moves to first or last cell in the same row
Alt + **PgUp** or **PgDn**	Moves to top or bottom cell in the column
OR Click: The mouse pointer in any cell you want to move to	

Select items

Mouse/menu	
To select a single cell:	Click: The left edge of the cell
To select a single row:	Click: To the left of the row, *or* Click: Anywhere in the relevant row Select: **Select Row** from the **Table** menu
To select a single column:	Click: The column's top gridline or border when the black arrow appears *or* Click: Anywhere in the relevant column Select: **Select Column** from the **Table** menu
To select multiple cells, rows or columns:	Drag: The mouse pointer across the cells, rows, or columns, *or* Select: A single cell, row, or column Hold down: The shift key and Click: Another cell, row, or column
To select an entire table:	Position: The cursor anywhere in the table Select: **Select Table** from the **Table** menu

Keyboard	
To select the next cell's contents:	Press: The **Tab** key
To select the preceding cell's contents:	Press: **Shift** + **Tab**
To extend a selection to adjacent cells:	Hold down: The **Shift** key and press an arrow key repeatedly
To select a column(s):	Click: In the column's top or bottom cell Hold down: The **Shift** key and press: The Up ↑ arrow or Down ↓ arrow key repeatedly
To extend a selection (or block):	Press: **Ctrl** + **Shift** + **F8** Press: The arrow keys to extend in the required direction Click: Outside the table Press: **Esc** to cancel selection mode
To remove the selection:	Press: **Shift** + **F8**

Change the column width

Mouse	Menu
Point to: The dividing line between the column and the adjacent column and press the left mouse button down *The pointer changes to a* [icon] *double-headed arrow* Drag: The column-dividing line to the left or right to increase or decrease the column width as appropriate Release: The mouse button	Click: In the column(s) to be changed Select: **Table Properties** from the **Table** menu, then select the **Column** tab Enter: The required column measurement in the **Preferred width** box Click: **OK**

To display column width measurements on the ruler:

- Click: In a cell and then hold down the **Alt** key as you drag the markers on the ruler

To make several columns or cells exactly the same width:

- Select: The columns or cells
- Select: **Autofit, Distribute Columns Evenly** from the **Table** menu, *or*
- Click: The [icon] **Distribute Columns Evenly** button on the **Tables and Borders** Tool Bar

To make the columns automatically fit the contents

- Click: The cursor insertion point inside the table
- Select: **Autofit** from the **Table** menu
- Click: **Autofit to Contents**

Change the row height

Mouse	Menu
Select: The row(s) to be changed Check: That you are in Print Layout View Drag: The row-dividing line (on the vertical ruler) up or down to increase or decrease the row height as appropriate. Row marker (dividing line) The pointer changes to a double-headed arrow and the Adjust Table Row tooltip appears Release: The mouse button	Select: The row(s) to be changed Select: **Table Properties** from the **Table** menu, then select the **Row** tab Enter: The required row measurement in the **Specify height** box Click: **OK**

To make several rows or cells exactly the same height:

- Select: The rows or cells
- Select: **Autofit**, **Distribute Rows Evenly** from the **Table** menu, *or*
- Click: The **Distribute Rows Evenly** button on the **Tables and Borders** Tool Bar

Insert columns and rows

- Position the insertion point: Immediately below the place where you wish to insert another column or row
- Select: **Insert** from the **Table** menu
- Select: **Columns to the Left** *or* **Columns to the Right** *or* **Rows Above** or **Rows Below**

OR:

Highlight: The column or row where you want to make an insertion Press: The right mouse button

- Select: **Insert Rows** or **Insert Columns**

Delete columns and rows

- Position the insertion point: At the place you wish to make the deletion
- Select: **Delete** from the **Table** menu
- Select: **Columns** *or* **Rows** as appropriate

OR:

Highlight: The column or row where you want to make a deletion Press: The right mouse button

- Select: **Delete Rows** or **Delete Columns**

Align text or data in a column or row

You can align text or data in the table, in each individual column or row, or in each individual cell, by selecting one of the Alignment buttons on the Formatting Tool Bar:

- Select: The entire table or column(s) or row(s) or cell(s) for which you want to set the alignment
- Click: The appropriate alignment button on the Formatting Tool bar

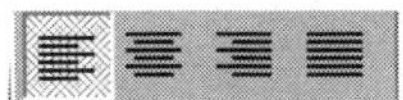

Remove borders/lines

Mouse	Menu:
◎ Select: **Select Table** from the **Table** menu or select the table by dragging the mouse across it to highlight all cells ◎ Click: The down arrow on the **Borders** button on the Formatting Tool Bar ◎ Select: The **No Border** option from the drop-down menu	Click: Anywhere inside the table Select: **Table Properties** from the **Table** menu Select: The **Table** tab Select: **Borders and Shading, Borders** Select: **None** in the **Setting:** section Click: **OK** (twice)
Note: You can use this method to remove lines from portions of the table by selecting only those cells, rows or columns you wish to edit.	

Position the table on the page

- Click: Anywhere inside the table
- Select: **Table Properties** from the **Table** menu
- Click: The **Table** tab
- Select: **Left, Centre** or **Right** from the **Alignment** section, or specify the distance to indent the table from the left margin in the **Indent from left** box
- Click: **OK**

Note: You can choose the **Options** button if you want to change the default cell margins or default cell spacing (ie the amount of space between cells in the table) but this will not be necessary for OCR/RSA examination purposes.

Use the **Table move handle** to move/drag the table to a different place on the page.

Use the **Table resize handle** to make the table larger or smaller

Merge cells

Select the cells you wish to join together, then, choose one of the following merge methods:

- Select: **Merge Cells** from the **Table** menu, *or*
- Click: The right mouse button and select: **Merge Cells**, *or*
- Select: The **Merge Cells** button from the **Table and Borders** Tool Bar

Split cells

Select the cell(s) to be split, then choose one of the following split cells methods:

- Select: **Split Cells** from the **Table** menu, *or*
- Click: The right mouse button; *and* select: **Split Cells**, *or.*
- Select: The **Split Cells** button from the Table and Borders Tool Bar

The **Split Cells dialogue box** appears on screen.

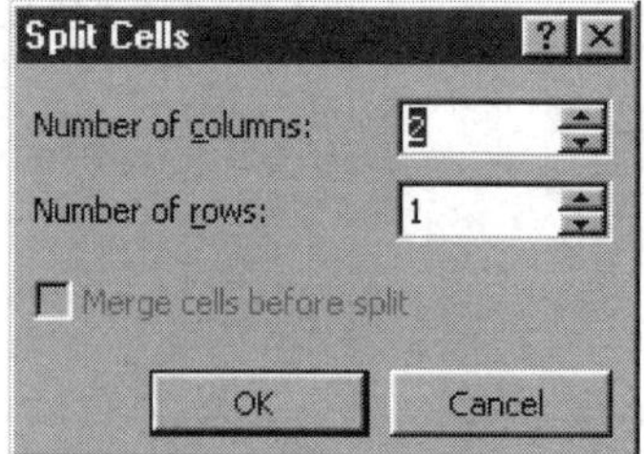

Figure 7.5 Split Cells dialogue box

- Enter: The number of columns or rows you want to split the selected cell(s) into.
- Click: **OK**

Sub-divided and multi-line column headings

A *multi-line column heading* means that the column heading appears on more than one line. You can either allow the words automatically to 'wrap' on to the next line, or press the return key to key in a word on the next line down.

EVENT	**START TIME**	**END TIME**	**ARENA**
(col 1)	**(col 2)**	**(col 3)**	**(col 4)**

A *sub-divided column heading* means that the column heading may be divided into two or more subheadings. Follow the instructions given for merging cells and/or splitting cells to display the required layout.

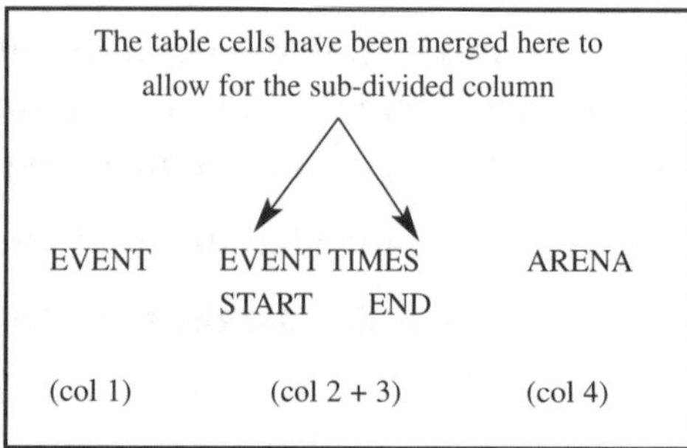

Exercise 7A – Practice Exercise

7.1 Use the **Insert Table** facility to create a table with 8 rows and 4 columns. Practise:

- moving around the table
- changing the column width and row height
- inserting a row and inserting a column, deleting a row and deleting a column
- entering data in the table
- selecting items in the table
- aligning data in each column to the left, right and centre
- merging and splitting table cells
- removing borders/lines from the table
- positioning the table on the page.

Repeat the above using the **Tables and Borders** facility.

7.2 Close the file without saving so you are ready to start the next exercise with a clear screen.

Exercise 7B

7.3 Starting with a new file, you are going to produce an unruled table with sub-divided and multi-line column headings. You can complete it using whichever method you prefer, and simply reproduce the table shown below (and skip step 7.4). However, if you need a bit more help, then you can follow the step-by-step instructions given in step 7.4. As usual, use Times New Roman and font size 12.

You will need to refer back to the instructions for table layouts given earlier in this unit for **insert table facility, align text or data in a column or row, merge cells, subdivided columns, remove borders/lines** etc.

NEW EMPLOYEES

EMPLOYEE NAME	**EMPLOYEE TITLE**	**CONTACT POINT**	
		EXT	**ROOM NO**
<u>Marketing and Sales</u>			
Hussain, Nadia	Marketing Assistant	257	403
Sunway, Mark	Sales Adviser	258	403
Bannistock, Alan	Telesales	68	225
<u>Administration Pool</u>			
Thurston, Lilian	Receptionist	16	180
Meredith, Sally	Office Supervisor	15	39
Burgoyne, Ivor	Mail Courier	8	39

Align the data in the EXT and ROOM NO columns to the right.

Align the data in the EMPLOYEE NAME and EMPLOYEE TITLE columns to the left.

7.4 Follow these step-by-step instructions if you need a bit more help reproducing the table layout shown at step 7.3. If you make a mistake as you are going along, use the **Undo** button to go back a step.

- Click: The Insert Table icon on the Standard Tool Bar and insert a table of 10 rows by 4 columns as shown below.

- Enter the data in each column and row as shown below, using bold for the headings. If necessary, increase the column width so that the text entries fit within each column, eg to fit Marketing Assistant in column 2. You do not need to do anything to make the underlined subheadings fit at this stage.

EMPLOYEE	**EMPLOYEE**	**CONTACT POINT**	
NAME	**TITLE**	**EXT**	**ROOM NO**
Marketing and Sales			
Hussain, Nadia	Marketing Assistant	257	403
Sunway, Mark	Sales Adviser	258	403
Bannistock, Alan	Telesales	68	225
Administration Pool			
Thurston, Lilian	Receptionist	16	180
Meredith, Sally	Office Supervisor	15	39
Burgoyne, Ivor	Mail Courier	8	39

Do not press return here

- Reduce the width of columns 3 and 4. Use the Merge Cells facility to merge the cells shown shaded in the table so that the layout appears as shown below.

EMPLOYEE NAME	**EMPLOYEE TITLE**	**CONTACT POINT**	
		EXT	**ROOM NO**
Marketing and Sales			
Hussain, Nadia	Marketing Assistant	257	403
Sunway, Mark	Sales Adviser	258	403
Bannistock, Alan	Telesales	68	225
Administration Pool			
Thurston, Lilian	Receptionist	16	180
Meredith, Sally	Office Supervisor	15	39
Burgoyne, Ivor	Mail Courier	8	39

You do not need to shade the cells yourself – the shading is simply to show you which cells are merged

- Insert a clear line space above and below the section headings as shown by the arrows below.
- Align the data in each section of the **EXT** column to the right. Perform this action separately for each section to prevent the underlined headings from being aligned to the right.
- Align the data in each section of the **ROOM NO** column to the right.
- Centre the data in the **CONTACT POINT** cell.

EMPLOYEE NAME	EMPLOYEE TITLE	CONTACT POINT	
		EXT	ROOM NO
Marketing and Sales			
Hussain, Nadia	Marketing Assistant	257	403
Sunway, Mark	Sales Adviser	258	403
Bannistock, Alan	Telesales	68	225
Administration Pool			
Thurston, Lilian	Receptionist	16	180
Meredith, Sally	Office Supervisor	15	39
Burgoyne, Ivor	Mail Courier	8	39

- Press: **Ctrl** + **Home** to move the cursor outside the table.
- Key in the title above the table **NEW EMPLOYEES**.
- Use the Select Table facility from the Table menu to select the entire table, then remove all table borders/lines.
- Press: **Ctrl** + **End** to move the cursor outside the table.
- Key in the paragraph shown below the table **A full induction programme** . . .

NEW EMPLOYEES

EMPLOYEE NAME	EMPLOYEE TITLE	CONTACT POINT	
		EXT	ROOM NO
Marketing and Sales			
Hussain, Nadia	Marketing Assistant	257	403
Sunway, Mark	Sales Adviser	258	403
Bannistock, Alan	Telesales	68	225
Administration Pool			
Thurston, Lilian	Receptionist	16	180
Meredith, Sally	Office Supervisor	15	39
Burgoyne, Ivor	Mail Courier	8	39

A full induction programme for all new employees will be arranged within the next month – details to follow.

7.5 Click on each section and check that it is in the correct font (Times New Roman font size 12) by checking the font and font Size on the Formatting Tool Bar. Save and print your document using the filename **EX7B**. Check your printout with the exercise above. If you find any errors, correct them on screen, save your document again and print again if necessary.

7.6 Leave **EX7B** on screen. Read the next information section headed **Sort items** carefully. Then, using the exercise on screen, practise the technique of sorting the items in the table.

Sort (rearrange) items

You can sort items in a table using the same principles and procedures that you learnt in Unit 6. Refer back to Page 66 to refresh your memory on sorting items.

You can either sort the whole table or a specific selection of cells, rows or columns. For example:

B2	Red	Box
T7	Blue	Tin
B4	Pink	Bowl

The table **before** sorting

T7	Blue	Tin
B4	Pink	Bowl
B2	Red	Box

The table **after** sorting by: **Column 2, Text,** and **Ascending** – items appear in alphabetical order of colour

A) Mary's containers		
B2	Red	Box
T7	Blue	Tin
B4	Pink	Bowl
B) John's containers		
T8	Orange	Tube
B5	Green	Basket
C6	Brown	Can

The table sections and rows **before** sorting

A) Mary's containers		
T7	Blue	Tin
B4	Pink	Bowl
B2	Red	Box
B) John's containers		
C6	Brown	Can
B5	Green	Basket
T8	Orange	Tube

The table **after** sorting first the rows in section **A)** and then the rows in section **B)** by **Column 2, Text,** and **Ascending** – items appear in alphabetical order of colour by section

Sorting items in a table

Select: Either the whole table, or the specific rows and/or columns that you want to sort (see previous instructions on selecting items in a table)

◎ Select: **Sort** from the **Table** Menu

The **Sort** dialogue box is displayed on screen.

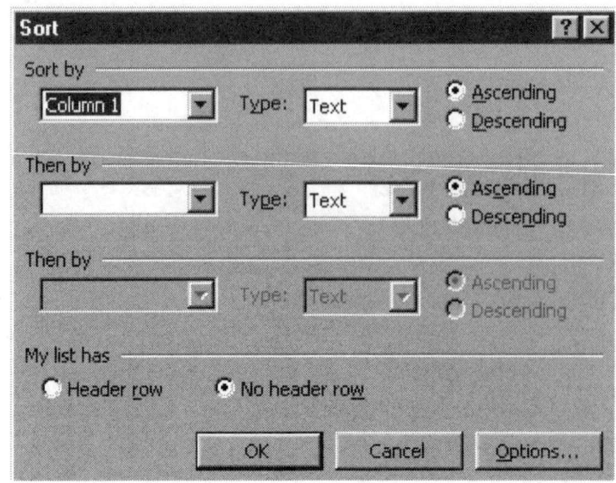

Figure 7.6 Sort dialogue box

◎ Select from the sort dialogue options as appropriate (see Unit 6, p. 66).

Exercise 7C

7.7 If **EX7B** is no longer as you originally saved it, close the file without saving then retrieve the correct version before carrying out the following amendments:

- ◎ Move the **Administration Pool** section so that it comes before the **Marketing and Sales** section (using cut and paste or the drag and drop method).

Practise using the **Sort** facility:

- ◎ Sort the **ROOM NO** within each section into exact ascending numerical order. Ensure that all the corresponding details are also moved.
- ◎ Sort the **EXT** within each section into exact descending numerical order. Ensure that all the corresponding details are also moved.
- ◎ Sort the **EMPLOYEE TITLE** within each section into exact alphabetical order. Ensure that all the corresponding details are also moved.

Complete a final sort:

- ◎ Sort the **EMPLOYEE NAME** within each section into exact alphabetical order. Ensure that all corresponding details are also moved.

7.8 Save and print your document using the filename **EX7C**. Check your printout with the key at the back of the book. If you find any errors, correct them on screen, save and print your document again if necessary.

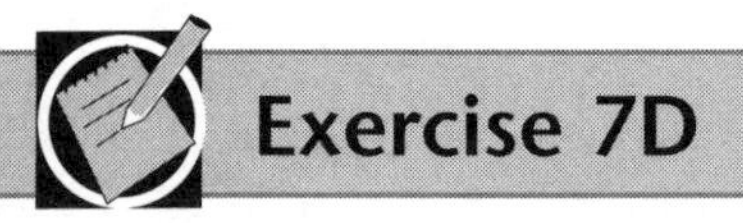

Exercise 7D

7.9 Starting with a new file, key in the following table. Save and print your document using the filename **EX7D**. Check your printout with the key at the back of the book. If you find any errors, correct them on screen, save and print your document again if necessary.

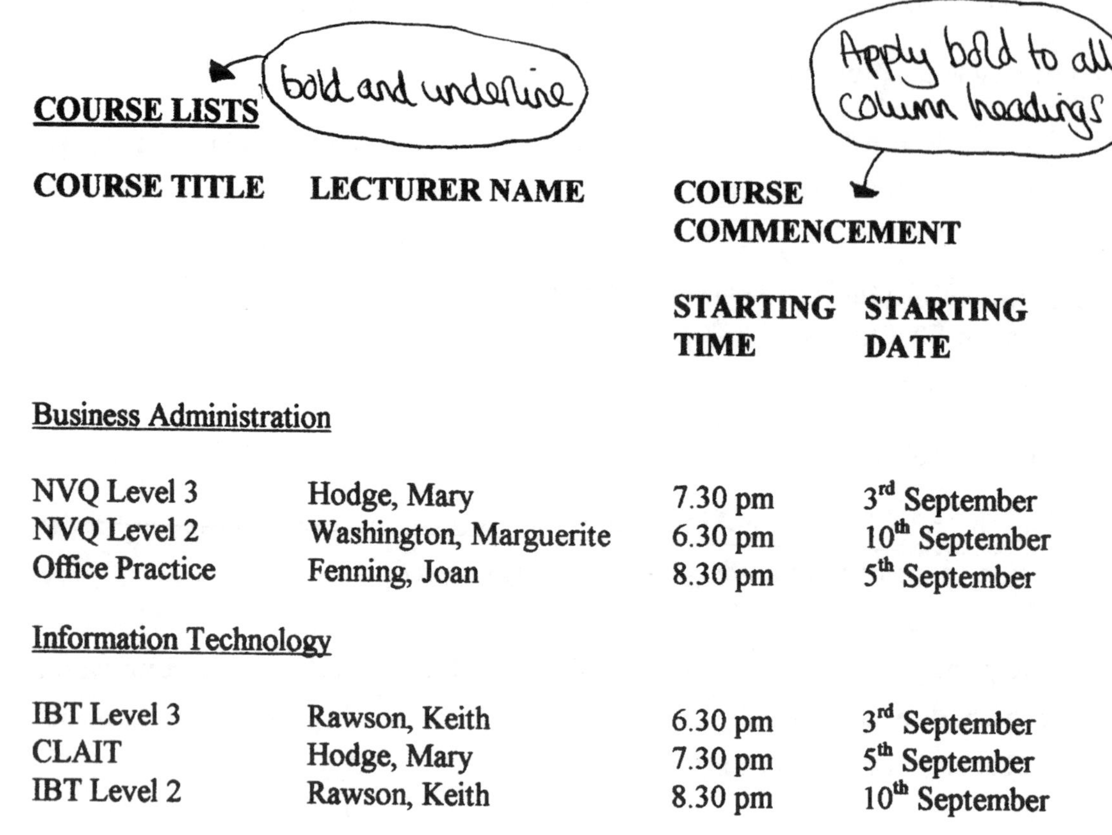

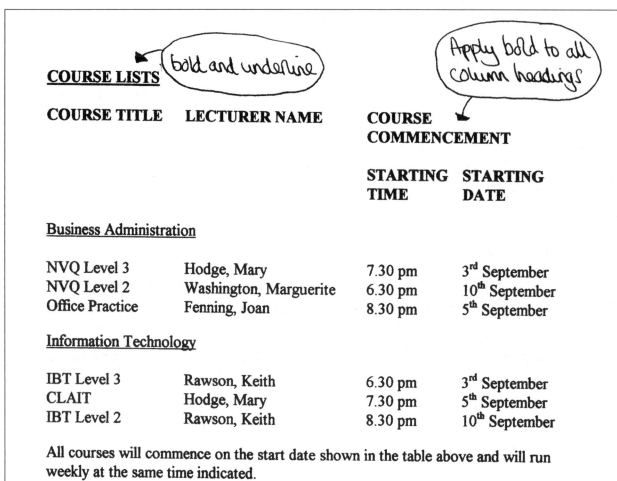

COURSE LISTS (bold and underline)

(Apply bold to all column headings)

COURSE TITLE	LECTURER NAME	COURSE COMMENCEMENT	
		STARTING TIME	STARTING DATE
Business Administration			
NVQ Level 3	Hodge, Mary	7.30 pm	3rd September
NVQ Level 2	Washington, Marguerite	6.30 pm	10th September
Office Practice	Fenning, Joan	8.30 pm	5th September
Information Technology			
IBT Level 3	Rawson, Keith	6.30 pm	3rd September
CLAIT	Hodge, Mary	7.30 pm	5th September
IBT Level 2	Rawson, Keith	8.30 pm	10th September

All courses will commence on the start date shown in the table above and will run weekly at the same time indicated.

SORT the items within each section into exact alphabetical order

DO NOT RULE

Exercise 7E

7.10 Starting with a new file, key in the following table. Save and print your document using the filename **EX7E**. Check your printout with the key at the back of the book. If you find any errors, correct them on screen, save and print your document again if necessary.

GREAT GARDEN ROADSHOW

DO NOT RULE

The G— G— R— planned to visit your area is listed below. Tickets are available on the day at the venue entrance.

ROADSHOW DATES		TOWN	VENUE
NUMBER OF DAYS	DATE		
Autumn roadshow events			
2	9 September	Huddersfield	Green Park
2	7 November	Bradford	Oakley Manor
1	16 October	Pudsey	Mountview Hall
Spring roadshow events			
2	16 April	Wakefield	Limes Park
1	21 March	Halifax	Piece Hall
2	6 March	Sheffield	Riverside Lodge
Summer roadshow events			
2	22 July	Skipton	Castle Grounds
1	14 August	Dewsbury	Lewisgate Mill Complex
2	8 June	Sheffield	Ennya Verona Centre

modify the layout so that
- the DATE column appears before the NUMBER OF DAYS column
- the Autumn roadshow events section appears after the Summer roadshow events section

sort into ascending DATE order within each section. Ensure corresponding details are also rearranged.

align all data in the TOWN and VENUE columns to the right

Exercise 7F

7.11 Starting with a new file, key in the following table. Save and print your document using the filename **EX7F**. Check your printout with the key at the back of the book. If you find any errors, correct them on screen, save and print your document again if necessary.

MISCELLANEOUS STOCK LIST

(DO NOT RULE)

The following items of stock need to be incorporated within the new computerised stock control programme.

DESCRIPTION	CODE	STOCK LEVEL NUMBERS	
		RE-ORDER LEVEL	CURRENT LEVEL
Male sportswear			
Tracksuit	T11	10	7
Socks, towelling	ST3	20	22
Swimming trunks	ST42	50	119
Jogging Pants	JP17	10	5
Female swimwear			
Swimming costume	SC12	15	12
Sarong, multi	SM9	20	17
Halter neck bikini	HB42	25	26
Shorts, lycra	SL72	50	57
Children's leisurewear			
Leotard	L6	10	12
Sweatband	S24	20	105
Jogging suit	JS14	10	9
Cycling shorts	CS10	20	28

modify the layout so that the RE-ORDER LEVEL column comes after the CURRENT LEVEL column

modify the layout so that the Male sportswear section comes after the Female swimwear section

sort into exact alphabetical order of DESCRIPTION within each section. Ensure that the corresponding details are also rearranged.

UNIT 8 STANDARD PARAGRAPHS

By the end of Unit 8, you should have learnt how to:

- **create standard paragraphs, phrases or portions of text which may be used frequently**
- **retrieve and insert standard paragraphs, phrases or portions of text into a document as required.**

Standard paragraphs (boilerplating)

Many letters or documents have some parts in them that are identical in content. This can mean keying in the same portions of text over and over again, eg company addresses, standard paragraphs or the salutation at the end of a letter. In Word 2000 you can store text or graphics that you use repeatedly and insert them as required into any document. This can obviously save you a great deal of keying-in time. The process is sometimes referred to as 'boilerplating'.

The method of saving standard paragraphs is exactly the same as saving any other document file. Using normal save procedures, you will be able to insert them into your main document as required. If you are inserting items that have been saved previously by someone else, you will need to identify the filename under which they have been stored. Often, a unique directory or folder is created to store standard paragraphs so that they can be easily retrieved.

Organisations often store a combination of standard paragraphs, phrases, portions of text and graphics, to generate standard letters quickly. Retrieving pre-stored paragraphs at relevant points allows operators to compose standard letters very quickly. Standard letters need to be well displayed. Your layout, line spacing and heading styles should be consistent. You may need to emphasise text (bold, underline etc), extract information from another task and also route copies.

Don't forget to insert the date in the correct position on letters and memos.

Standard paragraphs – document files

To create the standard paragraph file:

- Key in: The portion of text to be saved as a standard paragraph file

Save as a document file in the usual way:

- Select **Save As** from the **File** menu
- Key in: An appropriate filename

Note: If you use easily identifiable filenames, it will help you to retrieve the correct file. For example, **ENQUIRY** for a standard paragraph relating to customer enquiries. When a large number of paragraphs are stored, a numerical system may be used.

To insert the standard paragraph file into your document:
◎ Position the cursor: At the place where you want the standard paragraph file to be inserted ◎ Select: **File** from the **Insert** menu ◎ Check: That the correct directory or folder is displayed in the **Look in** box
Then retrieve the standard paragraph:
◎ Select: The document file you wish to insert ◎ Click: **OK**

8.1 You are going to create some standard paragraphs that may be useful for inserting into standard letters. Starting a new file, key in the following standard paragraph entry:

I am writing to thank you for the job application you submitted to us recently for the post of

8.2 Save the standard paragraph under the filename **APPLICATION**. Close the file.

8.3 Starting a new file for each standard paragraph entry, and with a clear screen, key in each portion of text shown in the left-hand column below. Save each file separately using the filename indicated in the right-hand column. Remember to close each file and start with a clear screen before creating and saving the next standard paragraph entry.

TEXT FOR EACH NEW STANDARD PARAGRAPH FILE	FILENAME
We would like to invite you to attend for an interview on	INTERVIEW
If you require any additional information, please do not hesitate to contact this office.	INFO
We regret to advise that on this occasion you have not been successful in your application.	REGRET
Please bring all your qualification certificates with you for verification purposes.	CERTIFICATES
You will be requested to give a short presentation to the interview panel. An OHP, projector and flipchart will be available.	PRESENTATION
If you would like more detailed feedback on your application, we shall be pleased to provide you with the written comments from the shortlisting panel.	FEEDBACK
Please report to the Main Reception at least 15 minutes before the start of the interview, where you will be greeted by a member of our staff.	ARRIVAL
Please find enclosed an information leaflet about the company along with a map of our location.	MAP
Thank you for the interest you have taken in our company.	THANK

8.4 You are now going to create some standard paragraphs that may be useful for inserting into memos. Create and save each of the following standard paragraph entries, using the filenames indicated. Remember to close each file and start with a clear screen before creating and saving the next standard paragraph entry.

TEXT FOR EACH NEW STANDARD PARAGRAPH FILE	FILENAME
I understand that you have a new member of staff joining your team	**NEW STAFF**
A full Induction programme has been arranged for all new members of staff and will be held	**INDUCTION**
Please contact the Health & Safety Officer to arrange an appointment for your new member of staff to go through the company policy.	**SAFETY**
I am enclosing a Welcome Pack. Please ensure that the acceptance slip is signed and returned to me confirming that both yourself and your new employee have reviewed the Pack.	**WELCOME**
Please ask your new member of staff to contact me on Extension 357 to confirm their personnel details for the company payroll.	**PAYROLL**

Exercise 8A

8.5 Starting with a clear screen, retrieve the file **Lettertemp**. Save as **EX8A** before keying in the text below and retrieve each of the following standard paragraph files as indicated.

> Our Ref: FML/gy34
>
> PERSONAL
>
> Mrs Jennifer Delaney
> 27 Fenniston Road
> BRADFORD
> BD16 2HG
>
> Dear Mrs Delaney
>
> Insert the paragraph stored as: **APPLICATION** Catering Manager.
>
> Insert the paragraph stored as: **REGRET** We did receive a very large number of applications for this particular post. Although you were a strong candidate, there were a number of other candidates who had significantly more experience and up-to-date qualifications. Insert the paragraph stored as: **FEEDBACK**
>
> I do hope that you will not be too disappointed with this outcome or deterred from applying for other positions which may be advertised.
>
> Insert the paragraph stored as: **THANK**
>
> Yours sincerely
>
> Fiona McLaughlin
> PERSONNEL OFFICER

8.6 Resave your document and print one copy. Check your printout with the key at the back of the book. If you find any errors, retrieve the document and correct them.

8.7 You will be able to practise retrieving the standard paragraphs you have created in the next unit. Exit the program if you have finished working or continue straight on to the next unit.

UNIT 9 ROUTING BUSINESS DOCUMENTS

By the end of Unit 9, you should have learnt how to:

- prepare business letters and memorandums
- print letters and memos on preprinted letterheads
- locate information in another document and insert it into a current document
- indicate routing of copies on business documents
- enumerate items.

Business letter and memo layout

Refer back to Unit 3 to refresh your memory on correct layout procedures for business letters and memorandums, and using either a preprinted letterhead/memohead or template.

Locate information from another document

Refer back to Unit 3 to refresh your memory on locating information from another document to insert into the current document.

Route copies

It is normal practice for the sender to keep one copy of a letter or memo for reference. Additional copies may be required for other people and this is usually indicated at the foot of the document.

Instructions may appear as:

Top and 2 copies please.
One file copy and one for
Sue Thompson. Indicate routing.

The routing indication is inserted at the bottom of the document (under any enclosure mark). For example:

Copy: Sue Thompson
File

When all the copies of the document have been printed, it is normal practice to indicate the destination of each copy by ticking, underlining in coloured pen, or highlighting.

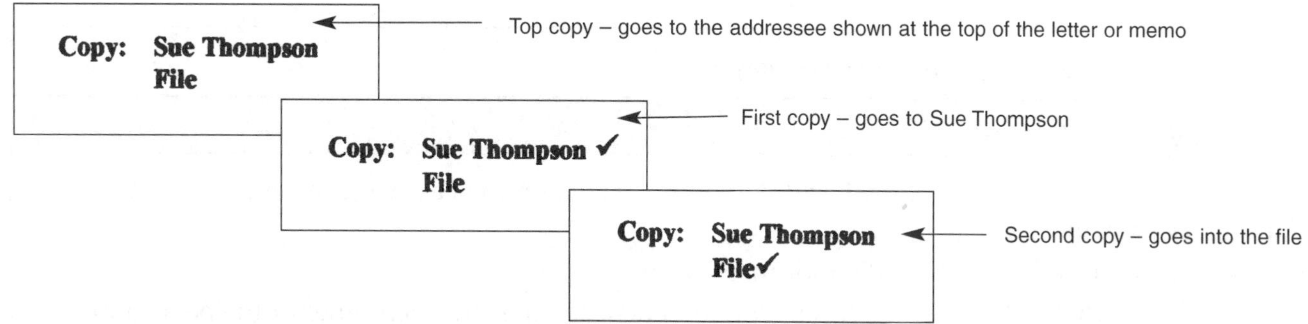
Copy: Sue Thompson
File
Top copy – goes to the addressee shown at the top of the letter or memo
Copy: Sue Thompson ✓
File
First copy – goes to Sue Thompson
Copy: Sue Thompson
File✓
Second copy – goes into the file

Enumeration

Word 2000 can quickly create enumerated or bulleted paragraphs. Enumeration shows sequence, while bullets emphasise separate items in a list. You can choose different styles of enumeration – capital letters, lower-case letters, numbers or Roman numerals, any of which can be followed by a bracket or a full stop or nothing. If you add, delete or reorder enumerated items, Word 2000 will automatically update the sequence for you. It is usual to leave one clear space between enumerated items.

Bulleted list:	*Enumerated list - numbers*	*Enumerated list - letters*
• Apples • Oranges • Pears • Peaches	1) Wash and dry the fruit carefully. 2) Peel, remove pips and pith, then arrange in quarters.	a) Wash and dry the fruit carefully. b) Peel, remove pips and pith, then arrange in quarters.

To create an enumerated list after keying in:

Mouse/Formatting Tool Bar method

- Key in: The paragraphs or items in the usual way
- Select: The paragraphs or items to which you want to add enumeration
- Click: The **Numbering** button on the Formatting Tool Bar

Note: To alter the format or display of the enumeration follow the mouse and menu instructions below

Mouse/menu

- Key in: The paragraphs or items in the usual way
- Select: The paragraphs or items to which you want to add enumeration
- Select: **Bullets and Numbering** from the **Format** menu
- Select: The **Numbered** tab
- Click: The style you require from the visual display options given (a blue outline appears on the selected box)
- Select: **Customize** if you want to modify the style further, ie change the font, number style, indent, alignment, position, or number to start from. *Note:* If you find that Word 2000 indents the enumerated paragraphs from the left margin, or applies some other formatting that you wish to alter, use the Customize option to enter the appropriate changes.
- Click: **OK**

To create an enumerated list as you key in:
Keyboard method
◎ Position the cursor: At the beginning of the paragraph to begin with the enumeration ◎ Key in: The enumeration (eg A) ◎ Press: **Tab** – to set the indent for the first line ◎ Press: **Ctrl** + **T** – to set the 'wrap around' indent for all subsequent lines of the paragraph ◎ Key in: The rest of the text Repeat the above for each enumerated paragraph. Word 2000 automatically inserts the next number.
To create an enumerated list displaying numbers or bullets:
Keyboard method
◎ Key in: **1)** followed by a space or a tab and the text you want. When you press ↵ (**return/enter**) to add the next paragraph or item, Word automatically inserts the next number ◎ Key in * instead of **1)** if you want to create a bulleted list *Note:* Using this method can sometimes cause more difficulties with line spacing between paragraphs or items, or with margin justification.
To finish the list:
Keyboard method
◎ Press ↵ (**return/enter**) twice. Press: **Backspace** to delete the last number in the list

Exercise 9A

9.1 Open the file **EX8A** and save as **EX9A**.

9.2 Delete the third paragraph.

9.3 Insert the following text and enumerated paragraphs after the second paragraph of the letter:

However, our Director of Resources, Karen Dawson, has asked me to draw your attention to several other vacancies which exist at the moment and which may be of interest. These are namely:

a) Catering Supervisor. This is a part time, permanent post based on Service Contract Scale 6-7.

b) Restaurant Manager. This is a full time, temporary post to cover maternity leave based on Management Contract Scale 9.

c) Catering Assistant. This is a f/t, 1-year fixed term post based on Service Contract Scale 3-4.

9.4 Indicate the routing of the letter – one copy to Customer Care Department and one copy for the file. In order to fit the letter on to a single page, either reduce the font size or select the Shrink to Fit option under Print Preview.

9.5 Save the document and print one copy. Check your printout with the key at the back of the book. If you find any errors, retrieve the document and correct them.

Exercise 9B

9.6 Starting with a clear screen, retrieve the file saved as **Memotemp**. Save as **EX9B** and key in the text shown below. Retrieve and insert the standard paragraphs where indicated.

9.7 Save your document and print one copy. Check your printout with the key at the back of the book. If you find any errors, retrieve the document and correct them.

(Use a justified right margin)

From: Fiona McLaughlin, Personnel Officer
To: Nasreen Begum, Customer Adviser (check from exercise 4A and amend if necessary)
Ref: FM/NB/6

NEW EMPLOYEE ← (bold)

(Insert the paragraph stored as NEW STAFF): George Cook. I would like to arrange for George, who is commencing his employment with you next week, to take part in the pilot mentoring scheme we have introduced recently. Please could you liaise with Sue Littlewood who has volunteered to act as mentor for George until he settles in.

(Insert the paragraph stored as WELCOME)

(Insert the paragraph stored as INDUCTION) on the first Tuesday of next month. The Induction programme will cover issues such as:

a) Background to, and organisational structure of, the co e (it's) personnel.

b) The main co policies, eg equal opportunities policy, grievance ~~policies~~ policy, etc.

c) The Annual Review and Appraisal Systems.

d) General info such as holiday entitlements, sickness and absence reporting, bus house styles, etc.

(Insert the paragraph stored as PAYROLL)

Top and 2 copies please, one for Sue Littlewood and one for the file. Indicate routing.

Exercise 9C

9.8 Starting with a clear screen, retrieve the file saved as **Lettertemp**. Save as **EX9C** and key in the text shown below. Retrieve and insert the standard paragraphs where indicated.

9.9 Resave your document and print one copy. Check your printout with the key at the back of the book. If you find any errors, retrieve the document and correct them.

9.10 Exit the program if you have finished working or continue straight on to the next unit.

(Use a ragged right margin)

Our ref: FM/RA/319

(mark the letter PRIVATE)

Mr Rory Andel
26 St Peter's Drive
LEEDS
LS5 2RM

Dr Mr A ———

Following yr recent application for the post of Catering Manager, (insert paragraph stored as INTERVIEW) Wed, 22 June at 2.30 pm. (Insert paragraph stored as ARRIVAL)

(Insert paragraph stored as PRESENTATION) This should last no longer than 5-ten minutes and should be ~~based on the~~ an explanation of 'How you intend to improve catering services'.

(Insert paragraph stored as CERTIFICATES) You may also choose to bring with you any other documentary evidence which demonstrates yr previous (experiance).

(Insert paragraph stored as MAP)

It would be helpful if you could confirm your attendance. If the interview time is (inconveineint), please let our Personnel Clerk, Hugh Winters, know as soon as poss.

Yrs scly

~~Frank~~ Fiona McLaughlin
Personnel Officer

(Top and 2 copies please, one file copy and one for Hugh Winters. Indicate routing)

UNIT 10 CONSOLIDATION 2

By the end of Unit 10, you will have revised and practised all the skills needed for the OCR/RSA Stage II Word Processing Part 2 award.

Look at your Progress Review Checklist and at your completed exercises to remind yourself of what you have learnt so far and to identify any weaknesses. Then complete the following exercises as revision.

Exercise 10A

Recall this document stored as **EX4C**. Save as **EX10A** and amend as shown below. Use single line spacing (except where indicated) and use a ragged right margin. Adjust the line length to 14 cm and number the pages at the bottom centre. Save the document and print one copy.

FAMILY LIFE

The family has been ~~referred to~~ described as a kinship group, ie, a group of persons directly

linked by kin connections, the adult members of which assume responsibility for

caring for children. Kinship connections are ~~based~~ centred on blood, marriage or adoption. (A)

~~Types of~~ Family Structures

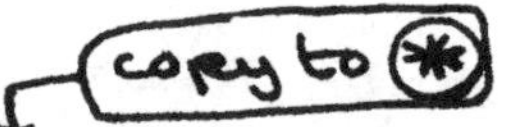

The traditional 'nuclear' family is where a husband and wife live with their children in the same household. ~~Sometimes this is described as the cereal packet family.~~ A recent study revealed that approximately one quarter of households in the United Kingdom consists of a married couple and their dependent children. Marriage rates increased during the first seventy years of this century, then declined during the following 25 yrs.
The 'extended' family is where two or more generations either live together in the same household or see each other on a regular basis, eg daily. (B)

There has been a significant rise in the number of 'one-parent' families. Over 22% of families with children are headed by a lone parent – nearly three times the proportion in 1971. This increase is believed to be linked to the rise in the divorce rate (around 40% of marriages end in divorce) and also in the number of births outside marriage (34% of babies are born to unmarried mothers, compared with 8% in 1971). In the 19th century, however, proportionately more children were affected by the death of a parent than are affected by divorce today.
There is also a rise in the number of 'reconstituted' families (step-families). Divorce, or the death of a spouse, can lead to a new family being formed as one or both partners bring children from their past relationships into the new family.

Another example of the way in which family structures are becoming more diverse is the 'same-sex' family. This would be where, for instance, a woman leaves her husband and takes her children to live with another woman. move to (A)

Many of today's families are subject to change and fluidity. Family members grow older, move in and out of different households through death, marriage, birth, divorce or simply personal choice. Some people now advocate that family life has to be viewed more as a temporary process, or a set of changing practices, rather than a permanent structure of relatively fixed roles and expectations.

~~*The Family in Society*~~ operator: change woman to female throughout this document

~~Although it is argued by some that the needs of pre-industrial society were met by the immobile extended family, historical research on family life in 17th century England by Peter Laslett, shows that the nuclear family, not the extended family, was the norm, and that considerable geographical mobility existed. However, a later study in 1851, found that the extended family was dominant and functioned as a 'mini-welfare state'.~~

~~From the middle of the 20th century the extended family was 're-discovered' in working class communities such as Bethnal Green and Hull.~~ The term 'dispersed extended family' was introduced to emphasise how families keep in touch with relatives through visits and the telephone.

The Symmetrical Family

move this section to the point marked Ⓑ

In 1975 the idea of the 'symmetrical' family was fashioned as Young and Wilmott put forward the view that relationships between husbands and wives had become far more balanced and egalitarian than in the past, with household chores and child care being increasingly shared. ~~It is apparent from~~ Earlier studies of working class families that marriage roles were highly segregated. Young and Wilmott's studies showed that 72% of husbands regularly helped with the housework and that domestic labour was no longer a solely female preserve. reveal

However, Ann Oakley in the 'Sociology of Housework', 1974, found ~~no evidence to support this view. Her studies revealed~~ that of the families she researched, only 15% of men had a high level of participation in housework. ~~This has been supported by the~~ Further research ~~of~~ by Jonathan Gershuny ~~which~~ shows that, although ~~it is possible that~~ there has been a moderate shift towards a 'symmetrical' pattern, the main burden of domestic work ~~definitely~~ continues to be carried by the woman.

Despite noted changes, there is evidence to suggest that roles in most marriages remain distinct and, according to feminists, are based on a inequality marked in power between husbands and wives.

The Twentieth Century Family 'Norm'

✱ Altho' divorce rates have risen & the diversity of family life has increased the "family based on a couple living with there children, and committed to a permanent relation=ship, is still the norm". The continuities of life family is, in fact, more striking than the discontinuities.

inset this paragraph only by 1.27cm at both left and right margins and use double line spacing

insert 20TH CENTURY FAMILIES as a header on every page

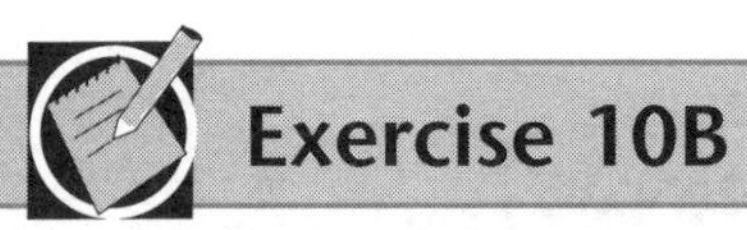

Exercise 10B

Key in the following table. Save the document as **EX10B** and print one copy.

DO NOT RULE

CONFERENCING FACILITIES

The Marketing Department ~~have~~ has compiled a list of venues suitable for hosting conferences, workshops or seminars.

[Further details can be obtained from Cynthia Driver, Marketing Manager.

VENUE	CONTACT	BOOKING PRICES	
		DAY 9am - 5pm	EVENING 6pm +
Facilities for up to 100 people			
Longmeadow Manor	Raham Ali	£175	£110
Richmond Hotel	Ben Jackson	£180	£135
Bedewell Park	Isla MacDonna	£200	£100
Meridian Centre	Franz Beier	£160	£95
Facilities for up to 50 people			
Park View Centre	Judy Leigh	£220	£100
Dorchester Hotel	Vanessa Wright	£200	£95
Newham Arts Centre	Peter Gannon	£250	£130
Queen's Hall	Shona Scholes	£150	£85
Facilities for up to 200 people			
Meridian Centre	F— B—	£300	£160
Fairview Lodge	Arshad Hussain	£280	£140
Bedewell Park	I— M—	£295	£150
TTR Mills Complex	Beth Browne	£285	£150

Please modify the layout so that:

- the Facilities for up to 100 people section comes after the Facilities for up to 50 people section
- the EVENING column comes before the DAY column

Please sort into exact alphabetical order of VENUE. Ensure corresponding details are rearranged.

Exercise 10C

Retrieve your memohead template file and save as **EX10C**. Key in the following document and insert the phrases/paragraphs as indicated. Save the document and print one copy.

From: Fiona McLaughlin, Personnel Officer
To: (insert name from Exercise 10B), Marketing Manager
Ref: FM/CO/34

(insert the paragraph stored as INDUCTION) next Fri. This will be of interest to you as (insert the paragraph stored as NEW STAFF) tomorrow, namely Ella Robertshaw.

I would (appprecaite) it if you could arrange Ella's work schedule so that she can be released from her normal duties to attend the Induction session, which will commence at 9 am and finish at approx 3.30 pm. Please could you confirm (Ellas) attendance with the Personnel Clerk, (Hugh Summers). (check with exercise 9C and amend if necessary)

(insert the paragraph stored as SAFETY)

(insert the paragraph stored as PAYROLL) This is particularly important as I understand that Ella may have changed her surname since the time of her interview as she postponed her employment start date with us because of her wedding arrangements. [When Ella arrives, please can you ensure that she is also given info on:

(use a ragged right margin)

a) Refectory opening times
b) Car parking arrangements
c) Staff newsletter services
d) Photocopying arrangements
e) E-mail addresses & telephone extensions for all staff
f) Intranet access & passwords

(Top plus 2 copies please, one for the Health and Safety Officer and one for file. Indicate routing.)

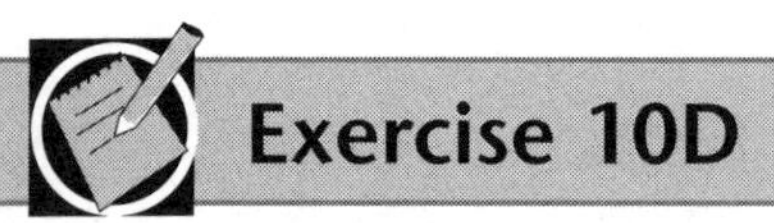

Exercise 10D

Recall this document stored as **EX10C**. Save as **EX10D** and amend as shown. Print one copy.

OFFTEC CORPORATE SERVICES

MEMORANDUM

use a justified right margin

From: Fiona McLaughlin, Personnel Officer
To: Cynthia Driver, Marketing Manager
Ref: FM/CD/34
Date: today's

NEW MEMBER OF STAFF

A full Induction programme has been arranged for all new members of staff and will be held next Friday. ~~This will be of interest to you as~~ I understand that you have a new member of staff joining your team tomorrow, namely Ella Robertshaw.

I would ~~appreciate it~~ be grateful if you could arrange Ella's work schedule so that she can ~~be released from her normal duties to~~ attend the Induction session, which will commence at 9.00 am and finish at approximately 3.30 pm. Please ~~could you~~ confirm Ella's attendance with the Personnel Clerk, Hugh Winters.

Please also contact the Health & Safety Officer to arrange an appointment for ~~your new member of staff~~ Ella to go through the company policy.

emphasise this paragraph

~~Please ask your new member of staff~~ It is important for Ella to contact me on Extension 357 to confirm ~~their~~ her personnel details for the company payroll. This is particularly important as I understand that ~~Ella~~ she may have changed her surname since the time of her interview as she postponed her employment start date with us because of her wedding arrangements.

Leave at least 25mm here

When Ella arrives, please can you ensure that she is also given information on:

sort into exact alphabetical order

a) Refectory opening times
b) Car parking arrangements
c) Staff newsletter services
d) Photocopying arrangements
e) E-mail addresses and telephone extensions for all company staff
f) Intranet access and passwords

inset this section 25 mm from left margin

~~Copy: Health and Safety Officer~~
~~File~~

I am afraid that I am currently out of stock of the standard Welcome pack, which we normally issue to all new employees. As soon as copies come back from the printers I will send one to you in the ~~internal~~ internal mail.

UNIT 11 EXAMINATION PRACTICE 2

By the end of Unit 11, you will have completed a mock examination for the OCR/RSA Stage II Word Processing Part 2 Award.

OCR/RSA Stage II Word Processing Part 2

This examination assesses your ability to produce documents such as: a notice; an article; lists of information; a table; and a standard document incorporating selected phrases, from handwritten and typewritten draft and from recalled text. The award demonstrates that you have acquired intermediate level skills in word processing.

The examination lasts for $1^3/_4$ hours and you must complete four documents, using a word processor. Printing is done outside this time.

Examinations are carried out in registered centres and are marked by OCR/RSA examiners. The centre will give you instructions regarding stationery. Letters must be produced on letterheads (either preprinted or a template) and memos may be produced on preprinted forms, by keying in entry details or by use of a template. The invigilator will give you instructions concerning the recalling of stored files.

Examination hints

When sitting your examination:

- you may use a manual prepared by the centre or the software manufacturer
- put your name, centre number and document number on each document
- check your work very carefully before printing – proofread, spellcheck
- assemble your printouts in the correct order at the end of the examination.

You are now ready to try a mock examination for Stage II Word Processing Part 2. Take care and good luck!

The list of assessment criteria for this mock examination is long and detailed. To be sure that you have reached the required standard to be entered for an examination, you need to work through several past papers and have these 'marked' by a tutor or assessor who is qualified and experienced in this field.

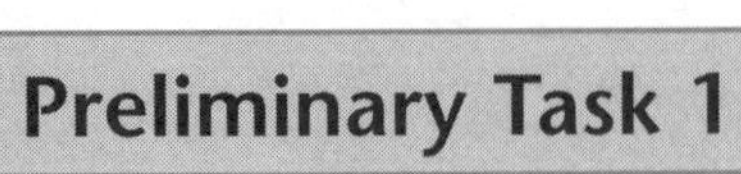

Preliminary Task 1

(Key in the following text and save as EX11A. No print needed.)

ELLIOTT HALL

You & yr family can enjoy a ~~great~~ [super] day out at E— H—. We have something for all ages, ranging from the informal / relaxing Italian-style gardens to the exciting [Jungle] adventure playground. ✓

Look at the attractions:

(Please key in in one column at left margin)

Italian-style gardens
Jungle adventure playground
Woodland walks
Estate church (17th century)
Guided tours of Hall
Lakeside walks
Himalayan ravine
Exhibition hall

Completed in 1775, E— H— is a perfect example of neo-classical architecture. Interior plasterwork was created under the direction of Robert Adam, whilst the influence of Thomas Chippendale is clearly ~~visible~~ seen in the fine furniture. // Edward Elliott, the 6th Lord Jerome, invited famous water-colourists [of his time] to capture the beauty of his beloved ~~Hall~~ [home] throughout the seasons; (there) work is displayed in the Gallery.

The silk-covered walls of the drawing rooms provide a fitting ~~arena~~ [backcloth] for the many portraits of the Elliott family. [The much-travelled members of the family (has) ~~provided~~ endowed present-day visitors with a magnificent collection of porcelain, needlework, carvings & other artefacts from around the world.

You will find E— H— between Wetherby and York, only five miles from the A1. A ~~regular~~ bus service operates 6 times a day between April and Sept from York.

Preliminary Task 2

Key in the following blocks of text and save them under the filename shown. DO NOT PRINT.

Thank you for the application form which you completed. I have taken note of yr details & yr particular requests. I am pleased to inform you that I have allocated stand(s) to meet yr requirements. — Save as PHRASE11A

Thank you for the application form which you completed. I regret to inform you that due to a high level of demand, I have been unable to allocate stands to you. — Save as PHRASE11B

Please let me have yr cheque by the last day of the month preceding the event. If I have not received yr cheque by this date, it will not be poss for your reservation to be held & yr stand(s) may be re-allocated. — Save as PHRASE11C

Vehicle access to an area near to the property for loading/unloading will be available 2 hours before the opening time. Standholders are requested not to begin 'packing up' until the given closing time. A period of 2 hours will be allowed for this process. — Save as PHRASE11D

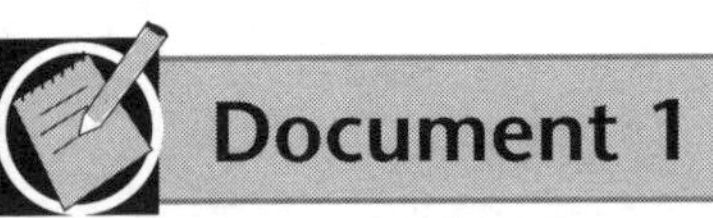

Document 1

Recall the document stored as UNIT11A and save as UNIT11DOC1. Amend as shown, using double line spacing except where indicated. Adjust line length to 15 cm. Use a justified right margin. Print one copy.

ELLIOTT HALL (bold)

Day Out 1999 Award Winner (bold)

Insert VISITOR INFORMATION as a header on every page

You and your family can enjoy a great day out at Elliott Hall. We have something for all ages, ranging from the relaxing ~~informal~~ formal Italian-style gardens to the exciting Jungle Book adventure playground. (Copy to Δ)

~~Look at~~ Find out about the attractions on offer by calling at the Visitor Centre and enjoy a delicious snack or 3-course meal in ~~the~~ Jerome's Diner. Δ

~~Italian-style gardens~~
~~Jungle Book adventure playground~~
~~Woodland walks~~
~~Estate church (17th century)~~
~~Guided tours of Hall~~
~~Lakeside walks~~
~~Himalayan ravine~~
~~Exhibition hall~~

Change Elliott to Alliott throughout this document

1st two paras in single line spacing

*

Completed in 1775, Elliott Hall is a perfect example of neo-classical architecture. Interior plaster work was created under the direction of Robert Adam, whilst the influence of Thomas Chippendale is clearly seen in the fine furniture.

Edward Elliott, the 6th Lord Jerome, invited famous ~~water colourists~~ landscape artists of his time to capture the beauty of his beloved home throughout the seasons; their work is displayed in the Gallery. The silk-covered walls of the drawing rooms provide a fitting backcloth for the many portraits of the Elliott family. ✓

The much-travelled members of the family have endowed present-day visitors with a magnificent collection of porcelain, needlework, carvings and other artefacts from around the world.

Single line spacing for these paragraphs

You will find Elliott Hall between Wetherby and York, only 5 miles from the A1. A bus service operates 6 times a day from York between April and September.

The grounds, gardens & adventure playground are open 7 days a week all year round (closed Christmas Day and Boxing Day).

The Hall and Exhibition Centre open daily from 11 am to 5.00 pm from 1 Apr to 30 Sept. Last admissions are at 4.00 pm.

Access is available between 9.00 am and 5 pm during the months Oct – March, and between 9.00 am and 8 pm during the months Apr – Sept.

Move to *

and woodlands
A gentle stroll through the gardens/brings you to the edge of the Himalayan ravine where you can see a spectacular waterfall cascading into an exotic dell filled by with plants, ferns and bamboos from the Himalayas. The ravine can be safely reached by a newly-constructed 'hairpin' walkway; the more adventurous and younger members of your group may wish to use the original, but rather somewhat steep, steps!

As you can imagine, The ravine was a favourite haunt of generations of Elliott children, and was particularly enjoyed by Marguerite, the wife of the 8th Lord Jerome, who often walked amongst the exotic flora recalling her days in the sub-continent during the height of the British Raj.

On leaving the Himalayan ravine, you will find yourself at the edge of the lake. The lake and it's wild fowl can be observed by following the circular path or by embarking on a boat trip in the 'Marguerite' – a Victorian-style launch. //A gentle ascent brings you back to the Hall, and Exhibition Centre, and Visitor Centre.

Δ

free is
Ample parking facilities are available and a free
users
wheelchair guide can be obtained by ringing 0131-3136828.

Single line-spacing

Numbers the pages please and start new page in a sensible place

Retrieve this document stored as EX11A. Save as UNIT11DOC2. Amend as indicated and print one copy.

Change ELLIOTT to ALLIOTT throughout the document

ELLIOTT HALL ← Centre, embolden and underline

~~You and your family can~~ Enjoy a great day out at Elliott Hall. We have something for all ages, ranging from the relaxing informal Italian-style gardens to the exciting Jungle adventure playground.

Inset by 25 mm from left margin

Leave at least 2 cm here

~~Look at the attractions~~:
ATTRACTIONS

Sort into alphabetical order

Italian-style gardens
Jungle adventure playground
Woodland walks
Estate church (17th century)
Guided tours of Hall
Lakeside walks
Himalayan ravine
Exhibition hall

THE HALL

Completed in 1775, Elliott Hall is a perfect example of neo-classical architecture. Interior plaster work was created under the direction of Robert Adam, whilst the influence of Thomas Chippendale is clearly seen in the fine furniture.

Edward Elliott, the 6th Lord Jerome, invited famous water-colourists of his time to capture the beauty of his beloved home throughout the seasons; their work is displayed in the Gallery. The silk-covered walls of the drawing rooms provide a fitting ~~backcloth~~ backdrop for the many portraits of the Elliott family.

The much-travelled members of the family have endowed ~~present-day~~ today's visitors with a magnificent collection of porcelain, needlework, carvings and other artefacts from around the world.

HOW TO FIND US

You will find Elliott Hall between Wetherby and York, only 5 miles from the A1. A bus service operates 6 times a day between April and September from York.

emphasise this paragraph

For further info on group discounts, education services, holiday activities and exhibitions, please telephone 0131-3136829.

Corporate dining facilities and Music Concerts during winter. Details available from the Events Coordinator on 0131-3136824.

Document 3

Key in the table below. Save as UNIT11DOC3 and print one copy. Do not rule the table.

Please modify layout so that Crafts section comes just below Music section, and VENUE column becomes the second column.

EVENTS CALENDAR

Check with the individual properties for further info about these and other events.

EVENT	DATE AND START	DURATION DAYS	VENUE
Music			
Jazz and BBQ	10.6.01	1	Mere House
Nostalgia Evening	3.5.01	2	Oakville Gardens
Lakeside ~~Symphonies~~ Symphony	7.5.01	6	Alliott Hall Lake
Moonlight Music	29.8.01	3	Ranleigh Park
Firework Fiesta	20.7.01	5	Chambers Hill
Barber of Seville	22.8.01	2	Mere House
Transport			
American Car Rally	4.5.01	3	Ranleigh Park
Austin Owners Rally	11.5.01	2	Alliott Hall Gardens
Vintage Motor Cycle Club	6.7.01	1	Mere Showground
MG Car Society	2.8.01	1	Ranleigh Park
Classic Cars	10.6.01	3	Mere Showground
Vintage Tractors	1.9.01	1	Mere Showground
Steam Fair	18.5.01	1	Alliott Hall Gardens
Historic Vehicles Rally	17.6.01	2	Alliott Hall Gardens
Crafts			
Flower Crafts	17.6.01	2	Oakville Gardens
Easter Crafts	27.3.01	1	Ranleigh Park
Yorkshire Day Fair	1.8.01	1	Oakville Gardens
Harvest Crafts	8.9.01	2	Ranleigh Park
~~Xmas~~ Christmas Tree Fair	10.12.01	2	Alliott Hall Gardens
Christmas Crafts	26.11.01	2	Alliott Hall Gardens

Arrange date in chronological order within each section. Ensure corresponding details are also re-arranged.

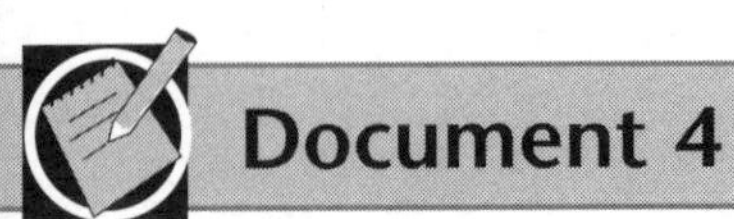

Document 4

Please key in the following document and insert phrases as indicated. Save as UNIT11DOC4 and print one copy.

Our ref MR/EVENTS/01/101

Mr J Napal
14 Townhead Green
Kirby Rushton
LEEDS
LS23 5BV

Dear Mr Napal

CHRISTMAS CRAFTS FAIR AT ALLIOTT HALL GARDENS

Insert phrase stored as PHRASE11A

The Christmas Crafts Fair is to be held at A— H— G— on 26 Nov and will last for 2 days. Stands are allocated for both days and, unfortunately, it is not poss to book for just 1 day.

Insert phrase stored as PHRASE11D

Refreshments will be available in Jerome's Diner throughout the day. Standholders are requested to park their vehicles at the lower end of the Hall's car park during the day in order to ensure easy access for the public.

Insert phrase stored as PHRASE11C

I hope that the Fair will prove an enjoyable and profitable investment of yr time.

Yrs sncly

Mollie Richards
Events Organiser

UNIT 12 INTRODUCTION TO MAIL MERGE

By the end of Unit 12, you should have learnt how to:

- **set up a mail merge operation**
- **create a mail merge main document (form letter)**
- **create a mail merge data file (data source)**
- **add, delete and amend records in a mail merge data file**
- **merge a mail merge main document and data file**
- **print merged documents.**

Mail merge (or mail shot)

Mail merge is the combining (merging) of data from two files into one file. The most common use of this feature is the production of 'personalised' letters which need to be sent out to a number of people on a mailing list. The mail merge feature would be useful to produce standard letters for all your customers or members but with their individual information inserted where appropriate. A generic letter would sound too impersonal, but to type out individual letters to everyone would be very time-consuming. Using mail merge makes it much easier and quicker to carry out this task.

The two files used to operate a mail merge are:

1 A **data file** - often a list of names, addresses and other details

(This file is called the 'data source' in Word 2000)

2 A **main document** – a letter or memo containing the generic text you want to send to all the people on your mailing list and a number of merge codes - merge codes are used to mark places where variable information from the data file will be inserted automatically

(This file is called the 'form letter' in Word 2000)

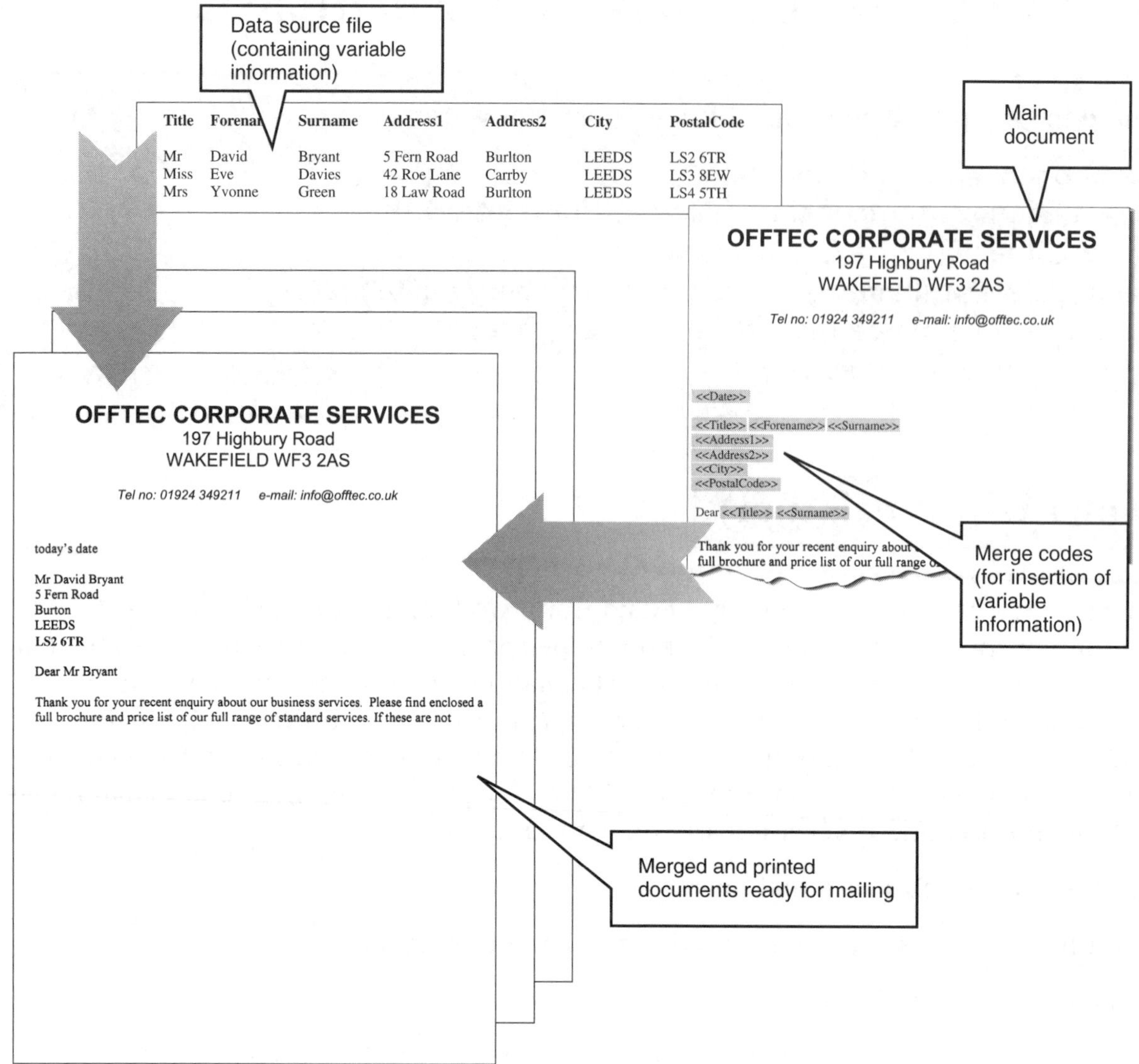

Figure 12.1 Mail merge

In the OCR/RSA Stage II Mail Merge Part 2 examination, you will normally be required to:

- retrieve, amend, sort and print one pre-stored data file
- create, sort and print a second data file
- create two main documents (one letter and one memo) to be merged with the above data files
- merge and print one set of individual mail merge documents from each data file, selecting on one criterion for one data file and on more than one criterion for the second data file.

Note: Although not required for the OCR/RSA examination, it is possible to merge and print address labels and envelopes from a mail merge data file.

Set up mail merge

These stages should be followed:

1 Create and name the main document (form letter) and key in the generic text.

2 Create the data file (data source) - sorting and printing a copy if necessary.

3 Insert merge codes in the main document (form letter) - printing a copy if necessary.

4 Merge the data source and main document, if necessary selecting records from the data source on one or more criteria.

5 View and then print the merged documents.

Word 2000's Mail Merge Helper dialogue box allows you to control the creation and manipulation of a mail merge task.

Create and name the main document (form letter)

The main document will contain text common to all recipients. The merge codes (indicating the position where personalised information is to be transferred from the data source) will be inserted at a later stage.

Mouse/menu

- Open: A **New** document
- Key in: The document text for your main document (letter or memo)
- Save: The main document using a suitable filename, eg **MAINDOC1** or **MAINDOC2** etc
- Select: **Tools, Mail Merge**

The **Mail Merge Helper** dialogue box is displayed on screen.

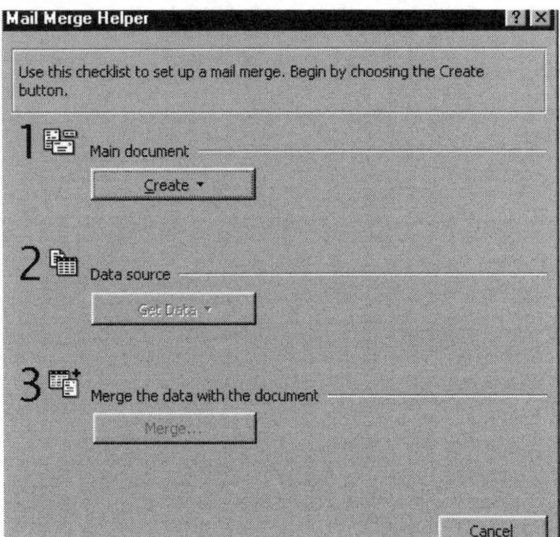

Figure 12.2 Mail Merge Helper dialogue box

- Click: **Create** in **Section 1 - Main Document**
- Select: **Form Letters** from the drop-down menu

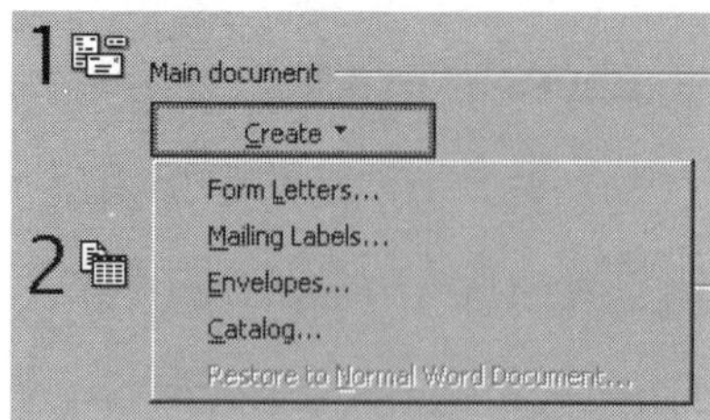

Figure 12.3 Create drop-down menu

The **Form Letters** dialogue box is displayed on screen.

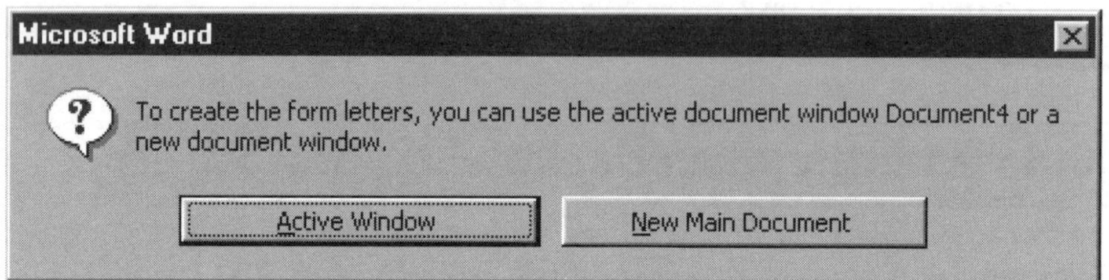

Figure 12.4 Form Letters dialogue box

- Click: **Active Window** – the Mail Merge Helper dialogue box is again displayed on screen (see Figure 12.2), ready for you to move to **Section 2 – Data Source**

The filename for the main document form letter is automatically displayed in Section 1 – Main Document

Exercise 12A

12.1 Following the instructions **Create and name the main document**, create a new main document by keying in the following letter and saving it using the filename **UNIT12MAIN**. Use Times New Roman and font size 12.

Our Ref: OIS/CS

Date of typing

Dear

Welcome to Offtec Investment Services, the financial investment branch of Offtec Corporate Services.

I have pleasure in enclosing a booklet giving details of our pensions and investment schemes as you requested. I am sure that you will find our terms and rates to be highly competitive.

I hope that you will be able to attend our introductory seminars where you will learn more about the important topic of making the most of your money. Dates and times are shown in the booklet.

Yours sincerely

Charles Seth
INVESTMENTS MANAGER

Enc

Create the data source

The data source will contain a record for each addressee. Each record will be made up of 'fields', eg **Name, Address, Postcode**. Each field should contain the same kind of information.

After keying in the main document and naming this as the form letter for the mail merge operation, you are prompted to move to Section 2 – Data Source in the Mail Merge Helper dialogue box.

With the **Mail Merge Helper** dialogue box on screen:

◎ Click: **Get Data** in **Section 2 - Data Source**

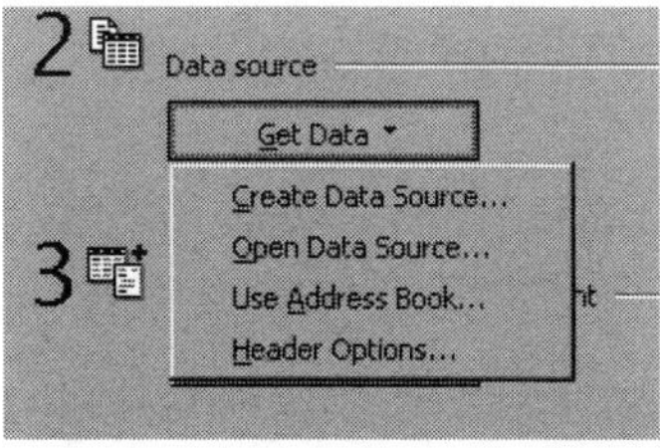

Figure 12.5 Get Data drop-down menu

◎ Select: **Create Data Source** from the drop-down menu

The **Create Data Source** dialogue box is displayed on screen.

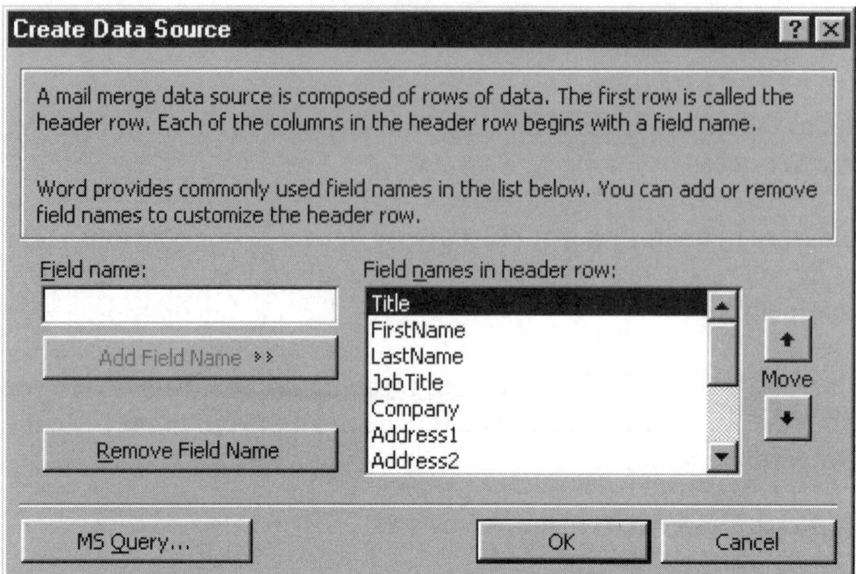

Figure 12.6 Create Data Source dialogue box

Word 2000 has already provided some commonly-used field names - these are displayed in the **Field names in header row** menu box, eg **Title, FirstName, LastName**. Your data source will be much easier to use if it contains only the field names you require for the data file you are creating. You can make the data file fit your requirements by carrying out the following actions:

◎ removing any field names you do not require
◎ adding any field names you do require
◎ confirming the field names when you have completed the first two steps.

You may not require some less common field names provided in Word 2000's menu box, eg **State**

To remove unwanted field names from the Data Source:

◎ Select: The **Field Name** that is not required in the menu box
◎ Click: **Remove Field Name**

Repeat until all unwanted field names are removed.

You may require a field name which is not displayed in Word 2000's menu box, eg **Category**

To add required field names to the Data Source:

◎ Key in: An appropriate name for the field in the **Field Name** box

Note: A field name must begin with a letter and must not contain spaces

◎ Click: **Add Field Name** to add your chosen field name to the list of **Field names in header row**

Repeat the above steps until all your additional fields have been named and each new field name has been added to the list.

Note: When you add a new field name to your data source, it is added at the bottom of the list of **Field names in header row.**

To move the field names into a different order:

The field names are transferred in the same order from the list in the menu box to the data form and to the data file when it is printed in table format. Your data file may be much easier to use if the field names are in a logical order. You can move the field names as follows:

- ◎ Select: The Field name to be moved
- ◎ Click: ↓ or ↑ on the **Move** section at right of the **Field names in header row** menu box to move the field names to the required position in the list

When you have set up your data file with the required field names and they are listed in the required order:

- ◎ Click: **OK** to confirm field names displayed

Save the data source

After confirming the field names selected for your data source, the Save As dialogue box is displayed on screen.

Select: An appropriate directory and drive in the **Save in** box
Key in: An appropriate name in the **File name** box
Click: **OK**

The **Save Data Source** dialogue box is displayed on screen.

Figure 12.7 Save Data Source dialogue box

To go straight to the Data Form and enter details for each record:

- ◎ Select: **Edit Data Source**

To add merge fields to the form letter:

- ◎ Select: **Edit Main Document**

Exercise 12A continued

12.2 With the main document **UNIT12MAIN** on screen, and the **Mail Merge Helper** dialogue box displayed, refer to the instructions under the **Create the data source** section and create a data source file to be merged later with the letter, removing and adding field names as follows:

a **Remove the following Field names:**

JobTitle
Company
State
Country
HomePhone
WorkPhone

b **Add the following Field name:**

Category

c **Practise changing the order of the field names in the Field names in Header row box. Arrange the Field names in the following order before proceeding:**

Title
FirstName
LastName
Address1
Address2
City
PostalCode
Category

12.3 Following the instructions **Save the Data Source**, save the data source you have just created as **UNIT12DATA1**.

The Mail Merge Helper dialogue box will be displayed on screen.

◎ Select **Edit Data Source** from the dialogue box.

Read the next two sections carefully, then go on to step 12.4.

Switch between the data source and the main document

When you have created a main document and a data source, the Mail Merge Helper dialogue box in Word 2000 links the two files together. During the mail merge operation, you will need to switch between the two files. Refer to the following instructions as you are learning to carry out the mail merge operation to learn the different methods.

Using the Mail Merge Helper dialogue box

◎ Click: The **Mail Merge Helper** button on the Mail Merge Helper Tool Bar

Figure 12.8 Mail Merge Tool Bar

The **Mail Merge Helper** dialogue box is displayed on screen.

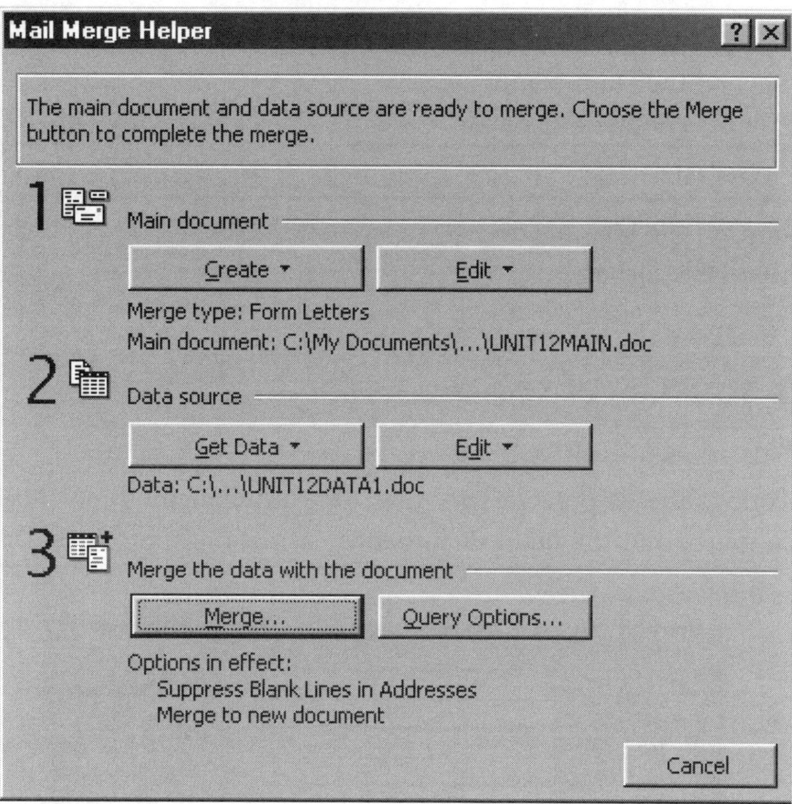

Figure 12.9 Mail Merge Helper dialogue box (after form letter and data source have been created)

To switch to the Main Document:

◎ Click: The **Edit** button in **Section 1 – Main Document**

To switch to the Data Source:

◎ Click: The **Mail Merge Helper** button on the Mail Merge Helper dialogue box

◎ Click: The **Edit** button in **Section 2 – Data Source**

Using the Database Tool Bar

Whilst in View Source (table format) mode, the **Database Tool Bar** is displayed on screen.

Figure 12.10 Database Tool Bar

To switch to the Main Document:

- Click: The **Mail Merge Main Document** button

To switch to the Data Source (Data Form):

- Click: The **Mail Merge Helper** button on the Mail Merge Helper dialogue box
- Click: The **Data Form** button

Using the Window option on the Main menu

To switch to the Main Document:

- Click: **Window** on the **Main** menu
- Select: The **Main Document** filename

To switch to the Data File:

- Click: **Window** on the **Main** menu
- Select: The **Data File** filename

Edit the data source (enter the record details)

Unless the Data Form is already on your screen, use one of the methods described in **Switching between the data source and the main document** to access the appropriate Data Source.

The **Data Form** is displayed on screen.

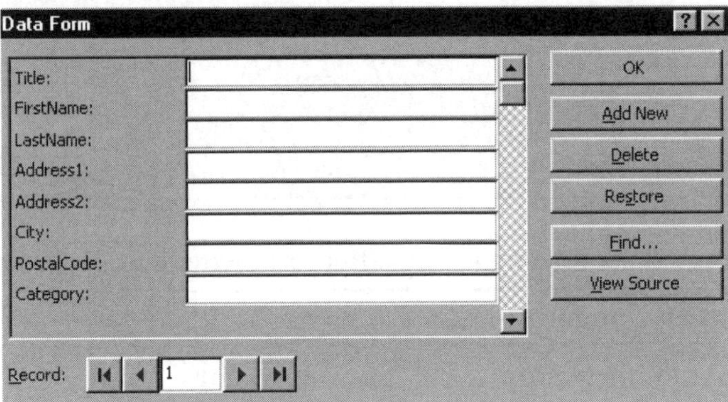

Figure 12.11 Data Form

1 Key in: The information for the first field (do not press the spacebar after keying in all the information)
2 Press: ↵ (return/enter) to enter the information and move to the next field
3 Repeat: Steps 1-2 until all fields for the first record are entered
4 Click: **Add New**
5 Repeat: Steps 1-3 for each record

When all records are entered:

- Click: **OK**

Options available in the data form	
Button	**Action**
Record	Move to another record by keying in the appropriate record number, *or* Click: **First Record, Previous Record, Next Record,** or **Last Record**
Delete	Deletes the current record
Restore	Reverses changes made to the current record
Find	Searches for specified data throughout records
View Source	Displays all records in the form of a table

Exercise 12A continued

12.4 Following the instructions under **Edit the data source**, enter the four records shown under **Exercise 12A – records for data source** into the Data Form (4 records).

Figure 12.12 Example of data form with first record completed

Exercise 12A – records for data source

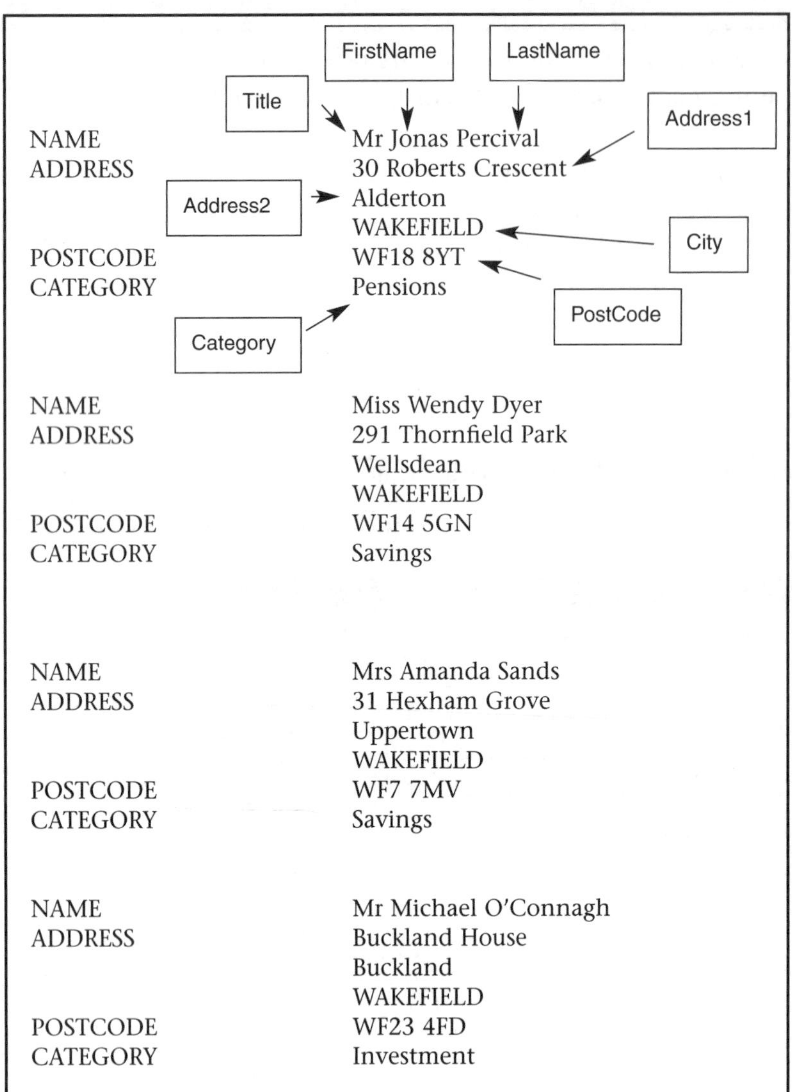

NAME Mr Jonas Percival
ADDRESS 30 Roberts Crescent
Alderton
WAKEFIELD
POSTCODE WF18 8YT
CATEGORY Pensions

NAME Miss Wendy Dyer
ADDRESS 291 Thornfield Park
Wellsdean
WAKEFIELD
POSTCODE WF14 5GN
CATEGORY Savings

NAME Mrs Amanda Sands
ADDRESS 31 Hexham Grove
Uppertown
WAKEFIELD
POSTCODE WF7 7MV
CATEGORY Savings

NAME Mr Michael O'Connagh
ADDRESS Buckland House
Buckland
WAKEFIELD
POSTCODE WF23 4FD
CATEGORY Investment

Remember not to press the spacebar after entering data into a field. Press return immediately after the last letter to avoid extra spaces when your letter is merged with the data file

Save and print the data source

You may be required to produce a printout of the records in your data source – at work as well as in examinations.

Using one of the methods described in **Switching between the data source and the main document**, access the appropriate Data Source.

- Click: The **View Source** button in the Data Form dialogue box

The Data Source file is displayed on screen. You may find some of the text wraps illogically in the boxes to allow all the information to be displayed. This format is acceptable in OCR/RSA examinations – you do not have to reformat the table layout.

- Select: **Print** from the **File** menu and print in the normal way
- Select: **Save** from the **File** menu to save the completed data file

Note: Before printing, use Print Preview to check that the data file will fit on the paper when printed. If it will not fit, you could reduce the left and right margins *or* change the Page Setup to Landscape.

Exercise 12A continued

12.5 Save and print one copy of the data file **UNIT12DATA1**. Check your work very carefully, comparing it with the printout check at the back of the book. If you find any errors, retrieve the data source and correct them now before proceeding further with your mail merge.

Insert merge codes in the main document

The main document and data source are linked through the Mail Merge Helper dialogue box when mail merge is set up. Word 2000 will transfer data from the data source to the main document, selecting the data by record and then by field. Merge codes in the main document indicate the position and type of the data which is to be transferred from the data source.

Using one of the methods described under **Switching between the data source and the main document** make sure that your Main Document Form Letter is displayed on screen and that the Mail Merge Tool Bar is also on screen.

Figure 12.13 Mail Merge Tool Bar

Note: the above Tool Bar should appear automatically when you open the Main Document Form Letter. However, if this Tool Bar is not present:

- Select: Tool Bars from the View menu
- Click: Mail Merge

A ✓ will appear to indicate that this Tool Bar is displayed.

1 Move the cursor: To the position where you wish to enter the first merge code in the main document
2 Click: The **Insert Merge Field** button on the Mail Merge Tool Bar
3 Select: The required field name from drop-down menu (Figure 12.14)
4 Repeat: Steps 1-3 for each subsequent merge field code required
5 Select: **Save** from the **File** menu to save the completed main document

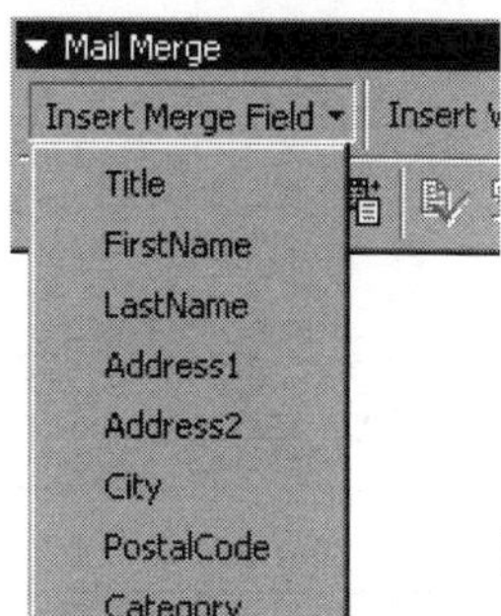

Figure 12.14 Field names drop-down menu

Formatting merge codes

Merge codes can be formatted after being inserted into the main document.

- Click: On the merge code text in your main document to check that the font size of the merge codes is the same as the remainder of the document
- Use: Bold, underline, italic etc if the data requires emphasis

Exercise 12A continued

12.6 Following the instructions under **Insert merge codes in main document**, ensure that the Main Document Form Letter saved as **UNIT12MAIN** is on screen, then insert merge codes in your main document as shown below. Check that the text of the merge codes is in the same font and size as the remainder of the letter.

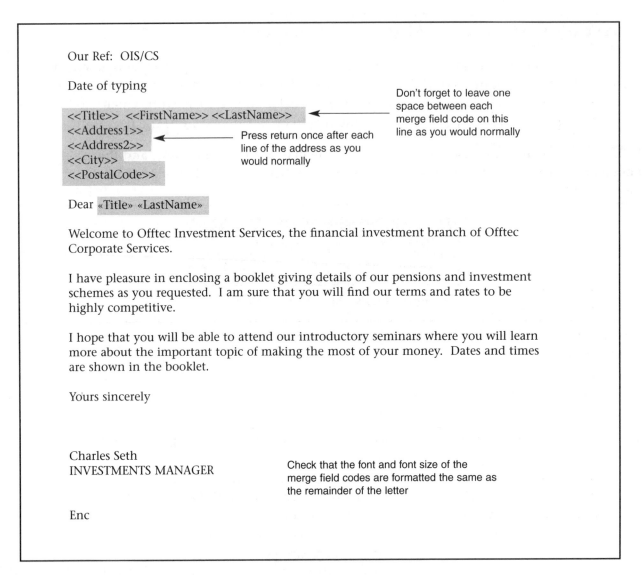

Our Ref: OIS/CS

Date of typing

<<Title>> <<FirstName>> <<LastName>>
<<Address1>>
<<Address2>>
<<City>>
<<PostalCode>>

Don't forget to leave one space between each merge field code on this line as you would normally

Press return once after each line of the address as you would normally

Dear «Title» «LastName»

Welcome to Offtec Investment Services, the financial investment branch of Offtec Corporate Services.

I have pleasure in enclosing a booklet giving details of our pensions and investment schemes as you requested. I am sure that you will find our terms and rates to be highly competitive.

I hope that you will be able to attend our introductory seminars where you will learn more about the important topic of making the most of your money. Dates and times are shown in the booklet.

Yours sincerely

Charles Seth
INVESTMENTS MANAGER

Check that the font and font size of the merge field codes are formatted the same as the remainder of the letter

Enc

Print the form letter

You may be required to produce a printout of the form letter - at work as well as in examinations.

With the form letter displayed on screen:

- Print in the normal way
- Select: **Save** from the **File** menu to save the completed main document

Exercise 12A continued

12.7 Resave the main document including the merge codes. Print a copy of the form letter. Check your work with the printout check at the back of the book. Correct any errors which you find before proceeding.

View the merged file

In the Main Document window:

- Click: The **View Merged Data** button on the Mail Merge Tool Bar

The first merged document is displayed on screen.

To view other records:

- Click: The arrow buttons on the Mail Merge Tool Bar, *or*
- Key in: The number of the required record in the box between the arrows

To return to the main document:

- Click: The **View Merged Data** button on the Mail Merge Tool Bar again

Print the merged file

To print all merged documents:

- Click: The **Merge to Printer** button on the Mail Merge Tool Bar

To print one merged letter, eg for checking purposes:

- Select: **Current page** in the **Page range** section of the Print dialogue box

Exercise 12A continued

12.8 Following the instructions under **View the merged file**, merge the main document and the data source. Check the merged documents carefully – four personalised letters should have been processed. If you need to make amendments, switch back to the main document to do this so that your amendments will apply to all the merged documents.

12.9 Print only the letter to Wendy Dyer. View Record 2 to display the letter and then select **Current Page** in the Print dialogue box. Check your printout of the letter to Wendy Dyer against the printout check at the back of the book. If you find any errors, switch back to the main document or the data file to correct them so that your amendments will apply to all the merged documents.

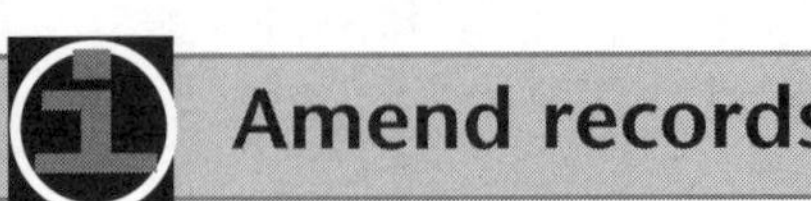

Amend records

It may be necessary for you to make amendments to the records in your data source as circumstances change, eg a change of address.

Method 1 – using the find record function in the data source

Word 2000 allows you to find a particular record without scanning through every record. This is useful for making amendments to individual records.

Using one of the methods described in **Switching between the data source and the main document** access the appropriate Data Source.

With the Data Form displayed on screen:

- Click: **Find**

***OR*, with the Data Source in View Source format, ie table format:**

- Click: The **Find Record** button on the Database Tool Bar

The Find in Field dialogue box is displayed on screen.

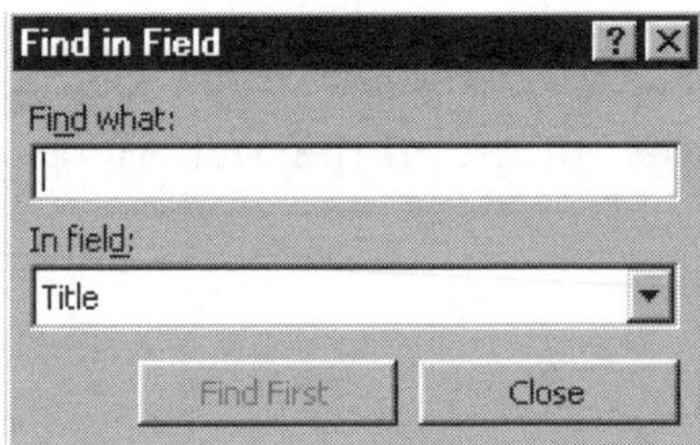

Figure 12.15 Find in Field dialogue box

- Key in: The data which you wish to amend in the **Find What:** box, eg Brown if you want to change this name to Browne
- Select: The field in which this is situated in the drop-down menu of the **In field** box, eg Name
- Click on: **Find First**

Note: Word 2000 will display the first record containing the specified data in the specified field. You should check other details such as address or date of birth within the record to help you to find the exact record you require as there may be several records with the name 'Brown'.

- Click: **Find Next** until you locate the correct record
- Click: **Close**
- Key in: The new (amended) data (overtyping the previous entry)
- Click: **Find** to select the next record to be amended
- Click: **OK** when all amendments to all records are completed

Method 2 – using the view source (table)

Word 2000 allows you to make amendments to records while they are displayed on screen in table format. This is useful if an additional field has been added and you wish to enter data into this field in each record. If the data is often the same, eg weekly or monthly, you could use the copy and paste facility to insert the data.

With the Data Form displayed on screen:

- Click: The **View Source** button in the **Data Form** dialogue box

The data source is displayed on screen in the form of a table.

- Amend the data as required, adding, deleting and changing as necessary
- Resave the file to save the changes

Exercise 12B

12.10 Display the Data Source saved as **UNIT12DATA1** on screen and resave as **UNIT12DATA2**. Using **Find record in the data source**, find the following records by keying in the LastName. Then amend the records as shown below:

	Mandy
NAME	Mrs ~~Amanda~~ Sands
ADDRESS	31 Hexham Grove
	Uppertown
	WAKEFIELD
POSTCODE	WF7 7MV
CATEGORY	Savings
NAME	Mr Michael O'Connagh
ADDRESS	~~Buckland House~~ The Manor House
	Buckland
	WAKEFIELD
POSTCODE	WF23 4FD
CATEGORY	Investment

Add and delete records

It may be necessary for you to add new records and also to delete records from your data source as circumstances change, eg an employee or member joining or leaving an organisation.

Using one of the methods described in **Switch between the data source and the main document**, access the appropriate Data Source.

To delete a record from the data source:

Find the appropriate record by using one of the Find options described under **Amending the records**:

With the Data Form for the record to be deleted displayed on screen.

- Click: The **Delete** button in the **Data Form** dialogue box

OR, with the View Source (Table) format on screen:

- Select: The Record to be deleted
- Click: The **Delete Record** button on the **Database** Tool Bar

To add a new record to the data source:

With the Data Form on screen (Figure 12.12):

- Click: **Add New** to move to a blank record
- Key in: The record details
- Click: **Add New**

With the View Source (Table) format on screen:

- Click: The **Add New Record** button on the Database Tool Bar
- Key in: The record details in the blank row created

Exercise 12B continued

12.11 Referring to the instructions **To delete a record from the data source**, delete the record for Jonas Percival.

12.12 Referring to the instructions **To add a new record to the data source**, add the following new members:

NAME	Dr Morag Usquaebae
ADDRESS	Flat 10A Royal Avenue HARROGATE
POSTCODE	HG2 9AS
CATEGORY	Investment
NAME	Mrs Jane Prior
ADDRESS	67 Ascot Lane Moordene LEEDS
POSTCODE	LS25 5DE
CATEGORY	Pensions
NAME	Miss Anna Muller
ADDRESS	1 Rowan Rise Alderton WAKEFIELD
POSTCODE	WF18 3DX
CATEGORY	Savings

12.13 Resave the data source and print one copy of the data file. Check this carefully with the printout check at the back of the book. If you find any errors, retrieve the data source and correct them.

Exercise 12C

12.14 Following the instructions under **View the merged file** and **Print the merged file**, merge and print letters to all six prospective clients of Offtec Investment Services. Check your documents against the printout checks at the back of the book. If you find any errors, retrieve the data source or the main documents and make any necessary corrections in these files so that amendments will be effective in all merged documents.

12.15 Exit the program if you have finished working or continue straight on to the next unit.

UNIT 13 MANIPULATING DATA IN MAIL MERGE

By the end of Unit 13, you should have learnt how to:

- add and delete fields in a mail merge data source
- sort a mail merge data source into alphabetical and numerical order
- select records by one or more criteria from a mail merge data source
- merge a main document with selected records
- print a main document merged with selected records.

Amend the data source fields

It may be necessary for you to make amendments to the data source fields so that you can store additional data or delete data that is no longer required.

Open the data source file you wish to amend in the usual way. The View Source (table format) is usually displayed. **If it is not displayed:**

- Click: The **View Source** button in the **Data Form** dialogue box (unless the date source file is already on screen)
- Check: That the Database Tool Bar (Figure 13.1) is displayed on screen

If it is not already displayed on screen:

- Select: **Tool Bars** from the **View** menu
- Select: **Database** (a ✓ will appear next to the word when it is selected)

The **Database Tool Bar** is displayed on the screen.

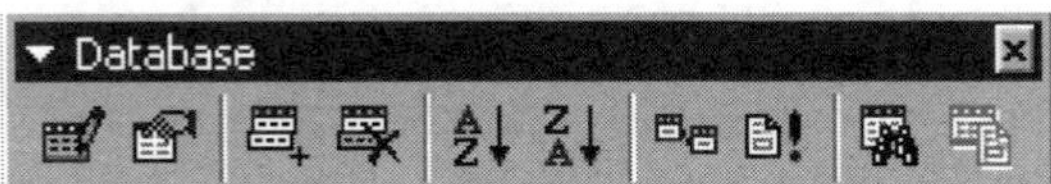

Figure 13.1 Database Tool Bar

- Click: The **Manage Fields** button on the Database Tool Bar

The Manage Fields dialogue box is displayed on screen.

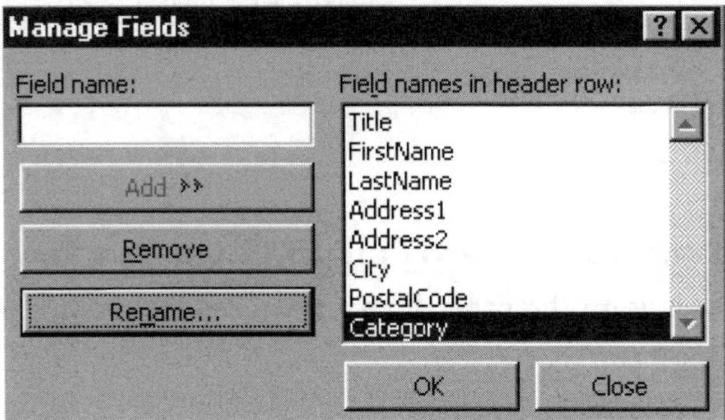

Figure 13.2 Manage Fields dialogue box

- Select: The field name you wish to amend in the **Field names in header row** box, *or*
- Key in: The field name you wish to amend in the **Field name** box

Options available in Manage Fields dialogue box	
Button	**Action**
Add	Add a new field name to the data source
Remove	Remove a field name from the data source
Rename	Rename an existing field in the data source
◎ Click: **OK** to confirm amendments	

Exercise 13A

13.1 Retrieve the data source file stored under the filename **UNIT12DATA2**. Save as **UNIT13DATA1**.

13.2 Following the instructions **Amend the data source fields**, refer to the data source printout and add an extra field name **Seminardate**.

13.3 Refer back to the instructions given in Unit 12 in **Amend records**, and complete Exercise 13A by amending all the records as shown and adding relevant data for the new field **Seminardate**. You may choose to amend the records in Data Form format or in View Source (Table) format.

Title	First Name	LastName	Address1	Address2	City	Postal Code	Category	Seminardate
Miss	Wendy	Dyer	291 Thornfield Park	Wellsdean	WAKEFIELD	WF14 5GN	Savings	23/10/00
Mrs	Mandy	Sands	31 Hexham Grove	Uppertown	LEEDS ~~WAKEFIELD~~	LS11 8AA ~~WF7 7MV~~	Savings	23/10/00
Mr	Michael	O'Connagh	The Manor House	Buckland	WAKEFIELD	WF23 4FD	Investment	10/09/00
Dr	Morag	Usquaebae	Flat 10A	Royal Avenue	HARROGATE	HG2 9AS	Investment	06/11/00
Mrs	Jane	Prior	67 Ascot Lane	Moordene	WAKEFIELD ~~LEEDS~~	WF7 7MV ~~LS25 5DE~~	Pensions	10/12/00
Miss	Anna	Muller	1 Rowan Rise	Alderton	WAKEFIELD	WF18 3DX	Pensions ~~Savings~~	28/10/00

13.4 Save the amended data source as **UNIT13DATA2**. Use Print Preview to check that the data source table will fit on the paper. If necessary, reduce the left and right margin settings under Page Setup to 2 cm.

Note: After reducing the margins, you may still find that text 'wraps around' in the headings. This form of presentation is acceptable in OCR/RSA examinations as the data source is a working document rather than a document which would be sent to customers or clients. In the examination, it is better to complete all the tasks correctly rather than waste time on trying to improve the appearance of the data source table.

13.5 Print one copy of the data file. Check your work very carefully, comparing it with the printout check at the back of the book. If you find any errors, retrieve the data source and correct them now before proceeding further with your mail merge.

Sort the data source

It may be necessary for you to sort the data source to present the information in a useful way.

Open the data source file you wish to amend in the usual way. The View Source (table format) is usually displayed. **If it is not displayed:**

- Click: The **View Source** button in the **Data Form** dialogue box
- Check: That the Database Tool Bar (Figure 13.1) is displayed on screen

If it is not displayed:

- Select: **Tool Bars** from the **View** menu
- Select: **Database** (a ✓ will appear next to the word when it is selected)

The Database Tool Bar is displayed on the screen (see Figure 13.1).

- Place the cursor: In the column representing the field by which the data source is to be sorted
- Click: The A↓Z **Sort ascending** or the Z↓A **Sort descending** button on the Database Tool Bar as appropriate

Exercise 13B

13.6 Retrieve the data source stored as **UNIT13DATA2** unless it is already on screen. Following the instructions under **Sort the data source**, sort the data into ascending (A-Z) alphabetical order of LastName and print one copy. Check your work with the printout check at the back of the book, and repeat the procedure if necessary.

13.7 Sort the data into descending (Z-A) order by **Seminardate** and print one copy. Check your work with the printout check at the back of the book and repeat the procedure if necessary.

13.8 Resave the data source and close the file.

Open the mail merge data source for use with a new main document

The main document and data source are linked when mail merge is set up. Word 2000 will transfer data from the data source to the main document, selecting the data by record and then by field. The Mail Merge Helper dialogue box helps you to link the two files together. You may use a previously created data source with a new main document to create different merged documents.

Open a new document and then follow the steps below:

- Select: **Tools, Mail Merge**

The Mail Merge Helper dialogue box is displayed on screen.

- Click: **Create Form Letters** in the **1 – Main Document** section of the Mail Merge Helper dialogue box
- Select: **Active window**

The Mail Merge Helper dialogue box is again displayed on screen.

- Click: **Get Data** in the **2 – Data Source** section of the Mail Merge Helper dialogue box
- Click: **Open Data Source**
- Select: The required **Data Source** from the listed files

The following dialogue box is displayed on screen.

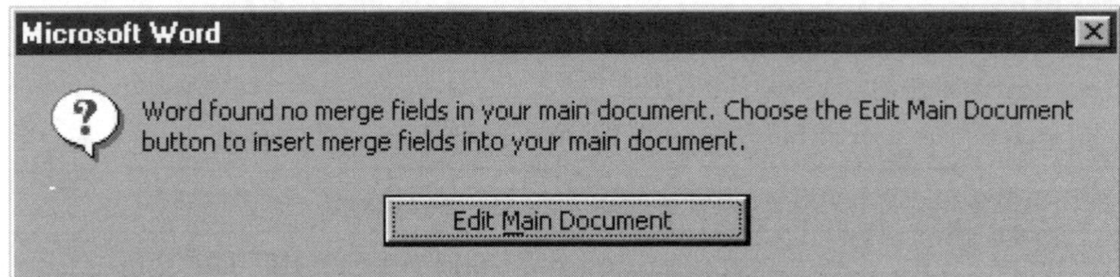

Figure 13.3 No Merge Fields dialogue box

- Select: **Edit Main Document**

Note: You should always save changes to your data source and to your main document. Whilst working on Exercises 13C to 13G, there is no need to save the merged documents. If your merged documents are not correct when you check them, changes should be made to the data source and/or main document so that when you re-operate the merge, they will all be correct.

Exercise 13C

13.9 Re-read the instructions given in Unit 12 under **Create and name the main document** and under **Open the mail merge data source** in this unit. You are going to start a new mail merge operation by using the active window as your main document. This will be merged with the data source stored as **UNIT13DATA2**. Follow the steps 13.10–13.12.

13.10 Open a new document. Select **File** from the **Insert** menu, and insert the letterhead file saved as **Lettertemp** into your document.

13.11 Following the instructions under **Open the mail merge data source for use with a new main document**, open the data source saved as **UNIT13DATA2**.

13.12 Key in the following letter using Times New Roman, font size 12. Referring back to the instructions in Unit 12 under **Insert merge codes in the main document**, insert merge codes in the letter where indicated by *, eg ***Title**.

Our Ref: OIS/CS

Date of typing

*Title *FirstName *LastName
*Address1
*Address2
*City
*PostalCode

Dear *Title *LastName

Introductory Seminar on *Category

Thank you for your interest in our Seminar. I hope that you found the information in our booklet of use to you. I am sure that when you attend the Seminar, you will be fascinated to hear what we can do to help you to secure your financial future.

When my assistant telephoned you, you confirmed that you would be able to attend the Seminar at the New Miller Inn on ***Seminardate**. The Seminar will commence at 7.00 pm and light refreshments will be served. Please bring along a friend or colleague if you wish. Simply return the enclosed reply card to confirm your attendance and add the name of the person who will accompany you.

Everyone who comes along to the Seminar will have free entry to our £2,000 Prize Draw. You may win a Mediterranean Cruise for two or £2,000 in cash!

I look forward to seeing you at the *Category Seminar on *Seminardate.

Yours sincerely

Charles Seth
INVESTMENTS MANAGER

Enc

13.13 Save the form letter you have just created as **UNIT13CMAIN**, and print one copy. Check your work with the printout check at the back of the book and correct any errors before proceeding.

13.14 Referring back to the instructions in Unit 12 under **View the merged file**, merge the main document and the data source. Check the merged documents carefully by clicking on

Next Record in the Mail Merge dialogue box – six personalised letters should have been processed.

Note: If you need to make any amendments, switch back to the main document to do this so that your amendments will apply to all of the merged documents. There is no need to print at this stage.

When the merged documents are correct, return to the main document by:

- Clicking on the **View Merged Data** button on the Mail Merge Tool Bar, *or*
- Selecting **Close** from the File menu (not saving changes)

Select specific records to be merged using one criterion

You may be requested to merge a form letter with a selection of the data source records which match one specific criterion.

- Click: The **Mail Merge Helper** button on the Mail Merge Tool Bar
- Click: The Query Options... **Query Options** button in Section 3

The **Query Options** dialogue box is displayed on screen.

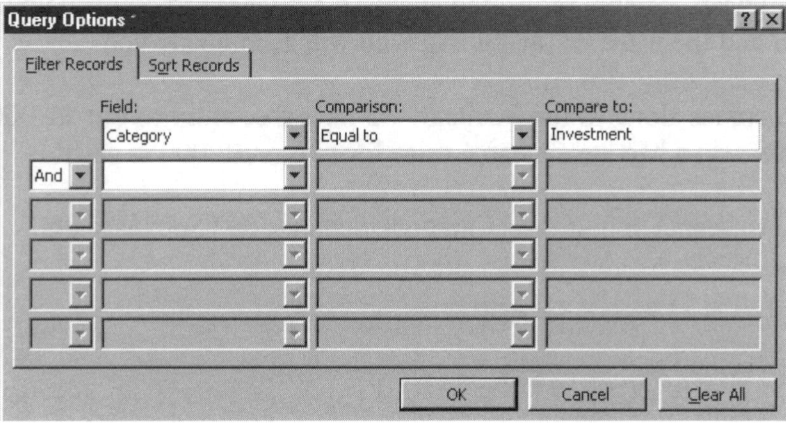

Figure 13.4 Query Options dialogue box

- Select: The field to which you want to apply a criterion from the drop-down menu in the **Field** box
- Select: **Equal to** from the drop-down menu in the **Comparison** box when you want to enter text or data against which records are matched and selected. (Other options such as **Less than, Greater than** and **Not equal to** are also available)
- Key in: The required criterion (the text or data to be used for selection) in the **Compare to** box
- Click: **OK**
- Click: **Merge** in **Section 3 – Merge the data with the document**

The **Merge** dialogue box is displayed on screen.

Figure 13.5 Merge dialogue box

- Select: **New Document** in the **Merge To** box
- Check: That **Don't print blank lines when data fields are empty** is selected (ie has a black circle in it)
- Click: The **Merge** button
- View: The merged file to check the selection is correct before printing
- Print, save and close the merged file

Exercise 13C continued

13.15 Referring to the instructions under **Select specific records to be merged using one criterion**, and/or using the instructions below, merge the main document with the records for **Investment** category clients only:

- Click: The **Mail Merge Helper** button on the Mail Merge Tool Bar
- Click: **Query Options** in Section 3 of the Mail Merge Helper dialogue box
- Select: **Category** from the Field drop-down menu
- Select: **Equal to** in the **Comparison** box
- Key in: **Investment** in the **Compare to** box
- Click: **OK**
- Click: **Merge** in Section 3 of the Mail Merge Helper dialogue box
- Select: **New Document** in the **Merge to** box of the Merge dialogue box
- Click: **Merge**

13.16 View the merged file to check the documents. There should be two letters – one to Mr Michael O'Connagh and one to Dr Morag Usquaebae. Scroll down the file to view and check both letters.

13.17 Print the merged file (two letters). Check your letters with the printout check at the back of the book. If you find any errors, switch back to the Mail Merge Helper dialogue box and then to the main document, data source or query options to correct your work so that your corrections will apply to all the letters. Close the file.

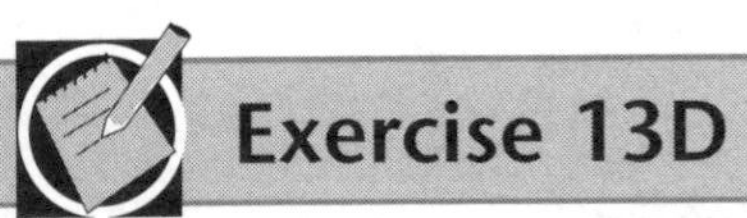

Exercise 13D

13.18 Retrieve the main document stored as **UNIT13CMAIN** and merge the main document with the records in the data source stored as **UNIT13DATA2** for members living in **WAKEFIELD** only.

13.19 View the merged file to check the documents. There should be four letters: to Miss Wendy Dyer, Mr Michael O'Connagh, Miss Jane Prior and Miss Anna Muller.

13.20 Print the merged file (four letters), and check your work with the printout check at the back of the book. If you find any errors, switch back to the Mail Merge Helper dialogue box and then to the main document, data source or query options to correct your work. Close the file without saving.

Select specific records to be merged using two criteria

You may be requested to merge a form letter with a selection of the data source records which match two (or more) specific criteria.

- Click: The **Mail Merge Helper** button on the Mail Merge Tool Bar
- Click: The **Query Options** button in Section 3

The Query Options dialogue box is displayed on screen (see Figure 13.4).

- Select: The appropriate field from the drop-down menu in the **Field** box
- Select: **Equal to** from the drop-down menu in the **Comparison** box (other options such as **Less than**, **Greater than** and **Not equal to** are also available)
- Key in: The required criterion in the **Compare To** box
- Repeat: The above procedure for the second criterion
- Click: **OK**
- Close: The Mail Merge Helper dialogue box
- View: The merged file to check the selection before printing (the number of selected records is displayed on the Mail Merge Tool Bar)

Exercise 13E

13.21 Retrieve the main document stored as **UNIT13CMAIN** and merge the main document with the records in the data source stored as **UNIT13DATA2** for **Savings** category clients whose **Seminar date** is **23/10/00**.

13.22 View the merged file to check the documents. There should be two letters – to Miss Wendy Dyer and Mrs Mandy Sands.

13.23 Print the merged file (two letters). Close the file without saving.

Exercise 13F

13.24 Using the same main document and data file, merge the main document with the records for **Pensions** members living in **WAKEFIELD**.

13.25 View the merged file to check the documents. There should be two letters – to Miss Anna Muller and Mrs Jane Prior.

13.26 Print the merged file (two letters). Close the file without saving.

Exercise 13G

13.27 Save the data source, created in Exercise 13A, as **UNIT13DATA3**. Following the instructions under **Amend the data source fields** remove the **Title** and **Category** fields from the data source:

- Switch to the data source if not already on screen
- Switch to View Source (Table) format
- Click: **Manage fields** on the Database Tool Bar
- Remove: The **Title** field
- Remove: The **Category** field

13.28 Print a copy of the data source. Check your work with the printout check at the back of the book. Resave the amended data source.

13.29 Exit the program if you have finished working or continue straight on to the next unit.

UNIT 14 CONSOLIDATION 3

By the end of Unit 14, you will have revised and practised all the techniques and skills needed for the OCR/RSA Stage II Mail Merge Part 2 Award.

Look at your Progress Review Checklist and at your completed exercises to remind yourself of what you have learnt so far and to identify any weaknesses. Then complete the following exercises as revision.

Exercise 14A

Please key in the following records as a datafile suitable for use with the memo in Exercise 14B. Save as EX14ADATA and print one copy.

Atkinson
Sharon
8 Windsmoor Gro
Holmehurst
ILKLEY
LS34 7DP
Customer Services

Molyneux
Diane
25 Ashurst Ave
Beech Heights
KEIGHLEY
BD22 2GE
Design

Inman
Pauline
24a Jackson Cross
Cross Lanes
SHIPLEY
BD24 9MV
Payroll

Jamil
Shamsa
17 Wheatwood St
East Head
BRADFORD
BD8 9EH
Telesales

Pazeerah
Asma
Belle Vue House
Craven Hill
BRADFORD
BD18 4OE
Customer Services

Forster
Norman
16 Tennyson Street
High Close
LEEDS
LS24 3SE
Technical

Leadbeater
Clive
20 Shaftesbury Dr
Park Lane Top
LEEDS
LS10 3LV
Technical

Stanley
Colin
16 Fountain Park Rd
Woodbottom
SHIPLEY
BD17 5NT
Telesales

MacLeod
Duncan
28 Bourne Rd
Holmehurst
ILKLEY
LS34 7DB
Design

Tomlinson
Allan
21 Devonshire Lane
Gloveley
KEIGHLEY
BD21 4DA
Payroll

Exercise 14B

Key in the standard document (memo) below to be merged with the data file created in Exercise 14A.

- Use the **Memotemp** memorandum head
- Use a ragged right margin
- Insert merge codes where indicated by *
- Save as **EX14BMAIN** and print one copy of the standard document
- Merge the standard document with the data source stored as **EX14ADATA** and filter the records to print memos to Technical Department staff only

MEMO

To: *FirstName *LastName, *Department Department
From: Barry Davidson, Training Officer

Staff Focus Group ← (emphasise heading)

Thank you for returning the tear-off slip from the latest [Bulletin] [Staff] and, more importantly, for volunteering to join the newly formed Staff Focus Group.

The aim of the Group is to ensure that we work towards achieving a reputation, based on real improvements, as a forward-thinking and caring employer. Your contribution as a representative of your department is very ~~important~~ valuable.

Our first meeting will be held at 4.00 pm on Thurs 20 October in the Training Room on Floor 5. I look forward to seeing you and working with you.

Exercise 14C

Please recall this datafile stored under EX14ADATA and save as EX14CDATA. Amend as indicated and then sort the amended datafile into alphabetical order of surname (LastName). Print one copy. This datafile will be required for Exercise 14D.

Please add fields to each record → Supervisor, Startdate, Scale

FirstName	LastName	Address1	Address2	City	PostalCode	Department	Supervisor	Startdate	Scale
Sharon	Atkinson	8 Windsmoor ~~Grove~~ Close	Holmehurst	ILKLEY	LS34 7DP	Customer Service[s]	S Smith	07/99	A3
Shamsa	Jamil	17 Wheatwood Street	East Head	BRADFORD	BD8 9EH	Telesales	M Fosse	06/98	A4
~~Clive~~ Callum	Leadbeater	20 Shaftesbury Drive	Park Lane Top	LEEDS	LS10 3LV	Technical	L Hoban	09/99	T2
Duncan	MacLeod	28 Bourne Road	Holmehurst	ILKLEY	LS34 7DB	Design	K Joy	04/97	T4
Diane	Molyneux	23 ~~25~~ Ashurst Avenue	Beech Heights	KEIGHLEY	BD22 2GE	Design	M Mohan	01/97	T3
Asma	Pazeerah	Belle Vue House	Craven Hill	BRADFORD	BD18 4OE	Customer Service[s]	A Burns	08/96	A4
~~Colin~~	~~Stanley~~	~~16 Fountain Park Road~~	~~Woodbottom~~	~~SHIPLEY~~	~~BD17 5NT~~	~~Telesales~~	~~M Fosse~~	~~11/98~~	~~A3~~
Allan	Tomlinson	21 Devonshire Lane	Gloveley	KEIGHLEY	BD21 4DA	Payroll	J Porter	11/98	A2
Pauline	Inman	24a Jackson Cross	Cross Lanes	SHIPLEY	BD24 9MV	Payroll	J Porter	10/98	~~A4~~ A3
Norman	~~Forster~~ Foster	16 Tennyson Street	High Close	LEEDS	LS24 3SE	Technical	P Pieterson	01/99	T2

Please delete this record

See separate sheet for additional records to be included in the datafile

Please add these records shown below to the datafile before sorting and printing.

Please put cities BRADFORD, KEIGHLEY, LEEDS in full throughout

Name	Address	Dept	Supervisor	Startdate	Scale
Sarah Arnold	10 Aire View, East Head, BFD, BD8 7HN	Cust Serv	S Smith	08/96	Scale A3
Martin Ford	Glen House, Gloveley, KLY, BD21 6DH	Telesales	M Fosse	07/97	
Nicky Marcou	10 Queens Dr, High Close, LDS, LS24 6PT	Telesales	V Barrett	06/98	
Penny Marr	1 Rosslyn View, Craven Hill, BFD, BD18 9LL	Cust Serv	A Burns	04/97	
Karen Jacques	Dean Cottage, Dean Bank, SHIPLEY, BD24 8LU	Design	M Mohan	11/97	Scale T4
Anna Nesovic	126 Manor St, Cross Lanes, SHIPLEY, BD24 5SH	Technical	P Pieterson	10/96	
Christopher Day	18 Barr Rd, Halton, SHIPLEY, BD24 5SA	Payroll	J Porter	12/97	Scale A4
Jenny Payne	1 Seed Hill, Wheatburn, LDS, LS18 3JJ	Design	K Joy	03/96	Scale T3
Audrey Thornton	3 Walker Pk, Parkway, BFD, BD16 1FW	Technical	I Jones	04/95	
Keith Thorpe	14 Pasture Lane, Beech Hts, KLY, BD22 1HC	Cust Servi	A Burns	07/98	Scale A2
Jeff Harvey	37 Ingfield, Ings Dale, KLY, BD19 7PC	Telesales	V Barrett	01/99	
Safina Zafar	51 Holly St, Lane Side, BFD, BD10 4CT	Technical	P Pieterson	10/98	Scale T2
Li Yeung	106 Bradford Rd, Easton, LDS, LS14 2MQ	Design	M Mohan	05/96	
Robert Sugden	Heather Glen, Dean Bank, SHIPLEY, BD24 3SS	Cust Serv	A Burns	05/99	Scale A5
Katie Stubbs	81 Delph Clo, Holmehurst, ILKLEY, LS34 4HT	Cust Serv	S Smith	10/99	
Claire Smalley	60 Colne Rd, Gloveley, KLY, BD21 7NL	Payroll	J Porter	06/98	
Louise Hare	54 Derwent St, Parkway, BFD, BD16 3WR	Technical	I Jones	02/96	Scale T2
Lucy Hall-Woods	42 Radfield Way, Halton, SHIPLEY, BD24 4JS	Design	K Joy	04/96	
Siobhan Doyle	28 Longcross Pl, High Close, LDS, LS24 4MJ	Technical	I Jones	06/99	
Michael Dowgill	82 Trinity Hill, Easton, LDS, LS14 6HY	Telesales	M Fosse	12/98	Scale A3

Exercise 14D

Key in the following standard document (letter) to be merged with the data file amended in Exercise 14C (**EX14CDATA**).

- Use the **Lettertemp** letterhead
- Insert merge codes at *
- Use a justified right margin
- Save as **EX14DMAIN** and print one copy of the standard document
- Merge with the data source saved as **EX14CDATA** and print letters:
  - to **Scale A3** employees in the **Customer Services Department**
  - to employees in the **Telesales Department** whose start date was **06/98**
  - to **Scale A3** employees under the supervision of **M Fosse**.

Our Ref: PSU/LK/Review/PREF *Startdate

*FirstName *LastName
*Address1
*Address2
*City
*PostalCode

Dear *FirstName

(Bold and underline)

*Department Department – Review of Salary Scales

The annual review of staffing and salary scales is now complete. All managers, supervisors & other staff have been involved in the appraisal procedure. I hope that you found yr own appraisal helpful & stimulating.

I am writing to inform you that, at the request of yr supervisor, * supervisor, yr post will be upgraded. As from the end of next month, yr Scale *scale (bold) post will be upgraded by one scale point. Yr increased salary will be paid at the end of the following month as pay is one month in arrears. [Yr supervisor and manager will discuss the responsibilities of yr post with you in the next two weeks. If you have any matters which you wish to discuss, please do so at this time.

Yrs sincerely

Leanne Kindersley

Personnel Unit Assistant

Copy: *Supervisor
*Department

UNIT 15 EXAMINATION PRACTICE 3

By the end of Unit 15, you will have completed a mock examination for the OCR/RSA Stage II Mail Merge Part 2 Award.

OCR/RSA Stage II Mail Merge Part 2

This examination assesses your ability to create, maintain and print data files and standard documents, and to print selected merged documents using merge facilities. The award demonstrates that you have acquired competence in operating mail merge.

The examination lasts for 1½ hours and you have to prepare and manipulate two data files and create two documents for use in two mail merge operations. Printing is done outside this time.

Examinations are carried out in registered centres and are marked by OCR/RSA examiners. The centre will give you instructions regarding stationery. Letters must be produced on letterheads (either preprinted or a template) and memos may be produced on preprinted forms, by keying in entry details or by use of a template. The invigilator will give you instructions concerning the recalling of stored files.

Examination hints

When sitting your examination:

- you may use a manual prepared by the centre or the software manufacturer
- put your name, centre number and document number on each document
- check your work very carefully before printing – proofread, spellcheck
- assemble your printouts in the correct order at the end of the examination.

You are now ready to try a mock examination for Stage II Mail Merge Part 2. Take care and good luck!

The list of assessment criteria for this mock examination is long and detailed. To be sure that you have reached the required standard to be entered for an examination, you need to work through several past papers and have these 'marked' by a tutor or assessor who is qualified and experienced in this field.

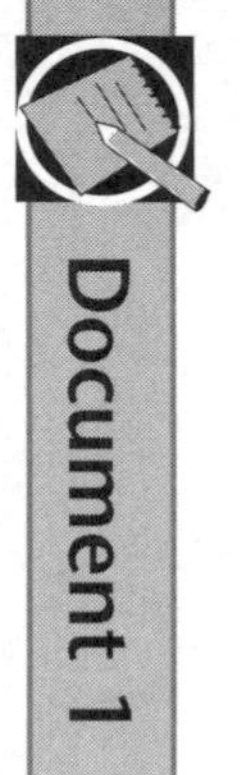

Document 1

Recall this datafile stored as EXI4CDATA and save as UNIT15DATA1. Add a new field and new records. Amend records as shown. Sort into alphabetical order by LastName. Save as UNIT15DATA1. Print one copy. The datafile will be used with Document 3.

FirstName	LastName	Address1	Address2	City	PostalCode	Department	Supervisor	Startdate	Scale	LeaveDays
~~Sarah~~ Sara	Arnold	10 Aire View	East Head	BRADFORD	BD8 7HN	Customer Service/S	S Smith	08/96	A3	29
Sharon	Atkinson	8 Windsmoor Close	Holmehurst	ILKLEY	LS34 7DP	Customer Service/S	S Smith	07/99	A3	25
Christopher	Day	18 Barr Road	Halton	SHIPLEY	BD24 5SA	Payroll	J Porter	12/97	A4	22
Michael	Dowgill	82 Trinity Hill	Easton	LEEDS	LS14 6HY	~~Telesales~~ Payroll	M Fosse	12/98	~~A3~~ A4	24
Siobhan	Doyle	28 Longcross Place	High Close	LEEDS	LS24 4MJ	Technical	I Jones	06/99	T2	25
Martin	Ford	Glen House	Gloveley	KEIGHLEY	BD21 6DH	Telesales	M Fosse	07/97	A3	22
Norman	Foster	16 Tennyson Street	High Close	LEEDS	LS24 3SE	Technical	P Pieterson	01/99	T2	25
Lucy	Hall-Woods	42 Radfield Way	Halton	SHIPLEY	BD24 4JS	Design	K Joy	04/96	T2	29
Louise	Hare	54 Derwent Street	Parkway	BRADFORD	BD16 3WR	Technical	I Jones	02/96	~~T2~~ T3	29
~~Jeff~~ Geoff	Harvey	~~37 Ingfield~~ 20 Green Ln	Ings Dale	KEIGHLEY	~~BD19 7PC~~ BD19 4LV	Telesales	V Barrett	01/99	A2	25
Pauline	Inman	24a Jackson Cross	Cross Lanes	SHIPLEY	BD24 9MV	Payroll	J Porter	10/98	A3	24
~~Karen~~	~~Jacques~~	~~Dean Cottage~~	~~Dean Bank~~	~~SHIPLEY~~	~~BD24 8LU~~	~~Design~~	~~M Mohan~~	~~11/97~~	~~T4~~	to be deleted
Shamsa	Jamil	17 Wheatwood Street	East Head	BRADFORD	BD8 9EH	Telesales	M Fosse	06/98	A4	25
Callum	Leadbeater	20 Shaftesbury Drive	Park Lane Top	LEEDS	LS10 3LV	Technical	L Hoban	09/99	T2	25

Please see separate sheets for additional records to be added and for amendments to existing records

Document 1 (continued)

FirstName	LastName	Address1	Address2	City	PostalCode	Department	Supervisor	Startdate	Scale	LeaveDays
Duncan	MacLeod	28 Bourne Road	Holmehurst	ILKLEY	LS34 7DB	Design	K Joy	04/97	T4	22
Nicky	Marcou	10 Queens Drive	High Close	LEEDS	LS24 6PT	Telesales	V Barrett	06/98	~~A3~~ A4	~~25~~ 26
Penny	Marr	1 Rosslyn View	Craven Hill	BRADFORD	BD18 9LL	Customer Service(s)	A Burns	04/97	A3	22
Diane	Molyneux	23 Ashurst Avenue	Beech Heights	KEIGHLEY	BD22 2GE	Design	M Mohan	01/97	T3	22
Anna	Nesovic	126 Manor Street	Cross Lanes	SHIPLEY	BD24 5SH	Technical	P Pieterson	10/96	T4	29
~~Jenny~~ Jennie	Payne	1 Seed Hill	Wheatburn	LEEDS	LS18 3JJ	Design	K Joy	03/96	T3	29
Asma	Pazeerah	Belle Vue House	Craven Hill	BRADFORD	BD18 4OE	Customer Service(s)	A Burns	08/96	A4	29
Claire	~~Smalley~~ Bacon	60 Colne Road	Gloveley	KEIGHLEY	BD21 7NL	Payroll	J Porter	06/98	A5	25
Katie	Stubbs	81 Delph Close	Holmehurst	ILKLEY	LS34 4HT	Customer Service(s)	S Smith	10/99	A5	29
Robert	Sugden	Heather Glen	Dean Bank	SHIPLEY	BD24 3SS	Customer Service(s)	A Burns	05/99	A5	29
~~Audrey~~	~~Thornton~~	~~3 Walker Park~~	~~Parkway~~	~~BRADFORD~~	~~BD16 1FW~~	~~Technical~~	~~I Jones~~	~~04/95~~	~~T3~~	~~30~~ (to be deleted)
Keith	Thorpe	14 Pasture Lane	Beech Heights	KEIGHLEY	BD22 1HC	Customer Service(s)	A Burns	07/98	A2	25
Allan	Tomlinson	21 Devonshire Lane	Gloveley	KEIGHLEY	BD21 4DA	Payroll	J Porter	11/98	A2	25
Li	Yeung	106 Bradford Road	Easton	LEEDS	LS14 2MQ	Design	M Mohan	05/96	~~T2~~ T3	28
Safina	Zafar	51 Holly Street	Lane Side	BRADFORD	BD10 4CT	Technical	P Pieterson	10/98	T2	24

Please see separate sheet for additional records

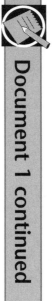

Document 1 continued

Please add these records before sorting and printing the database. Expand all abbreviations.

FirstName	LastName	Address1	Address 2	City	PostalCode	Department	Supervisor	StartDate	Scale	LeaveDays
Donna	Leyburn	6 High Place	High Close	LEEDS	LS24 3TU	Cust Serv	S Smith	07/96	A2	27
Janet	Browning	12 Hamlet Clo	Cross Lanes	SHIPLEY	BD24 8TD	Payroll	J Porter	06/96	A4	29
Anser	Azam	252 Lee Park	Parkway	BFD	BD16 8RT	Technical	I Jones	10/97	T3	23
Pauline	McIver	1 Rose View	Easton	LEEDS	LS14 1GP	Technical	L Hoban	10/97	T3	23
Michael	Bourne	20 Conrad St	Holmehurst	ILKLEY	LS34 6KL	Telesales	V Barrett	04/98	A3	24
Deborah	Palak	63 Pike Clo	Gloveley	KEIGHLEY	BD21 7DW	Design	K Joy	01/99	T2	22
Hassan	Lazar	72 Aireway	East Head	BRADFORD	BD8 6NQ	Telesales	M Fosse	05/97	A2	26
Laura	Downes	49 Chandler St	Ings Dale	KLY	BD19 4MJ	Cust Serv	J Porter	09/98	A4	25
Jeanne	Lund	14 Meadow Rd	Craven Hill	BFD	BD18 7PP	Cust Serv	A Burns	02/97	A3	23
Jacqui	Willson	64 Easton Ln	Cross Lanes	SHIPLEY	BD24 6DW	Telesales	V Barrett	04/98	A2	25
Maria	Paulo	Elm Cottage	Dean Bank	SHIPLEY	BD24 4JH	Telesales	M Fosse	01/99	A2	25
Margaret	Smythe	180 Solar Rd	Halton	SHIPLEY	BD24 7AS	Design	M Mohan	11/98	T2	24
Howard	Endsley	Moor House	Beech Heights	KLY	BD22 5CH	Design	M Mohan	12/97	T2	26
Emile	Amiens	16 Ringway	Wheatburn	LDS	LS18 8ST	Cust Serv	A Burns	10/96	A4	29
Suraya	Begum	84 Dalton Rd	Lane Side	BFD	BD10 6TW	Technical	L Hoban	08/98	T3	24

Document 2

Please key in the following records to create a data file for use with Document 4. Save as UNIT15DATA2 and print one copy.

Ms A Farooq
36 Overdale Mount
BARROWCROFT
BA4 7RQ
Macbeth

Mr E S Jowett
89 Leyden Ave
BURNCHESTER
BR9 4HC
Hamlet

Miss M T Salmon
1 Denwick Lane
FORDWICKTON
FN6 6KW
King Lear

Mr J C Stanley
Croft Edge
BARROWCROFT
BA4 8RS
Macbeth

Mrs R Qureshi
Pendle View
BURNCHESTER
BR10 7MP
Coriolanus

Miss K Kirkbright
10 Fielden Rd
FORDWICKTON
FN6 8EN
Macbeth

Mr L W Gregory
High Ridge Barn
BARROWCROFT
BA5 8GE
Much Ado about Nothing

Ms J Dalby
254 Barrowcroft Rd
BURNCHESTER
BR10 8TY
Romeo and Juliet

Mr S Brandt
55 Stones Park Grove
BARROWCROFT
BA4 6NB
Macbeth

Mrs A Ackroyd
72 Hill Top Rd
BARROWCROFT
BA5 7LO
Macbeth

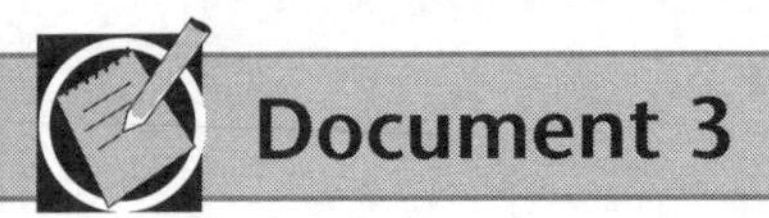

Document 3

Please key in this memo to be merged with UNIT15DATA1. Insert merge codes as shown and use a justified right margin. Print one copy of the standard document and memos to all Payroll Department employees.

MEMO

To: *FirstName *LastName

From: *Supervisor

Ref: *Department/Leave
Date:

ANNUAL LEAVE ← emboldden heading

Yr new Contract of Employment sets out a formula for calculating the total number of days of annual leave which are allocated to employees according to their scale and length of service.

According to our records, the month in which yr employment commenced was *StartDate and you are remunerated on Scale *Scale. Yr annual leave is *LeaveDays days. ← embolden this paragraph

Please complete the enclosed annual leave planner to indicate yr preferred allocation of yr leave days & let me have it before the end of next month (please insert date for last Friday of next month). After considering all employee requests and, of course, taking into a/c the need ~~for~~ to maintain staffing levels at all times, I will produce an annual leave plan for the department. [Whilst I will do my best to meet yr leave requests, I know that you will understand that this may not be possible in all cases. Leave planners which are returned after the date given above may not be accommodated.

Thank you.

Document 4

Please key in the following standard document to be merged with the datafile created in Document 2. Insert merge codes where indicated by *, and use an unjustified right margin. Print one copy of the standard document and also print documents to all employees living in Barrowcroft who gave the correct answer: Macbeth.

Ref: AL/BGT/Comp/*Answer

*Title *FirstName *LastName
* Address1
* City
* PostalCode

Dear *Title *LastName

Shakespeare Competition ← (CAPS and bold)

Thank you for returning the completed employee satisfaction questionnaire. Yr responses, together with those of all employees who also returned the questionnaire, will be forwarded to the management team. It is hoped that an employee focus group will be formed in the near future and you will be invited to become a member of this group.

However, the main purpose of this letter is to let you know that you have been successful in the Shakespeare competition which was linked to the questionnaire. Yr answer was correct: the quote was taken from Shakespeare's play *Answer.

(Please embolden)

The Northern Theatre Group is to perform this play at the *CITY GRAND THEATRE & you have won 2 tickets in the Dress Circle for the performance on Sat 27 Nov at 8.00 pm. You will also rec a 2-course dinner with wine in the Forum Restaurant at the theatre before the performance. We have made restaurant bookings and reserved theatre tickets for other employees who were also successful in the competition. / Our co has established links with the Grand Theatre through sponsorship & corporate entertainment. I am sure that you will thoroughly enjoy yr evening. Please call in to the Marketing Unit to collect yr tickets within the next few days.

Yrs sncly

Alyson Lindley
Marketing Assistant

Progress Review Checklist

Unit	Topic	Date completed	Comments
1	Proofreading text		
	Typographical and spelling errors		
	Spelling and grammar check		
	AutoCorrect		
	Formatting/emphasising text		
	Margin alignment		
	Line spacing		
	Change the document line length		
	Change margin settings		
	Indent a portion of text		
	Change the typing line length		
2	Grammatical and punctuation errors		
	Abbreviations		
	Correction signs		
	Insert additional text into a document		
	Page numbering continuation sheets – page breaks		
	Consistency of presentation		
	Add characters not available on the keyboard		
3	Business letter layout		
	Special marks and enclosure marks		
	Using pre-printed forms or templates		
	Memorandum layout		
	Confirming facts – locating information from another document		
	Automatic date insertion		
4	Consolidation 1		
5	Examination Practice 1 – OCR/RSA Stage II Text Processing Part 1		
6	Changing the typing line length, indenting text, insetting margins		
	Rearranging text		
	Find and replace text		
	Headers and footers		
	Allocating space		
	Sort items		

Unit	Topic	Date completed	Comments
7	Tables		
	Insert Table facility		
	Tables and Borders facility		
	Sub-divided and multi-line headings		
	Sort (rearrange) items in a table		
8	Standard paragraphs		
	Creating standard paragraphs/phrases		
	Inserting standard paragraphs/phrases		
9	Routing business documents		
	Indicating routing and printing copies		
	Enumeration		
	Producing letters and memos using standard paragraphs/phrases		
	Producing letters and memos using pre-printed forms and templates		
10	Consolidation 2		
11	Examination Practice 2 – OCR/RSA Stage II Word Processing Part 2		
12	Mail merge – main document		
	Create data source		
	Enter records in data source		
	Insert merge codes in the main document		
	Merge main document and data file		
	Print merged documents		
	Add, delete and amend records		
13	Mail merge – amend data source fields		
	Sort data source		
	Select records using one criterion		
	Select records using two criteria		
	Merge main document and selected records		
	Print merged documents		
14	Consolidation 3		
15	Examination Practice 3 – OCR/RSA Stage II Mail Merge Part 2		

Glossary

Action	Keyboard	Mouse	Menu
Accents (combination keys)	Select: **International characters** from the **Help** index to see the combinations Hold down/Press keys: As shown *See also*: Symbols		
Alignment of text	*See*: Ragged right margin, Centre text, Justified right margin		
Allocate clear lines	Press: ↵ once for each line required, plus one		
Allocate vertical space			**Format**, **Paragraphs**, **Indents and Spacing** Key in: The measurement required in the **Before** spin box
AutoCorrect			**Tools**, **AutoCorrect**
AutoFormat	Press: **Alt** + **Ctrl** + **K**		**Format**, **AutoFormat**
Blocked capitals	Press: **Caps Lock** key		
Bold text	Press: **Ctrl** + **B**	Click: **B** on the Formatting Tool Bar	**Format**, **Font**
Borders		Click: [button] on the Formatting Tool Bar	**Format**, **Borders and Shading**
Bulleted lists		Click: [button] on the Formatting Tool Bar	**Format**, **Bullets and Numbering** Select: **Bulleted** Click: On the required style
Capitalise letters	Press: **Ctrl** + **Shift** + **A**		**Format**, **Change Case**, **Uppercase**
Case of letters (to change)	Press: **Shift** + **F3**		**Format**, **Change Case**
Centre text	Press: **Ctrl** + **E**	Click: [button] on the Formatting Tool Bar	**Format**, **Paragraph**, **Indents and Spacing**, **Alignment**, **Centred**
Close a file (clear screen)	Press: **Ctrl** + **W**		**File**, **Close**
Copy a block of text Highlight text to be copied	Press: **Ctrl** + **C**	Click: [button] on the Standard Tool Bar *or* Press: Right mouse button and Select: **Copy**	**Edit**, **Copy**
Position cursor where text is to be copied to	Press: **Ctrl** + **V**	Click: [button] on the Standard Tool Bar *or* Press: Right mouse button and select: **Paste**	**Edit**, **Paste**
Cursor movement Move cursor to required position Move to top of document Move to end of document Move left word by word Move right word by word Move to end of line Move to start of line Move to top/bottom of paragraph Move up/down one screen	Use arrow keys: → ↑ ← ↓ Press: **Ctrl** + **Home** Press: **Ctrl** + **End** Press: **Ctrl** + ← Press: **Ctrl** + → Press: **End** Press: **Home** Press: **Ctrl** + ↑ *or* **Ctrl** + ↓ Press: **PgUp** *or* **PgDn**	Click: Left mouse button in required position	
Cut text	*See*: Delete/cut a block of text		
Date insertion	Press: **Alt** + **Shift** + **D**		**Insert**, **Date and Time**

Action	Keyboard	Mouse	Menu
Delete/cut a block of text	Select: Text to be deleted Press: ← (**Del**) *or* Select: Text to be deleted Press: **Ctrl** + **X**	Select: Text to be deleted/cut Click: [scissors icon] on the Formatting Tool Bar	Select: Text to be deleted/cut Select: **Edit**, **Cut** *or* Press: Right mouse button; select: **Cut**
Delete/cut a character	Move cursor to correct character; Press: **Del** *or* Move cursor to right of incorrect character; Press:← (**Del**)		
Delete/cut a word	Move cursor to end of word: Press: ← (**Del**) *or* Select: Word to be deleted Press: **Ctrl** + **X**	Select: Word to be deleted/cut Click: [scissors icon] on the Formatting Tool Bar	Select: Word to be deleted/cut Select: **Edit**, **Cut** *or* Press: Right mouse button; select: **Cut**
Enumeration	Key in: The enumeration e.g. A) Press: The **Tab** key Key in: The rest of the text Repeat for each enumerated paragraph	Click: [numbering icon] on the Formatting Tool Bar	**Format**, **Bullets and Numbering** Select: **Numbered** Click: On the required style
Exit the program	Press: **Alt** + **F4**	Click: Control button at right of Title Bar	**File**, **Exit**
Find text	Press: **Ctrl** + **F**		**Edit**, **Find**
Font size Next larger point size Next smaller point size	Press: **Ctrl** + **Shift** + **P** Choose desired size Press: **Ctrl** +] Press: **Ctrl** + [	Click: [10 ▾] on the Formatting Tool Bar Choose desired size	**Format**, **Font** Choose desired size
Font typeface style	Press: **Ctrl** + **Shift** + **F** Choose desired font	Click: [Times New Roman] on the Formatting Tool Bar Choose desired font	**Format**, **Font** Choose desired font
Fractions	*See*: Symbols/Accents/Fractions		
Go to (a specified page)	Press: **Ctrl** + **G** *or* **F5**		**Edit**, **Go To ...**
Grammar tool	Press: **F7**	Click: [spelling icon] on the Standard Tool Bar	**Tools**, **Spelling and Grammar**
Headers and Footers To delete:	 Select: The actual text or page number Press: ← (**Del**)		Select: **View**, **Header and Footer** Key in: The header text and/or footer text
Help function and Office Assistant	Press: **F1** (for Contents) Press: **Shift** + **F1** (for **What's This?** – context-sensitive help)	Click: [?] on the Formatting Tool Bar for the **Office Assistant**	**Help**
Highlight/shade text		Click: [highlight icon] on the Formatting Tool Bar	**Format**, **Borders and Shading**, **Shading**
Indent function Indent at left to next tab stop Indent at left to previous tab stop	 Press: **Ctrl** + **M** Press: **Ctrl** + **Shift** + **M**	Click: [indent icon] on the Formatting Tool Bar	**Format**, **Paragraph**, **Indents and Spacing**

Action	Keyboard	Mouse	Menu
Indent as a hanging paragraph Unindent and return to standard margin	Press: **Ctrl** + **T** Press: **Ctrl** + **Q**	Click: [icon] on the Formatting Tool Bar *Using ruler* first-line indent left indent first-line and left indent right indent	
Insert special character/symbols			To insert a symbol: Position cursor: Where you want the character/symbol to appear Select: **Insert**, **Symbol**
Insert text	Simply key in the missing character(s) at the appropriate place – the existing text will 'move over' to make room for the new text. If **OVR** is displayed (overtyping), Press: **Ins(ert)** key to remove		
Italics	Press: **Ctrl** + **I**	Click: [icon] on the Formatting Tool Bar	**Format**, **Font**
Justified right margin	Press: **Ctrl** + **J**	Click: [icon] on the Formatting Tool Bar	**Format**, **Paragraph**, **Indents and Spacing**, **Alignment**, **Justified**
Line break (to insert)	Press: **Shift** + ↵		
Line length – to change	Select text. Display horizontal ruler. Move margin markers to required position on ruler		
Line spacing – to set	Press: **Ctrl** + **1** (single) Press: **Ctrl** + **2** (double) Press: **Ctrl** + **0** (to add or delete a line space)		**Format**, **Paragraph**, **Indents and Spacing**, **Line Spacing**
Mail merge – add record		**Switch to Data Form** Click: **Add New** Key in: The record Click: **Add New** *or* **Switch to View Source** Click: **Add New** Record Key in: The record	
Mail merge – amend fields		**Switch to View Source** Click: [icon] on the Database Tool Bar	
Mail merge – create data source	Select: **Tools**, **Mail Merge**, **Get Data** in Section 2, **Create Data Source**		
Mail merge – create main document	Select: **Tools**, **Mail Merge**, **Create** in Section 1, **Form Letters**, **Active Window**		
Mail merge – delete record		Select: **Switch to Data Form** Select: **Find Record** Click: **Delete** *or* Select: **Switch to View Source** Select: The required record Select: **Delete**	
Mail merge – enter records		**Switch to Data Form** Key in: The record Select: **Add New**	

Action	Keyboard	Mouse	Menu
Mail merge – find record		**Switch to Data Form** Click: **Find** Click: Key in: The data Select: **In Field** Click: **Find First** *or* **Switch to Data Form** Click: **View Source** Click:	
Mail merge – insert merge codes		**Switch to Main Doc** Click: **Insert Merge Field** on Mail Merge Tool Bar Select: The required filename	
Mail merge – open data source		Select: **Tools**, **Mail Merge** Click: **Get Data** in Section 2 Select: **Open Data Source**	
Mail merge – print merged file		Click:	
Mail merge – select records		Select: **Query Options** in the **Mail Merge Helper** dialogue box Select: The required field Key in: The required options	
Mail merge – sort data source		**Switch to View Source** Place the cursor: In the appropriate column Click: or	
Mail merge – switch between Data Source and Main Document		Click: Select: **Edit** in Section 1 or 2 *or* Click: or on the Database Tool Bar	**Window**, **Main Doc** **Window**, **Datafile**
Mail merge – view merged file		**Switch to Main Doc** Click:	
Margins (to change)	Use the mouse pointer to drag the left and/or right margin boundaries to the appropriate place on the horizontal ruler. Press: The **Alt** key at the same time to view the measurements on screen		**File**, **Page Setup**, **Margins**
Move around document	*See*: Cursor movement		
Move a block of text Select: Text to be moved Position cursor where text is to be moved to	Press: **F2** *or* **Ctrl** + **X** Press: **Ctrl** + **V** *or* ↵	Click: on the Standard Tool Bar Click: on the Standard Tool Bar *drag and drop moving:* Select: Text to be moved Click: Left mouse button in middle of text and keep held down Drag: Selection to required location Release: Mouse button	**Edit**, **Cut** **Edit**, **Paste** *or* Press: Right mouse button Select: **Cut** Press: Right mouse button Select: **Paste**
Open an existing file	Press: **Ctrl** + **O**	Click: on the Standard Tool Bar	**File**, **Open**
Open a new file	Press: **Ctrl** + **N**	Click: on the Standard Tool Bar	**File**, **New**
Page break (to insert)	Press: **Ctrl** + ↵		**Insert**, **Break**, **Page break**
Page numbering	Press: **Alt** + **Shift** + **P**		**Insert**, **Page Numbers**
Page Setup			**File**, **Page Setup** Choose from **Margins**, **Paper Size**, **Paper Source and Layout**

Action	Keyboard	Mouse	Menu
Paragraphs – splitting/joining	*Make a new paragraph (ie split a paragraph into two):* Move cursor to first letter of new paragraph: Press: ↵ twice *Join two consecutive paragraphs into one:* Move cursor to first letter of new paragraph: Press: ← (**Del**) twice (backspace delete key) Press: **Space Bar** (to insert a space after full stop)		
Print out hard copy	Press: **Ctrl + P**	Click: [printer icon] on the Standard Tool Bar	**File**, **Print**
Print Preview	Press: **Ctrl + F2**	Click: [print preview icon] on the Standard Tool Bar	**File**, **Print Preview** Select: **Zoom** *or* **Full Page**
Ragged right margin	Press: **Ctrl + L**	Click: [align left icon] on the Formatting Tool Bar	**Format**, **Paragraph**, **Indents and Spacing**, **Alignment**, **Left**
Remove text emphasis First, select the emphasised text to be changed back to normal text	Press: **Ctrl + Space Bar** *or* Press: **Ctrl + Shift + Z**	Click: Appropriate emphasis button on the Formatting Tool Bar (to deselect)	**Format**, **Paragraph**, **Indents and Spacing**
Repeat typing or actions (redo)	Press: **F4** to repeat previous action *or* Press: **Ctrl + Y**	Click: [redo icon] on the Formatting Tool Bar To redo (repeat) sets of actions, drag down the **Redo** drop-down list – select the group of actions you wish to repeat	**Edit**, **Repeat Typing**
Replace text	Press: **Ctrl + H**		**Edit**, **Replace**
Replace text – typeover Word will fit the replacement	1 Select: The incorrect text and then type in the correct entry 2 Move cursor: To incorrect entry Press: The **Ins** key (typeover on) and overtype with correct entry Press: The **Ins** key again (typeover off) to stop overtyping of text		
Restore deleted text	Press: **Ctrl + Z**	Click: [undo icon] on the Formatting Tool Bar	**Edit**, **Undo Typing**
Ruler – to display			**View**, **Ruler**
Save work to disk Save a file for the first time Save an active file which has been saved previously Save all open files	Press: **F12** Press: **Ctrl + S** *or* Press: **Shift + F12**	Click: [save icon] on the Standard Tool Bar	**File**, **Save As**, **Enter Filename** Select: Correct Directory/Drive Click: **OK** **File**, **Save** **File**, **Save All**
Scroll bars (to view)			**Tools**, **Options**, **View** Select: Horizontal Scroll Bar and Vertical Scroll Bar options
Search for text	*See* Find text		
Select text One character (or more) One word To end of line Start of line A full line A paragraph Whole document Any block of text Remove selection	Press: **Shift** + → *or* ← Press: **Shift** + **Ctrl** + → *or* ← Press: **Shift** + **End** Press: **Shift** + **Home** Press: **Shift** + **End** *or* **Home** — Press: **Ctrl** + **A** —	Click and drag pointer across text Double-click on word Click and drag pointer right or down Click and drag pointer left or up Click in selection border Double-click in selection border Triple-click in selection border Position pointer at start of text and Hold down **Shift**. Then, position pointer at end of text and click Click in any white space	

Action	Keyboard	Mouse	Menu
Sort (rearrange) items			Select: The items or text to be sorted Select: **Table**, **Sort**
Spaced capitals	Press: **Caps Lock** key. Leave one space after each letter. Leave three spaces after each word		
Spellcheck	Press: **F7**	Click: [icon] on the Standard Tool Bar	**Tools**, **Spelling and Grammar**
Standard Paragraph Files To create/store standard paragraphs: To insert standard paragraphs into your document:	Key in: The portion of text to be saved as a standard paragraph file Save it in a separate file using normal **Save** procedures Position the cursor: Where you want the standard paragaph to be inserted Select: **File** from the **Insert** menu Select/key in: The appropriate filename		
Status Bar			**Tools**, **Options**, **View** Select: Status Bar option
Switch on and load Word		Double-click: **Microsoft Word Icon**	Select: **MS Word from Start**
Symbols	*See*: Insert special characters/symbols		
Symbols/Accents/ Fractions			**Insert**, **Symbol** Select: The required font Click: On the required symbol Select: **Insert**, **Close**
Tables Insert table Tables and borders		Click: [icon] on the Standard Tool Bar Click: [icon] on the Standard Tool Bar	**Table**, **Insert Table** **Table**, **Draw Table**
Underline text Single underline Double underline	Press: **Ctrl** + **U** Press: **Ctrl** + **Shift** + **W** Press: **Ctrl** + **Shift** + **D**	Click: [icon] on the Formatting Tool Bar	**Format**, **Font**, **Underline**
Undo mistakes, typing or actions	Press: **Ctrl** + **Z**	Click: [icon] on the Standard Tool Bar. To undo sets of actions, drag down the **Undo** drop-down list; select: The group of actions you wish to undo	**Edit**, **Undo Typing**
Units of measurement			**Tools**, **Options**, **General**, **Measurement Units** Select: Desired unit from drop-down menu
View magnified pages		Click: [100%] on the Standard Tool Bar Click: **Magnifies** on Print Preview	**View**, **Zoom**
View – normal view	Press: **Ctrl** + **F2**	Click: The [icon] **Normal View** button at left of document window	**View**, **Normal**
View – outline view		Click: The [icon] **Outline View** button at left of document window	**View**, **Outline**
View – page layout view		Click: The [icon] **Print Layout View** button at left of document window	**View**, **Page Layout**
View – Print Preview	Press: **Ctrl** + **F2**	Click: [icon] on the Standard Tool Bar	**File**, **Print Preview** Select: **Zoom** *or* **Full Page**
Widow/orphan control			**Format**, **Paragraph**, **Line and Page Breaks**

Unit 1
Exercise 1C

DIGITAL RADIO

The portable radio has definitely come a long way since the advent of its early ancestor, the wireless. Once a popular youth culture of the 50's, known as the ghetto blaster in the 80's, the radio of the 90's now accommodates new achievements in digital technology. With the development of paper-thin transistor cards, portable radios are smaller and lighter than ever before. *Sometimes the weight of the batteries can be more than that of the radio itself.*

Digital technology also offers enhanced sound quality and clearer reception with radios retuning themselves to receive a station when listeners are on the move. Graphics and other display information, such as phone numbers, are being advertised on the more sophisticated and expensive models.

It is easy to appreciate the benefits of replacing the old manual tuning dial through the more accurate digital display. As with digital television, compressed signals enable each waveband to carry more information than the old analogue systems.

Digital radio allows listeners more opportunities to experience many more radio stations.

Another breakthrough has been the windup radio. Cranking a handle for a few seconds powers an internal generator inside the radio, eliminating the need for electricity or battery power. The wind up radio is particularly useful for radio access in remote foreign parts where electricity or battery power is unavailable or when it is simply inconvenient.

Unit 1
Exercise 1D

DIGITAL RADIO

The portable radio has definitely come a long way since the advent of its early ancestor, the wireless. Once a popular youth culture of the 50's, known as the ghetto blaster in the 80's, the radio of the 90's now accommodates new achievements in digital technology. With the development of paper-thin transistor cards, portable radios are smaller and lighter than ever before. Sometimes the weight of the batteries can be more than that of the radio itself.

Digital technology also offers enhanced sound quality and clearer reception with radios retuning themselves to receive a station when listeners are on the move. Graphics and other display information, such as phone numbers, are being advertised on the more sophisticated and expensive models.

It is easy to appreciate the benefits of replacing the old manual tuning dial through the more accurate digital display. As with digital television, compressed signals enable each waveband to carry more information than the old analogue systems.

Digital radio allows listeners more opportunities to experience many more radio stations.

> Another breakthrough has been the windup radio. Cranking a handle for a few seconds powers an internal generator inside the radio, eliminating the need for electricity or battery power. The wind up radio is particularly useful for radio access in remote foreign parts where electricity or battery power is unavailable or when it is simply inconvenient.

Unit 1
Exercise 1E

TRAVEL HEALTH

Every year thousands of holidaymakers suffer unnecessarily from the effects of travelling or too much sun. Yet, many holiday illnesses are relatively easy to prevent, using a combination of common sense and adequate preparation.

Travel Sickness

Symptoms – nausea, dizziness, vomiting.

To combat air, boat or car travel sickness ensure you take medication at least half an hour before setting off to give it sufficient time to work. Check the instructions on the packet as some products cause drowsiness and are not recommended for drivers.

Prickly Heat

Symptoms – red, itchy, spotty rash.

Although there is no specific remedy for this you can prevent it by keeping as cool as possible. Prickly heat is caused by sweat temporarily clogging the skin around the sweat glands. Wear light, loose cotton clothes and apply a soothing, mildly astringent body lotion all over and an antiperspirant to vulnerable areas.

Sunburn

Symptoms – very red, painful skin, blisters can develop in bad cases.

Drink plenty of water and use calamine lotion on the skin. Prevention is better than cure so use a high factor sun cream which protects against both UVB and UVA rays which are responsible for sunburn.

Heatstroke

Symptoms – body is uncomfortably hot, faintness, nausea.

Avoid direct sunlight and drink as much water as you can. Avoid tea, coffee and alcohol which cause dehydration and worsen symptoms. Try to stay in a place with air conditioning or access a fan, loosen clothing and seek proper attention from someone with appropriate medical experience.

Unit 1
Exercise 1F

OFFTEC CORPORATE SERVICES

MEMORANDUM

Unit 1
Exercise 1G

OFFTEC CORPORATE SERVICES
197 Highbury Road
WAKEFIELD WF3 2AS

Tel no: 01924 349211   e-mail: info@offtec.co.uk

Unit 2
Exercise 2A

THE WAY IN PROGRAMME

INTRODUCTION AND INFORMATION

The Way In Programme is designed so that learners can select a number of skills from the miscellaneous programmes listed below.

Art and Design
Brickwork
Plumbing
Woodwork
Painting and Decorating
Mathematics
English
Computers

After taking into account previous experience and interests, each learner can make up their own individual programme. Learners can study what they want and we guarantee that tutors are specially trained to meet learner needs and draw on learner strengths. The Way In Programme offers nationally recognised qualifications and later an opportunity to progress onto a vocational programme. Each learner is given a personal plan immediately and specific support is provided for students with learning difficulties.

Tutor support

Tutors can help with spoken and written English and with understanding and carrying out basic calculations, etc.

This work is integrated into the practical skills to enhance understanding and competence.

Computers

Many jobs need some understanding of computers nowadays. It is possible for students to spend approximately 2 hours per week learning keyboard skills and acquiring some knowledge of the everyday use of computers necessary in offices and in industry. Local organisations and manufacturers may provide short work placements towards the end of the year in June or July.

Unit 2
Exercise 2B

THE WAY IN PROGRAMME

INTRODUCTION AND INFORMATION

The Way In Programme is designed so that learners can select a number of vocationally related skills from the miscellaneous programmes listed below.

Art and Design
Health and Social Care
Brickwork
Plumbing
Painting and Decorating
Woodwork
Hairdressing
Numeracy
Literacy
Computers

After taking into account previous experience and interests, each learner can make up their own individual programme. Learners can study what they want and we guarantee that tutors are specially trained to meet learner needs and draw on learner strengths.

The Way In Programme offers nationally recognised qualifications and later an opportunity to progress onto a vocational programme. Each learner is given a personal plan immediately and specific support is provided for students with learning difficulties.

TUTOR SUPPORT

Tutors can help with spoken and written English and with understanding and carrying out basic calculations, etc. This work is integrated into the practical skills to enhance understanding and competence. Spelling, attention to detail, vocabulary, numeracy and commercial awareness are developed in a realistic manner.

1

Unit 2
Exercise 2B continued

COMPUTERS

Many jobs need some understanding of computers nowadays. It is possible for students to spend approximately 2 hours per week learning keyboard skills and acquiring some knowledge of the everyday use of computers in offices and in industry.

Local organisations and manufacturers may provide short work placements towards the end of the year in June or July.

ADVICE AND GUIDANCE

Our advisers give advice and offer guidance on all aspects of education and training throughout the year. Prospective students can drop in at any time. Facilities are available for confidential interviews.

ASSISTANCE WITH COSTS

Many students on full-time courses are eligible for help with travel and child care costs. Although it is not possible to guarantee a place for everyone, the majority of students are given the opportunity of placing their child or children in the College's own nursery.

APPLICATION AND ENROLMENT

Details available from the Guidance Unit.

2

Unit 2
Exercise 2C

SPECIAL OFFERS ON NEW PRODUCTS

AUTUMN SEASON

In response to the feedback our salesmen have received from customers, we are proud to announce the following new products. These will be available from 1 August and a 10% reduction on prices will be offered through to the end of November.

HOW TO ORDER

Simply complete order forms and forward in the usual way.

Hazelnut dessert in 125g square pots; packs of 4, 6 packs per box. A popular new flavour to add to the range; £6.00 per box, RRP £1.49.

Peach and mango yoghurt in 150g round pots; packs of 6, 6 packs per box. An exotic addition to your Bonavitale yoghurt range; £8.00 per box, RRP £1.75.

Organic chocolate dessert in 125g square pots; packs of 4, 6 packs per box. An old favourite brought up to date; £7.10 per box, RRP £1.69.

Geisha soy sauce in 100ml bottles; packs of 6, 4 packs per box. A delicious new version of an old Japanese speciality; £11.00 per box, RRP £0.65.

Decaffeinated Ceylon tea in 40-bag cartons; packs of 24, 24 packs per box. A refreshing drink for your health-conscious customers; £18.73 per box; RRP £1.00.

PLEASE NOTE: VAT AT 17.5% TO BE ADDED TO ALL ITEMS.

Unit 2
Exercise 2D

MEMORANDUM

To: Paul Brüllow, Administration Unit
From: Michèle Dupré, Training Unit
Ref: TU/MD/0097/WP
Date: Today's date

TRAINING PROGRAMMES FOR NEW SOFTWARE

Further to our discussion 3 days ago, I am writing to confirm the dates, times, venue and topics for training. At each session, there will be sufficient space for 6 employees in the IT Training Room (D10) and not 4 as I stated earlier.

Please let me have names and unit details of employees allocated to each 1¼ - 1½ hour session when you have drawn up a rota.

Tuesday 4 October	1300 hrs	Mail Merge
Tuesday 11 October	1330 hrs	Tables
Wednesday 19 October	1300 hrs	Templates
Wednesday 26 October	1330 hrs	Symbols
Tuesday 1 November	1330 hrs	International correspondence

Detailed training schemes are attached.

During training needs analysis, more than 95% of operators identified the last 2 topics on the above list as unfamiliar to them. In addition, 86% said that they would use black pen or, worse still, ignore them, when faced with symbols to be reproduced such as Ö, ç, ¥ and ¢!

Encs

Unit 2
Exercise 2E

SPECIAL OFFERS ON NEW PRODUCTS

AUTUMN SEASON

In response to the feedback our salesmen have received from customers, we are proud to announce the following new products. These will be available from 1 August and a 10% reduction on prices will be offered through to the end of November.

HOW TO ORDER

Simply complete order forms and forward in the usual way.

Hazelnut dessert in 125g square pots; packs of 4, 6 packs per box. A popular new flavour to add to the range; £6.00 per box, RRP £1.49.

Peach and mango yoghurt in 150g round pots; packs of 6, 6 packs per box. An exotic addition to your Bonavitale yoghurt range; £8.00 per box, RRP £1.75.

Organic chocolate dessert in 125g square pots; packs of 4, 6 packs per box. An old favourite brought up to date; £7.10 per box, RRP £1.69.

Geisha soy sauce in 100ml bottles; packs of 6, 4 packs per box. A delicious new version of an old Japanese speciality; £11.00 per box, RRP £0.65.

Decaffeinated Ceylon tea in 40-bag cartons; packs of 24, 24 packs per box. A refreshing drink for your health-conscious customers; £18.73 per box; RRP £1.00.

NEW TELEPHONE ORDER LINE

Our telephone order line is now open between:

8.00 am - 8.00 pm Monday – Wednesday
8.00 am - 6.00 pm Thursday – Sunday

Please give your customer number and telephone number including area code when placing an order.

1

Unit 2
Exercise 2E continued

Remember, delivery is FREE within a 30-mile radius. Between 30 miles and 70 miles, there is a carriage charge of £25.00. Distances over a 70-mile radius are charged at £40.00 per delivery.

For delivery days, see schedule on Page 310 of catalogue.

MINIMUM ORDER – £200.00.

PLEASE NOTE: VAT AT 17.5% TO BE ADDED TO ALL ITEMS.

TELEPHONE 01342-564329

2

Unit 3
Exercise 3A

OFFTEC CORPORATE SERVICES
197 Highbury Road
WAKEFIELD WF3 2AS

Tel no: 01924 349211 e-mail: info@offtec.co.uk

Our ref LB/tw

Today's date

URGENT

Mr Raymond Burns
Burns Installation Ltd
37 Ellerdale Crescent
NORWICH
NR3 2PS

Dear Mr Burns

Thank you for your e-mail received yesterday, which has been passed to me by a colleague.

I am pleased to enclose a catalogue detailing our wide range of consultancy services. As you are aware, we are a forward looking company and all our consultants are trained to the highest standards. Our experts can provide you with a number of business solutions, all of which can be tailored to meet your needs and available resources.

Also enclosed is an information pack about our organisation. The pack includes testimonials from some of our satisfied customers who have used our services in the past and are happy to recommend them to other manufacturers.

We would be pleased to discuss your requirements in more detail with you and can arrange for a preliminary consultation should you wish to explore opportunities further. **This would place you under no obligation.**

I look forward to hearing from you shortly.

Yours sincerely

Linda Braithwaite
Senior Consultant

Encs

Unit 3
Exercise 3B

OFFTEC CORPORATE SERVICES
197 Highbury Road
WAKEFIELD WF3 2AS

Tel no: 01924 349211 e-mail: info@offtec.co.uk

Our ref MD/ZA

Today's date

PERSONAL

Mrs Ruth Ayre
Bramwell Lodge Park
Nelson Road
LEICESTER
LE22 4RS

Dear Mrs Ayre

I have recently received a catalogue in which you have placed an advertisement offering special discounts for companies wishing to take advantage of weekend breaks at your Park.

We are hoping to send approximately 12 sales consultants for a 2-night team-building event and are looking for suitable accommodation. I would appreciate it if you could forward some additional information about the miscellaneous facilities and resources that you can provide to business clients.

As financial arrangements are not immediately apparent from the brochure, could you also advise on the available discount and whether we could pay by account.

Please address all further correspondence to my secretary, Janet Patel, whose card is enclosed.

Yours sincerely

Mahsood Dabhad
Personnel Manager

Enc

Unit 3
Exercise 3C

OFFTEC CORPORATE SERVICES

MEMORANDUM

URGENT – BY HAND

From: Linda Braithwaite, Senior Consultant
To: Marion Jones, Business Adviser
Ref: LB/tw/mj
Date: today's

CONSULTATION APPOINTMENT

I have been contacted by Mr Raymond Burns from Burns Installation Ltd. Mr Burns is anxious to have a preliminary consultation with one of our business advisers at the earliest opportunity.

I have already sent out our standard promotion pack, but you may wish to also forward our new marketing leaflet, "**Business Solutions for Tomorrow**", prior to your visit.

If you feel it would be necessary or beneficial for me to accompany you, I am only available on (date of Thursday of next week). Would it be possible for you to confirm a visit date before the end of this week as my diary tends to fill up fairly quickly? I should be grateful if you would give Mr Burns' visit your immediate attention as his company has a number of important links with some of our existing clients.

Unit 3
Exercise 3D

OFFTEC CORPORATE SERVICES

MEMORANDUM

From: Mahsood Dabhad, Personnel Manager
To: Linda Braithwaite, Senior Consultant
Ref: MD/ZA/LB3
Date: today's

SALES TEAM WEEKEND AWAY

I have contacted 3 possible venues which would be appropriate for the team-building weekend event you are hoping to hold for the Sales Team, commencing (date of 3rd Friday of next month).

In order that I can confirm places, I would appreciate it if you could supply me with a list of names (and signatures) of those staff who will definitely be participating, along with any special dietary requirements they may have.

Accommodation will normally be 2 staff to a room, although I acknowledge that it may be necessary for some staff to have their own separate room. The Staff Development Committee has agreed that all expenses for the event will be paid for by the company, apart from drinks and snacks from the bar.

Please let me know if you would like me to select a venue on your behalf or if you would prefer to look at the brochures yourself first.

Unit 4
Exercise 4A

OFFTEC CORPORATE SERVICES
197 Highbury Road
WAKEFIELD WF3 2AS

Tel no: 01924 349211 e-mail: info@offtec.co.uk

Our ref: NB/RTS

Your ref: WF/227

Today's date

For the attention of Mr Will Fry, General Manager

Peterson Tools Ltd
Mount View Business Park
Mount View Road
HUDDERSFIELD
HD7 2BS

Dear Sirs

Thank you for your recent correspondence concerning the photocopying machine we supplied to you earlier this month and which has since developed a number of faults. We have now obtained a full report from the manufacturer's own engineer who has confirmed that the goods are not repairable.

We understand that the engineer supplied you with a temporary replacement machine to service your immediate requirements until we had the opportunity to make you an offer. Under the terms of your guarantee we are able to offer you a brand new replacement or, alternatively, we will credit your account with the total amount paid. I am advised by our Stock Department that we could deliver and install a new copier in approximately 2 week's time. If this is acceptable I would appreciate it if you could add your signature to the enclosed form and return it in the envelope provided. **As a gesture of goodwill we are prepared to offer you a 2½% discount off the price of the goods to compensate for the inconvenience caused.**

I look forward to hearing from you shortly.

Yours sincerely

Nasreen Begum
Customer Care Manager

Enc

Unit 4
Exercise 4B

OFFTEC CORPORATE SERVICES

MEMORANDUM

From: Nasreen Begum, Customer Care Manager
To: Jim Gannon, Finance Officer
Ref: NB/RTS/JG17
Date: today's

CUSTOMER DISCOUNT

We have arranged to give Peterson Tools Ltd a discount of 2½% against the cost of a new photocopier, which they have ordered from us today as a replacement for a previous machine bought from us earlier this month which was faulty.

The order number is: RB200031ZX.

Please can you credit their account with the appropriate amount and confirm, in writing, their new balance to their General Manager, Mr Will Fry.

I have arranged for the new copier to be delivered to their premises on (date of Friday of next week). I would appreciate it if the necessary documentation could be processed immediately to avoid any further complaint from this customer.

Unit 4
Exercise 4C

FAMILY LIFE

The family has been referred to as a kinship group, ie, a group of persons directly linked by kin connections, the adult members of which assume responsibility for caring for children. Kinship connections are based on blood, marriage or adoption.

Types of Family

The traditional 'nuclear' family is where a husband and wife live with their children in the same household. Sometimes this is described as the cereal packet family. A recent study revealed that approximately one quarter of households in the United Kingdom consists of a married couple and their dependent children.

The 'extended' family is where two or more generations either live together in the same household or see each other on a regular basis, eg daily.

There has been a significant rise in the number of 'one-parent' families. Over 22% of families with children are headed by a lone parent – nearly three times the proportion in 1971. This increase is believed to be linked to the rise in the divorce rate (around 40% of marriages end in divorce) and also in the number of births outside marriage (34% of babies are born to unmarried mothers, compared with 8% in 1971).

There is also a rise in the number of 'reconstituted' families (step-families). Divorce, or the death of a spouse, can lead to a new family being formed as one or both partners bring children from their past relationships into the new family.

Another example of the way in which family structures are becoming more diverse is the 'same-sex' family. This would be where, for instance, a woman leaves her husband and takes her children to live with another woman.

Many of today's families are subject to change and fluidity. Family members grow older, move in and out of different households through death, marriage, birth, divorce or simply personal choice. Some people now advocate that family life has to be viewed more as a temporary process, or a set of changing practices, rather than a permanent structure of relatively fixed roles and expectations.

The Family in Society

Although it is argued by some that the needs of pre-industrial society were met by the immobile extended family, historical research on family life in 17th century England by Peter Laslett, shows that the nuclear family, not the extended family, was the norm, and that considerable geographical mobility existed. However, a later study in 1851, found that the extended family was dominant and functioned as a 'mini-welfare state'.

From the middle of the 20th century the extended family was 're-discovered' in working class communities such as Bethnal Green and Hull. The term 'dispersed

1

Unit 4
Exercises 4C continued

extended family' was introduced to emphasise how families keep in touch with relatives through visits and the telephone.

The Symmetrical Family

In 1975 the idea of the 'symmetrical' family was fashioned as Young and Wilmott put forward the view that relationships between husbands and wives had become far more balanced and egalitarian than in the past, with household chores and child care being increasingly shared. It is apparent from earlier studies of working class families that marriage roles were highly segregated. Young and Wilmott's studies showed that 72% of husbands regularly helped with the housework and that domestic labour was no longer a solely female preserve.

However, Ann Oakley in the 'Sociology of Housework', 1974, found no evidence to support this view. Her studies revealed that of the families she researched, only 15% of men had a high level of participation in housework. This has been supported by the further research of Jonathan Gershuny which shows that, although it is possible that there has been a moderate shift towards a 'symmetrical' pattern, the main burden of domestic work definitely continues to be carried by the woman.

2

Unit 5
Document 1

OFFTEC CORPORATE SERVICES
197 Highbury Road
WAKEFIELD WF3 2AS

Tel no: 01924 349211 e-mail: info@offtec.co.uk

Our ref: JA:JP:dtv32

Today's date

PERSONAL

Mr Jordan Parry
264 Mayview Street
SKIPTON
BD25 1TN

Dear Mr Parry

I am writing with regard to your recent job application for the post of Sales Adviser (Temporary) with our company. I am pleased to advise you that you have been shortlisted for the post and the panel would like to invite you to attend for an interview on *(date of first Wednesday of next month)* at 2.30 pm. If this time is inconvenient, please let me know as soon as possible.

It will be necessary for you to bring your qualification certificates with you for verification purposes. The interview will last for approximately 30-45 minutes during which you will be given an opportunity to ask questions about the organisation and discuss various aspects of the post. **You will also be asked to give a short presentation of 5-10 minutes summarising your previous experience and outlining your plans for developing the post.** In the meantime, I shall contact your referees to obtain their written references.

Please report to the main reception at 2.15 pm. A map showing the location of the company is enclosed.

Yours sincerely

Jennifer Allwood
Personnel Assistant

Enc

Unit 5
Document 2

OFFTEC CORPORATE SERVICES

MEMORANDUM

From: Jennifer Allwood, Personnel Assistant
To: Marion Jones, Business Adviser
Ref: JA:MJ:dtv32
Date: today's

TEMPORARY SALES ADVISER: POST DTV32

The date for interviewing candidates for the above post is now set for *(date of first Wednesday of next month).*

We will be interviewing a total of three applicants between 1.30 pm – 4.30 pm and I believe you will be chairing the panel. I am enclosing the applications and CVs of each candidate for you to look over and bring to the interview with you.

I also propose to hold a separate pre-interview meeting next week to agree the interview questions to be asked and to discuss methods of scoring. Please can you e-mail me with the days and times you are available.

We also need to confirm financial arrangements for the post, as I understand from Payroll that there have been recent changes to the Sales Team's rates of commission and claimable expenses.

Encs

Unit 5
Document 3

PAINTING WITH SPECIAL EFFECTS

There are a number of different painting techniques, which can be applied to enhance the interior design of a room by giving a special effect. To create a soft, subtle effect, stick with colours from the same colour family. For a more dramatic effect, experiment with strong, contrasting colours. You can use ordinary paint, rather than a special effect paint, but remember that these will not be semi-transparent and will dry much more quickly. Before applying any of the special effects referred to below, you will first need to apply a background colour using ordinary emulsion paint.

SPONGING

A natural sponge is the best type of sponge for this technique. Use the appropriate size for the surface to be sponged, ie a large sponge for walls and a smaller sponge for corners, woodwork or furniture. Be careful not to overload the sponge with paint – wipe off any excess first and practise on a piece of spare card. Dip the frilly side of your dampened sponge into the paint and dab the sponge on to your surface at different angles to obtain a random, freckle-like print. Try not to concentrate on isolated areas which will appear patchy, but rather to obtain an overall effect across the surface as a whole.

If you are using several colours, allow sufficient time for the first colour to dry thoroughly before applying the next. If you make a mistake, leave to dry, before re-applying the background paint or simply wipe over and re-sponge.

RAG ROLLING

Different rag rolling effects can be obtained by using a chamois, an old lace curtain, or even a 'scrunched up' plastic bag. Using a brush or roller, apply the paint evenly over a small section of the surface area. Then, while the paint is still wet, dampen your bunched ragging tool and roll it roughly across the surface to 'rag off' the paint in a random pattern. If you are covering a large area, rag one block, then immediately paint an adjacent block, using a roller or brush to blend the two areas together before ragging the join. Stand back from your work every now and again to make sure that you are blending the blocks together so that there are no obvious separate patches or marks where the wet edges have dried.

Keep re-bunching your ragging tool and apply the rag at different angles to obtain a random effect. If the rag becomes clogged, rinse it through quickly, squeeze out any excess water, and continue.

1

Unit 5
Document 3 continued

DRAGGING

Apply the paint evenly in strips of approximately 60 cm width. Then, dip a clean dragging brush into the paint, wipe excess on to a rag, then drag the brush (using the flat side) downwards through the paint. After each stroke, it is advisable to wipe the brush with a rag to avoid a build up of paint. If the brush becomes clogged, rinse it through quickly, dry on a rag, and continue.

This is quite a difficult technique to apply to very large areas, such as walls, and is best applied to smaller areas such as doors, window frames, cupboards, etc. When dragging wood, always ensure you drag in the same direction as the natural grain. When dragging a panelled door, drag each individual panel before doing the surrounding areas.

COLOUR WASHING

Use a special colourwash brush or a very soft, large decorating brush. Dip the brush into the paint, remove any excess, and apply to the surface in a haphazard criss-cross manner, at different angles. For the first coat, you should deliberately miss some patches. When the first coat is dry, apply a second coat of paint (either using the same colour or an alternative) in the same manner, going over the patches you missed earlier, to give a soft build up of colour. If the paint starts to dry and spreading it becomes difficult it may be necessary to either moisten the brush with water or dampen the walls with a wet roller.

You can experiment with thinning the paint to achieve a more gradual colour build up and translucent effect – try 2 parts paint to 1 part water, It is best to work systematically across the surface and complete a whole wall at a time to create a soft, clouding effect. Stand back from your work every now and again to make sure that there are no obvious patches or marks where the wet edges have dried.

2

Unit 6
Exercise 6A

THE WAY IN PROGRAMME

INTRODUCTION AND INFORMATION

The Way In Programme is designed so that learners can select a number of vocationally related skills from the miscellaneous programmes listed below.

Art and Design
Health and Social Care
Brickwork
Plumbing
Painting and Decorating
Woodwork
Hairdressing
Numeracy
Literacy
Computers

After taking into account previous experience and interests, each learner can make up their own individual programme. Learners can study what they want and we guarantee that tutors are specially trained to meet learner needs and draw on learner strengths.

The Way In Programme offers nationally recognised qualifications and later an opportunity to progress onto a vocational programme. Each learner is given a personal plan immediately and specific support is provided for students with learning difficulties.

TUTOR SUPPORT

Tutors can help with spoken and written English and with understanding and carrying out basic calculations, etc. This work is integrated into the practical skills to enhance understanding and competence. Spelling, attention to detail, vocabulary, numeracy and commercial awareness are developed in a realistic manner.

1

Unit 6
Exercise 6A continued

COMPUTERS

Many jobs need some understanding of computers nowadays. It is possible for students to spend approximately 2 hours per week learning keyboard skills and acquiring some knowledge of the everyday use of computers in offices and in industry.

Local organisations and manufacturers may provide short work placements towards the end of the year in June or July.

ADVICE AND GUIDANCE

Our advisers give advice and offer guidance on all
aspects of education and training throughout the year.
Prospective students can drop in at any time.
Facilities are available for confidential interviews.

ASSISTANCE WITH COSTS

Many students on full-time courses are eligible for help with travel and child care costs. Although it is not possible to guarantee a place for everyone, the majority of students are given the opportunity of placing their child or children in the College's own nursery.

APPLICATION AND ENROLMENT

Details available from the Guidance Unit.

2

Unit 6
Exercise 6B

SPECIAL OFFERS ON NEW PRODUCTS

<u>AUTUMN SEASON</u>

In response to the feedback our salesmen have received from customers, we are proud to announce the following new products. These will be available from 1 August and a 10% reduction on prices will be offered through to the end of November.

MINIMUM ORDER – £200.00.

<u>HOW TO ORDER</u>

Simply complete order forms and forward in the pre-paid envelope.

Geisha soy sauce in 100ml bottles; packs of 6, 4 packs per box. A delicious new version of an old Japanese speciality; £11.00 per box, RRP £0.65.

Decaffeinated Ceylon tea in 40-bag cartons; packs of 24, 24 packs per box. A refreshing drink for your health-conscious customers; £18.73 per box; RRP £1.00.

Hazelnut dessert in 125g square tubs; packs of 4, 6 packs per box. A popular new flavour to add to the range; £6.00 per box, RRP £1.49.

Peach and mango yoghurt in 150g round tubs; packs of 6, 6 packs per box. An exotic addition to your Bonavitale yoghurt range; £8.00 per box, RRP £1.75.

Pure chocolate dessert in 125g square tubs; packs of 4, 6 packs per box. An old favourite brought up to date; £7.10 per box, RRP £1.69.

PLEASE NOTE: VAT AT 17.5% TO BE ADDED TO ALL ITEMS.

<u>NEW TELEPHONE ORDER LINE</u>

TELEPHONE 01342-564329

Our telephone order line is now open between:

8.00 am - 8.00 pm Monday – Wednesday
8.00 am - 6.00 pm Thursday – Saturday
10.00 am – 4.00 pm Sunday

Please give your customer number and telephone number including area code when placing an order.

1

Unit 6
Exercise 6B continued

<u>DELIVERY</u>

Remember, delivery is <u>FREE</u> within a 30-mile radius. Between 30 miles and 70 miles, there is a carriage charge of £25.00. Distances over a 70-mile radius are charged at £40.00 per delivery. For delivery days, see schedule on Page 310 of catalogue.

<u>NEW PURE JUICES</u>

Watch out for our new range of pressed and bottled natural pure juices made from fresh fruits and vegetables.

Nature's Fayre is a new company which guarantees that its products are manufactured from pure produce grown in the best possible conditions. Processing takes place within 2 – 3 hours of harvesting when the active nutrients are at their peak.

NO SUGAR, ALCOHOL, CHEMICALS OR PRESERVATIVES ARE ADDED.

A <u>10% discount</u> will be given to all customers ordering immediately from our latest catalogue.

Take the opportunity to stock up your shelves NOW. These juices promise to be very popular.

TELEPHONE 01342-564329

Please give your customer number and telephone number including area code when placing an order.

2

Unit 6
Exercise 6C

Your name Exercise 6C Centre No

THE WAY IN PROGRAMME

INTRODUCTION AND INFORMATION

The Way In Programme is designed so that learners can select a number of vocationally related skills from the miscellaneous programmes listed below.

Art and Design
Health and Social Care
Brickwork
Plumbing
Painting and Decorating
Woodwork
Hairdressing
Numeracy
Literacy
Computers

After taking into account previous experience and interests, each learner can make up their own individual programme. Learners can study what they want and we guarantee that tutors are specially trained to meet learner needs and draw on learner strengths.

The Way In Programme offers nationally recognised qualifications and later an opportunity to progress onto a vocational programme. Each learner is given a personal plan immediately and specific support is provided for students with learning difficulties.

TUTOR SUPPORT

Tutors can help with spoken and written English and with understanding and carrying out basic calculations, etc. This work is integrated into the practical skills to enhance understanding and competence. Spelling, attention to detail, vocabulary, numeracy and commercial awareness are developed in a realistic manner.

COMPUTERS

Many jobs need some understanding of computers nowadays. It is possible for students to spend approximately 2 hours per week learning keyboard skills and acquiring some knowledge of the everyday use of computers in offices and in industry.

Local organisations and manufacturers may provide short work placements towards the end of the year in June or July.

1

Unit 6
Exercise 6C continued

Your name Exercise 6C Centre No

ADVICE AND GUIDANCE

Our advisers give advice and offer guidance on all aspects of education and training throughout the year. Prospective students can drop in at any time. Facilities are available for confidential interviews.

ASSISTANCE WITH COSTS

Many students on full-time courses are eligible for help with travel and child care costs. Although it is not possible to guarantee a place for everyone, the majority of students are given the opportunity of placing their child or children in the College's own nursery.

APPLICATION AND ENROLMENT

Details available from the Guidance Unit.

2

Unit 6
Exercise 6D

Your name Exercise 6D Centre No

THE WAY IN PROGRAMME

INTRODUCTION AND INFORMATION

The Way In Programme is designed so that students can select a number of vocationally related skills from the miscellaneous programmes listed below.

Art and Design
Brickwork
Computers
Hairdressing
Health and Social Care
Literacy
Numeracy
Painting and Decorating
Plumbing
Woodwork

After taking into account previous experience and interests, each learner can make up their own individual programme. Students can study what they want and we guarantee that tutors are specially trained to meet learner needs and draw on learner strengths.

Local organisations and manufacturers may provide short work placements towards the end of the year in June or July.

Students have been able to gain valuable experience with the following local organisations. All of the companies listed below have indicated that they would be happy to take students on placements again in the future.

Carey, Roy, Howard & Co
Cross & Wilkinson Ltd
Designs on You (Hair and Beauty)
Fernville House
Inn Place
Lancaster & Derby Building Society
Sugden Electronics Ltd
Wools Direct
Yorkshire Elevators Plc

The Way In Programme offers nationally recognised qualifications and later an opportunity to progress onto a vocational programme. Each learner is given a personal plan immediately and specific support is provided for students with learning difficulties.

1

Unit 6
Exercise 6D continued

Your name Exercise 6D Centre No

TUTOR SUPPORT

Tutors can help with spoken and written English and with understanding and carrying out basic calculations, etc. This work is integrated into the practical skills to enhance understanding and competence. Spelling, attention to detail, vocabulary, numeracy and commercial awareness are developed in a realistic manner.

COMPUTERS

Many jobs need some understanding of computers nowadays. It is possible for students to spend approximately 2 hours per week learning keyboard skills and acquiring some knowledge of the everyday use of computers in offices and in industry.

APPLICATION AND ENROLMENT

Details available from the Guidance Unit.

ADVICE AND GUIDANCE

After taking into account previous experience and interests, each learner can make up their own individual programme. Students can study what they want and we guarantee that tutors are specially trained to meet learner needs and draw on learner strengths.

Our advisers give advice and offer guidance on all aspects of education and training throughout the year. Prospective students can drop in at any time. Facilities are available for confidential interviews.

ASSISTANCE WITH COSTS

Many students on full-time courses are eligible for help with travel and child care costs. Although it is not possible to guarantee a place for everyone, the majority of students are given the opportunity of placing their child or children in the College's own nursery.

2

Unit 6
Exercise 6E

Your name Exercise 6E Centre No 1

SPECIAL OFFERS ON NEW PRODUCTS

AUTUMN SEASON

In response to the feedback our salesmen have received from customers, we are proud to announce the following new products. These will be available from 1 August and a 10% reduction on prices will be offered through to the end of November.

MINIMUM ORDER – £200.00.

HOW TO ORDER

Simply complete order forms and forward in the pre-paid envelope.

Geisha soy sauce in 100ml bottles; packs of 6, 4 packs per box. A delicious new version of an old Japanese speciality; £11.00 per box, RRP £0.65.

Decaffeinated Ceylon tea in 40-bag cartons; packs of 24, 24 packs per box. A refreshing drink for your health-conscious customers; £18.73 per box; RRP £1.00.

Hazelnut mousse in 125g square tubs; packs of 4, 6 packs per box. A popular new flavour to add to the range; £6.00 per box, RRP £1.49.

Peach and mango yoghurt in 150g round tubs; packs of 6, 6 packs per box. An exotic addition to your Bonavitale yoghurt range; £8.00 per box, RRP £1.75.

Pure chocolate mousse in 125g square tubs; packs of 4, 6 packs per box. An old favourite brought up to date; £7.10 per box, RRP £1.69.

PLEASE NOTE: VAT AT 17.5% TO BE ADDED TO ALL ITEMS.

NEW TELEPHONE ORDER LINE

TELEPHONE 01342-564329

Our telephone order line is now open between:

8.00 am - 8.00 pm Monday – Wednesday
8.00 am - 6.00 pm Thursday – Saturday
10.00 am – 4.00 pm Sunday

Please give your customer number and telephone number including area code when placing an order.

Autumn Catalogue

Unit 6
Exercise 6E continued

Your name Exercise 6E Centre No 2

DELIVERY

Remember, delivery is FREE within a 30-mile radius. Between 30 miles and 70 miles, there is a carriage charge of £25.00. Distances over a 70-mile radius are charged at £40.00 per delivery. For delivery days, see schedule on Page 310 of catalogue.

NEW PURE JUICES

Watch out for our new range of pressed and bottled natural pure juices made from fresh fruits and vegetables.

Nature's Fayre is a new company which guarantees that its products are manufactured from pure produce grown in the best possible conditions. Processing takes place within 2 – 3 hours of harvesting when the active nutrients are at their peak.

NO SUGAR, ALCOHOL, CHEMICALS OR PRESERVATIVES ARE ADDED.

A 10% discount will be given to all customers ordering immediately from our latest catalogue.

Take the opportunity to stock up your shelves NOW. These juices promise to be very popular.

TELEPHONE 01342-564329

Please give your customer number and telephone number including area code when placing an order.

Autumn Catalogue

Unit 7
Exercise 7C

NEW EMPLOYEES

EMPLOYEE NAME	EMPLOYEE TITLE	CONTACT POINT	
		EXT	ROOM NO
<u>Administration Pool</u>			
Burgoyne, Ivor	Mail Courier	8	39
Meredith, Sally	Office Supervisor	15	39
Thurston, Lilian	Receptionist	16	180
<u>Marketing and Sales</u>			
Bannistock, Alan	Telesales	68	225
Hussain, Nadia	Marketing Assistant	257	403
Sunway, Mark	Sales Adviser	258	403

A full induction programme for all new employees will be arranged within the next month – details to follow.

Unit 7
Exercise 7D

<u>COURSE LISTS</u>

COURSE TITLE	LECTURER NAME	COURSE COMMENCEMENT	
		STARTING TIME	STARTING DATE
<u>Business Administration</u>			
NVQ Level 2	Washington, Marguerite	6.30 pm	10th September
NVQ Level 3	Hodge, Mary	7.30 pm	3rd September
Office Practice	Fenning, Joan	8.30 pm	5th September
<u>Information Technology</u>			
CLAIT	Hodge, Mary	7.30 pm	5th September
IBT Level 2	Rawson, Keith	8.30 pm	10th September
IBT Level 3	Rawson, Keith	6.30 pm	3rd September

All courses will commence on the start date shown in the table above and will run weekly at the same time indicated.

Unit 7
Exercise 7E

GREAT GARDEN ROADSHOW

The Great Garden Roadshow planned to visit your area is listed below. Tickets are available on the day at the venue entrance.

ROADSHOW DATES		**TOWN**	**VENUE**
DATE	**NUMBER OF DAYS**		
Spring roadshow events			
6 March	2	Sheffield	Riverside Lodge
21 March	1	Halifax	Piece Hall
16 April	2	Wakefield	Limes Park
Summer roadshow events			
8 June	2	Sheffield	Ennya Verona Centre
22 July	2	Skipton	Castle Grounds
14 August	1	Dewsbury	Lewisgate Mill Complex
Autumn roadshow events			
9 September	2	Huddersfield	Green Park
16 October	1	Pudsey	Mountview Hall
7 November	2	Bradford	Oakley Manor

Unit 7
Exercise 7F

MISCELLANEOUS STOCK LIST

The following items of stock need to be incorporated within the new computerised stock control programme.

DESCRIPTION	**CODE**	**STOCK LEVEL NUMBERS**	
		CURRENT LEVEL	**RE-ORDER LEVEL**
Female swimwear			
Halter neck bikini	HB42	26	25
Sarong, multi	SM9	17	20
Shorts, lycra	SL72	57	50
Swimming costume	SC12	12	15
Male sportswear			
Jogging pants	JP17	5	10
Socks, towelling	ST3	22	20
Swimming trunks	ST42	119	50
Tracksuit	T11	7	10
Children's leisurewear			
Cycling shorts	CS10	28	20
Jogging suit	JS14	9	10
Leotard	L6	12	10
Sweatband	S24	105	20

Unit 8

Exercise 8A

OFFTEC CORPORATE SERVICES
197 Highbury Road
WAKEFIELD WF3 2AS

Tel no: 01924 349211 e-mail: info@offtec.co.uk

Our Ref: FML/gy34

Today's date

PERSONAL

Mrs Jennifer Delaney
27 Fenniston Road
BRADFORD
BD16 2HG

Dear Mrs Delaney

I am writing to thank you for the job application you submitted to us recently for the post of Catering Manager.

We regret to advise that on this occasion you have not been successful in your application. We did receive a very large number of applications for this particular post. Although you were a strong candidate, there were a number of other candidates who had significantly more experience and up-to-date qualifications. If you would like more detailed feedback on your application, we shall be pleased to provide you with the written comments from the shortlisting panel.

I do hope that you will not be too disappointed with this outcome or deterred from applying for other positions which may be advertised.

Thank you for the interest you have taken in our company.

Yours sincerely

Fiona McLaughlin
PERSONNEL OFFICER

Exercise 9A

OFFTEC CORPORATE SERVICES
197 Highbury Road
WAKEFIELD WF3 2AS

Tel no: 01924 349211 E-mail:info@offtec.co.uk

Our Ref: FML/gy34

Today's date

PERSONAL

Mrs Jennifer Delaney
27 Fenniston Road
BRADFORD
BD16 2HG

Dear Mrs Delaney

I am writing to thank you for the job application you submitted to us recently for the post of Catering Manager.

We regret to advise that on this occasion you have not been successful in your application. We did receive a very large number of applications for this particular post. Although you were a strong candidate, there were a number of other candidates who had significantly more experience and up-to-date qualifications. If you would like more detailed feedback on your application, we shall be pleased to provide you with the written comments from the shortlisting panel. However, our Director of Resources, Karen Dawson, has asked me to draw your attention to several other vacancies which exist at the moment and which may be of interest. These are namely:

a) Catering Supervisor. This is a part time, permanent post based on Service Contract Scale 6-7.

b) Restaurant Manager. This is a full time, temporary post to cover maternity leave based on Management Contract Scale 9.

c) Catering Assistant. This is a full time, 1-year fixed term post based on Service Contract Scale 3-4.

Thank you for the interest you have taken in our company.

Yours sincerely

Fiona McLaughlin
PERSONNEL OFFICER

Copy: Customer Care Department
File

Copy: Customer Care Department ✓
File

Copy: Customer Care Department
File ✓

Unit 9
Exercise 9B

OFFTEC CORPORATE SERVICES

MEMORANDUM

From: Fiona McLaughlin, Personnel Officer
To: Nasreen Begum, Customer Care Manager
Ref: FM/NB/6
Date: today's

NEW EMPLOYEE

I understand that you have a new member of staff joining your team: George Cook.

I would like to arrange for George, who is commencing his employment with you next week, to take part in the pilot mentoring scheme we have recently introduced. Please could you liaise with Sue Littlewood who has volunteered to act as mentor for George until he settles in.

I am enclosing a Welcome Pack. Please ensure that the acceptance slip is signed and returned to me confirming that both yourself and your new employee have reviewed the Pack.

A full Induction programme has been arranged for all new members of staff and will be held on the first Tuesday of next month. The Induction programme will cover issues such as:

a) Background to, and organisational structure of, the company and its personnel.

b) The main company policies, eg equal opportunities policy, grievance policy, etc.

c) The Annual Review and Appraisal Systems.

d) General information such as holiday entitlements, sickness and absence reporting, business house styles, etc.

Please ask your new member of staff to contact me on Extension 357 to confirm their personnel details for the company payroll.

Enc

Copy: Sue Littlewood
File

Copy: Sue Littlewood ✓
File

Copy: Sue Littlewood
File ✓

Unit 9
Exercise 9C

OFFTEC CORPORATE SERVICES
197 Highbury Road
WAKEFIELD WF3 2AS

Tel no: 01924 349211 e-mail: info@offtec.co.uk

Our ref: FM/RA/319

Today's date

PRIVATE

Mr Rory Andel
26 St Peter's Drive
LEEDS
LS5 2RM

Dear Mr Andel

Following your recent application for the post of Catering Manager, we would like to invite you to attend for an interview on Wednesday, 22 June at 2.30 pm. Please report to the Main Reception at least 15 minutes before the start of the interview, where you will be greeted by a member of our staff.

You will be requested to give a short presentation to the interview panel. An OHP, projector and flipchart will be available. This should last no longer than 5-10 minutes and should be an explanation of 'How you intend to improve catering services'.

Please bring all your qualification certificates with you for verification purposes. You may also choose to bring with you any other documentary evidence which demonstrates your previous experience.

Please find enclosed an information leaflet about the company along with a map of our location.

It would be helpful if you could confirm your attendance. If the interview time is inconvenient, please let our Personnel Clerk, Hugh Winters, know as soon as possible.

Yours sincerely

Fiona McLaughlin
Personnel Officer

Encs

Copy: Hugh Winters
File

Copy: Hugh Winters ✓
File

Copy: Hugh Winters

Unit 10
Exercise 10A

FAMILY LIFE

The family has been described to as a kinship group, ie, a group of persons directly linked by kin connections, the adult members of which assume responsibility for caring for children. Kinship connections are based on blood, marriage or adoption. Many of today's families are subject to change and fluidity. Family members grow older, move in and out of different households through death, marriage, birth, divorce or simply personal choice. Some people now advocate that family life has to be viewed more as a temporary process, or a set of changing practices, rather than a permanent structure of relatively fixed roles and expectations.

Family Structures

The traditional 'nuclear' family is where a husband and wife live with their children in the same household. A recent study revealed that approximately one quarter of households in the United Kingdom consists of a married couple and their dependent children. Marriage rates increased during the first 70 years of this century, then declined during the following 25 years.

The 'extended' family is where 2 or more generations either live together in the same household or see each other on a regular basis, eg daily. The term 'dispersed extended family' was introduced to emphasise how families keep in touch with relatives through visits and the telephone.

There has been a significant rise in the number of 'one-parent' families. Over 22% of families with children are headed by a lone parent – nearly 3 times the proportion in 1971. This increase is believed to be linked to the rise in the divorce rate (around 40% of marriages end in divorce) and also in the number of births outside marriage (34% of babies are born to unmarried mothers, compared with 8% in 1971). In the 19th century, however, proportionately more children were affected by the death of a parent than are affected by divorce today.

There is also a rise in the number of 'reconstituted' families (step-families). Divorce, or the death of a spouse, can lead to a new family being formed as one or both partners bring children from their past relationships into the new family.

Another example of the way in which family structures are becoming more diverse is the 'same-sex' family. This would be where, for instance, a female leaves her husband and takes her children to live with another female.

The Symmetrical Family

In 1975 the idea of the 'symmetrical' family was fashioned as Young and Wilmott put forward the view that relationships between husbands and wives had become far more balanced and egalitarian than in the past, with household chores and child care being increasingly shared. Earlier studies of working class families reveal that marriage roles were highly segregated. Young and Wilmott's studies showed that 72% of husbands regularly helped with the housework and that domestic labour was no longer a solely female preserve. However, Ann Oakley in

Unit 10
Exercise 10A continued

the 'Sociology of Housework', 1974, found that of the families she researched, only 15% of men had a high level of participation in housework. Further research by Jonathan Gershuny shows that, although there has been a moderate shift towards a 'symmetrical' pattern, the main burden of domestic work continues to be carried by the female.

Despite noted changes, there is evidence to suggest that roles in most marriages remain distinct and, according to feminists, are based on a marked inequality in power between husbands and wives.

The 20th Century Family 'Norm'

The traditional 'nuclear' family is where a husband and wife live with their children in the same household. Although divorce rates have risen and the diversity of family life has increased the 'family based on a couple living with their children and committed to a permanent relationship is still the norm'. The continuities of family life are, in fact, more striking than the discontinuities.

Unit 10
Exercise 10B

CONFERENCING FACILITIES

The Marketing Department has compiled a list of venues suitable for hosting conferences, workshops or seminars.

Further details can be obtained from Cynthia Driver, Marketing Manager.

VENUE	CONTACT	BOOKING PRICES	
		EVENING 6pm+	**DAY 9am-5pm**
Facilities for up to 50 people			
Dorchester Hotel	Vanessa Wright	£95	£200
Newham Arts Centre	Peter Gannon	£130	£250
Park View Centre	Judy Leigh	£100	£220
Queen's Hall	Shona Scholes	£85	£150
Facilities for up to 100 people			
Bedewell Park	Isla MacDonna	£100	£200
Longmeadow Manor	Reham Ali	£110	£175
Meridian Centre	Franz Beier	£95	£160
Richmond Hotel	Ben Jackson	£135	£180
Facilities for up to 200 people			
Bedewell Park	Isla MacDonna	£150	£295
Fairview Lodge	Arshad Hussain	£140	£280
Meridian Centre	Franz Beier	£160	£300
TTR Mills Complex	Beth Browne	£150	£285

Unit 10
Exercise 10C

OFFTEC CORPORATE SERVICES

MEMORANDUM

From: Fiona McLaughlin, Personnel Officer
To: Cynthia Driver, Marketing Manager
Ref: FM/CD/34
Date: today's

A full Induction programme has been arranged for all new members of staff and will be held next Friday. This will be of interest to you as I understand that you have a new member of staff joining your team tomorrow, namely Ella Robertshaw.

I would appreciate it if you could arrange Ella's work schedule so that she can be released from her normal duties to attend the Induction session, which will commence at 9.00 am and finish at approximately 3.30 pm. Please could you confirm Ella's attendance with the Personnel Clerk, Hugh Winters.

Please contact the Health and Safety Officer to arrange an appointment for your new member of staff to go through the company policy.

Please ask your new member of staff to contact me on Extension 357 to confirm their personnel details for the company payroll. This is particularly important as I understand that Ella may have changed her surname since the time of her interview as she postponed her employment start date with us because of her wedding arrangements.

When Ella arrives, please can you ensure that she is also given information on:

a) Refectory opening times
b) Car parking arrangements
c) Staff newsletter services
d) Photocopying arrangements
e) E-mail addresses and telephone extensions for all company staff
f) Intranet access and passwords

Copy: Health and Safety Officer
File

Copy: Health and Safety Officer ✓
File

Copy: Health and Safety Officer
File ✓

Unit 10
Exercise 10D

OFFTEC CORPORATE SERVICES

MEMORANDUM

From: Fiona McLaughlin, Personnel Officer
To: Cynthia Driver, Marketing Manager
Ref: FM/CD/34
Date: today's

NEW MEMBER OF STAFF

I understand that you have a new member of staff joining your team tomorrow, namely Ella Robertshaw. A full Induction programme has been arranged for all new members of staff and will be held next Friday.

I would be grateful if you could arrange Ella's work schedule so that she can attend the Induction session, which will commence at 9.00 am and finish at approximately 3.30 pm. Please confirm Ella's attendance with the Personnel Clerk, Hugh Winters. Please also contact the Health and Safety Officer to arrange an appointment for Ella to go through the company policy.

It is important for Ella to contact me on Extension 357 to confirm her personnel details for the company payroll. This is particularly important as I understand that she may have changed her surname since the time of her interview as she postponed her employment start date with us because of her wedding arrangements.

When Ella arrives, please can you ensure that she is also given information on:

a) Car parking arrangements
b) E-mail addresses and telephone extensions for all company staff
c) Intranet access and passwords
d) Photocopying arrangements
e) Refectory opening times
f) Staff newsletter services

I am afraid that I am currently out of stock of the standard Welcome pack, which we normally issue to all new employees. As soon as copies come back from the printers I will send one to you in the internal mail.

Unit 11
Document 1

VISITOR INFORMATION

ALLIOTT HALL

Day Out 1999 Award Winner

You and your family can enjoy a great day out at Alliott Hall. We have something for all ages, ranging from the relaxing formal Italian-style gardens to the exciting Jungle Book adventure playground.

Find out about the attractions on offer by calling at the Visitor Centre and enjoy a delicious snack or 3-course meal in Jerome's Diner.

You will find Alliott Hall between Wetherby and York, only 5 miles from the A1. A bus service operates 6 times a day from York between April and September.

The grounds, gardens and adventure playground are open 7 days a week all year round (closed Christmas Day and Boxing Day). Access is available between 9.00 am and 5.00 pm during the months October to March, and between 9.00 am and 8.00 pm during the months April to September.

The Hall and Exhibition Centre open daily from 11.00 am to 5.00 pm from 1 April to 30 September. Last admissions are at 4.00 pm

Completed in 1775, Alliott Hall is a perfect example of neo-classical architecture. Interior plaster work was created under the direction of Robert Adam, whilst the influence of Thomas Chippendale is clearly seen in the fine furniture.

The much-travelled members of the family have endowed present-day visitors with a magnificent collection of needlework, porcelain, carvings and other artefacts from around the world.

Edward Alliott, the 6th Lord Jerome, invited famous water-colourists of his time to capture the beauty of his beloved home throughout the seasons; their work is displayed in the Gallery. The silk-covered walls of the drawing rooms provide a fitting backcloth for the many portraits of the Alliott family.

1

Unit 11
Document 1 continued

VISITOR INFORMATION

A gentle stroll through the gardens and woodlands brings you to the edge of the Himalayan ravine where you can see a spectacular waterfall cascading into an exotic dell filled with plants, ferns and bamboos from the Himalayas. The ravine can be safely reached by a newly-constructed 'hairpin' walkway; the more adventurous and younger members of your group may wish to use the original, but rather steep, steps!

The ravine was a favourite haunt of generations of Alliott children, and was particularly enjoyed by Marguerite, the wife of the 8th Lord Jerome, who often walked amongst the exotic flora recalling her days in the sub-continent during the height of the British Raj.

On leaving the Himalayan ravine, you will find yourself at the edge of the lake. The lake and its wildfowl can be observed by following the circular path or by embarking on a boat trip in the 'Marguerite' – a Victorian-style launch.

A gentle ascent brings you back to the Hall, Exhibition Centre and Visitor Centre.

You and your family can enjoy a great day out at Alliott Hall. We have something for all ages, ranging from the relaxing formal Italian-style gardens to the exciting Jungle Book adventure playground.

Ample free parking is available and a free wheelchair users' guide can be obtained by ringing 0131-3136828.

2

Unit 11
Document 2

ALLIOTT HALL

Enjoy a great day out at Alliott Hall. We have something for all ages, ranging from the relaxing informal Italian-style gardens to the exciting Jungle adventure playground.

ATTRACTIONS

Estate church (17th century)
Exhibition hall
Guided tours of Hall
Himalayan ravine
Italian-style gardens
Jungle adventure playground
Lakeside walks
Woodland walks

Corporate dining facilities and Music Concerts during winter. Details available from the Events Coordinator on 0131-3136824.

THE HALL

Completed in 1775, Alliott Hall is a perfect example of neo-classical architecture. Interior plaster work was created under the direction of Robert Adam, whilst the influence of Thomas Chippendale is clearly seen in the fine furniture.

Edward Alliott, the 6th Lord Jerome, invited famous water-colourists of his time to capture the beauty of his beloved home throughout the seasons; their work is displayed in the Gallery. The silk-covered walls of the drawing rooms provide a fitting backdrop for the many portraits of the Alliott family.

The much-travelled members of the family have endowed today's visitors with a magnificent collection of porcelain, needlework, carvings and other artefacts from around the world.

HOW TO FIND US

You will find Alliott Hall between Wetherby and York, only 5 miles from the A1. A bus service operates 6 times a day between April and September from York.

For further information on group discounts, education services, holiday activities and exhibitions, please telephone 0131-3136829.

Unit 11
Document 3

EVENTS CALENDAR

Check with the individual properties for further information about these and other events.

EVENT	VENUE	DATE AND DURATION	
		START	DAYS
Music			
Nostalgia Evening	Oakville Gardens	3.5.01	2
Lakeside Symphony	Alliott Hall Lake	7.5.01	6
Jazz and BBQ	Mere House	10.6.01	1
Firework Fiesta	Chambers Hill	20.7.01	5
Barber of Seville	Mere House	22.8.01	2
Moonlight Music	Ranleigh Park	29.8.01	3
Crafts			
Easter Crafts	Ranleigh Park	27.3.01	1
Flower Crafts	Oakville Gardens	17.6.01	2
Yorkshire Day Fair	Oakville Gardens	1.8.01	1
Harvest Crafts	Ranleigh Park	8.9.01	2
Christmas Crafts	Alliott Hall Gardens	26.11.01	2
Christmas Tree Fair	Alliott Hall Gardens	10.12.01	2
Transport			
American Car Rally	Ranleigh Park	4.5.01	3
Austin Owners Rally	Alliott Hall Gardens	11.5.01	2
Steam Fair	Alliott Hall Gardens	18.5.01	1
Classic Cars	Mere Showground	10.6.01	3
Historic Vehicles Rally	Alliott Hall Gardens	17.6.01	2
Vintage Motor Cycle Club	Mere Showground	6.7.01	1
MG Car Society	Ranleigh Park	2.8.01	1
Vintage Tractors	Mere Showground	1.9.01	1

Unit 11
Document 4

OFFTEC CORPORATE SERVICES
197 Highbury Road
WAKEFIELD WF3 2AS

Tel no: 01924 349211 e-mail: info@offtec.co.uk

Our ref MR/EVENTS/01/101

Today's date

Mr J Napal
14 Townhead Green
Kirby Rushton
LEEDS
LS23 5BV

Dear Mr Napal

CHRISTMAS CRAFTS FAIR AT ALLIOTT HALL GARDENS

Thank you for the application form which you completed. I have taken note of your details and your particular requests. I am pleased to inform you that I have allocated stand(s) to meet your requirements.

The Christmas Crafts Fair is to be held at Alliott Hall Gardens on 26 November and will last for 2 days. Stands are allocated for both days and, unfortunately, it is not possible to book for just 1 day.

Vehicle access to an area near to the property for loading/unloading will be available 2 hours before the opening time. Standholders are requested not to begin 'packing up' until the given closing time. A period of 2 hours will be allowed for this process.

Refreshments will be available in Jerome's Diner throughout the day. Standholders are requested to park their vehicles at the lower end of the Hall's car park during the day in order to ensure easy access for the public.

Please let me have your cheque by the last day of the month preceding the event. If I have not received your cheque by this date, it will not be possible for your reservation to be held and your stand(s) may be reallocated.

I hope that the Fair will prove an enjoyable and profitable investment of your time.

Yours sincerely

Mollie Richards
Events Organiser

Unit 12
Exercise 12A–UNIT12DATA1

Title	FirstName	LastName	Address1	Address2	City	PostalCode	Category
Mr	Jonas	Percival	30 Roberts Crescent	Alderton	WAKEFIELD	WF18 8YT	Pensions
Miss	Wendy	Dyer	291 Thornfield Park	Wellsdean	WAKEFIELD	WF14 5GN	Savings
Mrs	Amanda	Sands	31 Hexham Grove	Uppertown	WAKEFIELD	WF7 7MV	Savings
Mr	Michael	O'Connagh	Buckland House	Buckland	WAKEFIELD	WF23 4FD	Investment

Unit 12
Exercise 12A – Main document

Our Ref. OIS/CS

Date of typing

«Title» «FirstName» «LastName»
«Address1»
«Address2»
«City»
«PostalCode»

Dear «Title» «LastName»

Welcome to Offtec Investment Services, the financial investment branch of Offtec Corporate Services.

I have pleasure in enclosing a booklet giving details of our pensions and investment schemes as you requested. I am sure that you will find our terms and rates to be highly competitive.

I hope that you will be able to attend our introductory seminars where you will learn more about the important topic of making the most of your money. Dates and times are shown in the booklet.

Yours sincerely

Charles Seth
INVESTMENTS MANAGER

Enc

Unit 12
Exercise 12A – Merged letter

Our Ref: OIS/CS

Date of typing

Miss Wendy Dyer
291 Thornfield Park
Wellsdean
WAKEFIELD
WF14 5GN

Dear Miss Dyer

Welcome to Offtec Investment Services, the financial investment branch of Offtec Corporate Services.

I have pleasure in enclosing a booklet giving details of our pensions and investment schemes as you requested. I am sure that you will find our terms and rates to be highly competitive.

I hope that you will be able to attend our introductory seminars where you will learn more about the important topic of making the most of your money. Dates and times are shown in the booklet.

Yours sincerely

Charles Seth
INVESTMENTS MANAGER

Enc

Unit 12
Exercise 12B – UNIT12DATA2

Title	FirstName	LastName	Address1	Address2	City	PostalCode	Category
Miss	Wendy	Dyer	291 Thornfield Park	Wellsdean	WAKEFIELD	WF14 5GN	Savings
Mrs	Mandy	Sands	31 Hexham Grove	Uppertown	WAKEFIELD	WF7 7MV	Savings
Mr	Michael	O'Connagh	The Manor House	Buckland	WAKEFIELD	WF23 4FD	Investment
Dr	Morag	Usquaebae	Flat 10A	Royal Avenue	HARROGATE	HG2 9AS	Investment
Mrs	Jane	Prior	67 Ascot Lane	Moordene	LEEDS	LS25 5DE	Pensions
Miss	Anna	Muller	1 Rowan Rise	Alderton	WAKEFIELD	WF18 3DX	Savings

Unit 12
Exercise 12C – Merged document

Our Ref: OIS/CS

Date of typing

Miss Wendy Dyer
291 Thornfield Park
Wellsdean
WAKEFIELD
WF14 5GN

Dear Miss Dyer

Welcome to Offtec Investment Services, the financial investment branch of Offtec Corporate Services.

I have pleasure in enclosing a booklet giving details of our pensions and investment schemes as you requested. I am sure that you will find our terms and rates to be highly competitive.

I hope that you will be able to attend our introductory seminars where you will learn more about the important topic of making the most of your money. Dates and times are shown in the booklet.

Yours sincerely

Charles Seth
INVESTMENTS MANAGER

Enc

Letters also to:
Mrs Mandy Sands; Mr Michael O'Connagh; Dr Morag Usquaebae; Mrs Jane Prior; Miss Anna Muller.

Unit 13
Exercise 13A – UNIT13DATA2

Title	FirstName	LastName	Address1	Address2	City	PostalCode	Category	Seminardate
Miss	Wendy	Dyer	291 Thornfield Park	Wellsdean	WAKEFIELD	WF14 5GN	Savings	23/10/00
Mrs	Mandy	Sands	31 Hexham Grove	Uppertown	LEEDS	LS11 8AA	Savings	23/10/00
Mr	Michael	O'Connagh	The Manor House	Buckland	WAKEFIELD	WF23 4FD	Investment	10/09/00
Dr	Morag	Usquaebae	Flat 10A	Royal Avenue	HARROGATE	HG2 9AS	Investment	06/11/00
Mrs	Jane	Prior	67 Ascot Lane	Moordene	WAKEFIELD	WF7 7MV	Pensions	10/12/00
Miss	Anna	Muller	1 Rowan Rise	Alderton	WAKEFIELD	WF18 3DX	Pensions	28/10/00

Unit 13B
Exercise 13B – Sorted by Last Name

Title	FirstName	LastName	Address1	Address2	City	PostalCode	Category	Seminardate
Miss	Wendy	Dyer	291 Thornfield Park	Wellsdean	WAKEFIELD	WF14 5GN	Savings	23/10/00
Miss	Anna	Muller	1 Rowan Rise	Alderton	WAKEFIELD	WF18 3DX	Pensions	28/10/00
Mr	Michael	O'Connagh	The Manor House	Buckland	WAKEFIELD	WF23 4FD	Investment	10/09/00
Mrs	Jane	Prior	67 Ascot Lane	Moordene	WAKEFIELD	WF7 7MV	Pensions	10/12/00
Mrs	Mandy	Sands	31 Hexham Grove	Uppertown	LEEDS	LS11 8AA	Savings	23/10/00
Dr	Morag	Usquaebae	Flat 10A	Royal Avenue	HARROGATE	HG2 9AS	Investment	06/11/00

Unit 13
Exercise 13B – Sorted by Seminar Date

Title	FirstName	LastName	Address1	Address2	City	PostalCode	Category	Seminardate
Mrs	Jane	Prior	67 Ascot Lane	Moordene	WAKEFIELD	WF7 7MV	Pensions	10/12/00
Dr	Morag	Usquaebae	Flat 10A	Royal Avenue	HARROGATE	HG2 9AS	Investment	06/11/00
Miss	Anna	Muller	1 Rowan Rise	Alderton	WAKEFIELD	WF18 3DX	Pensions	28/10/00
Miss	Wendy	Dyer	291 Thornfield Park	Wellsdean	WAKEFIELD	WF14 5GN	Savings	23/10/00
Mrs	Mandy	Sands	31 Hexham Grove	Uppertown	LEEDS	LS11 8AA	Savings	23/10/00
Mr	Michael	O'Connagh	The Manor House	Buckland	WAKEFIELD	WF23 4FD	Investment	10/09/00

Unit 13
Exercise 13C – Main Document

OFFTEC CORPORATE SERVICES
197 Highbury Road
WAKEFIELD WF3 2AS

Tel no: 01924 349211 E-mail: info@offtec.co.uk

Our Ref: OIS/CS

Date of typing

«Title» «FirstName» «LastName»
«Address1»
«Address2»
«City»
«PostalCode»

Dear «Title» «LastName»

Introductory Seminar on «Category»

Thank you for your interest in our Seminar. I hope that you found the information in our booklet of use to you. I am sure that when you attend the Seminar, you will be fascinated to hear what we can do to help you to secure your financial future.

When my assistant telephoned you, you confirmed that you would be able to attend the Seminar at the New Miller Inn on **«Seminardate»**. The Seminar will commence at 7.00 pm and light refreshments will be served. Please bring along a friend or colleague if you wish. Simply return the enclosed reply card to confirm your attendance and add the name of the person who will accompany you.

Everyone who comes along to the Seminar will have free entry to our £2,000 Prize Draw. You may win a Mediterranean Cruise for two or £2,000 in cash!

I look forward to seeing you at the «Category» Seminar on «Seminardate».

Yours sincerely

Charles Seth
INVESTMENTS MANAGER

Enc

Unit 13
Exercise 13C – Merged letter

OFFTEC CORPORATE SERVICES
197 Highbury Road
WAKEFIELD WF3 2AS

Tel no: 01924 349211 e-mail: info@offtec.co.uk

Our Ref: OIS/CS

Date of typing

Mr Michael O'Connagh
The Manor House
Buckland
WAKEFIELD
WF23 4FD

Dear Mr O'Connagh

Introductory Seminar on Investment

Thank you for your interest in our Seminar. I hope that you found the information in our booklet of use to you. I am sure that when you attend the Seminar, you will be fascinated to hear what we can do to help you to secure your financial future.

When my assistant telephoned you, you confirmed that you would be able to attend the Seminar at the New Miller Inn on **10/09/00**. The Seminar will commence at 7.00 pm and light refreshments will be served. Please bring along a friend or colleague if you wish. Simply return the enclosed reply card to confirm your attendance and add the name of the person who will accompany you.

Everyone who comes along to the Seminar will have free entry to our £2,000 Prize Draw. You may win a Mediterranean Cruise for two or £2,000 in cash!

I look forward to seeing you at the Investment Seminar on 10/09/00.

Yours sincerely

Charles Seth
INVESTMENTS MANAGER

Enc

Letters also to:
Dr Morag Usquaebae
Flat 10A
Royal Avenue
HARROGATE
HG2 9AS
Category: Investment
Seminar Date: 06/11/00

Unit 13
Exercise 13D – Merged letter

OFFTEC CORPORATE SERVICES
197 Highbury Road
WAKEFIELD WF3 2AS

Tel no: 01924 349211 e-mail: info@offtec.co.uk

Our Ref: OIS/CS

Date of typing

Miss Wendy Dyer
291 Thornfield Park
Wellsdean
WAKEFIELD
WF14 5GN

Dear Miss Dyer

Introductory Seminar on Savings

Thank you for your interest in our Seminar. I hope that you found the information in our booklet of use to you. I am sure that when you attend the Seminar, you will be fascinated to hear what we can do to help you to secure your financial future.

When my assistant telephoned you, you confirmed that you would be able to attend the Seminar at the New Miller Inn on **23/10/00**. The Seminar will commence at 7.00 pm and light refreshments will be served. Please bring along a friend or colleague if you wish. Simply return the enclosed reply card to confirm your attendance and add the name of the person who will accompany you.

Everyone who comes along to the Seminar will have free entry to our £2,000 Prize Draw. You may win a Mediterranean Cruise for two or £2,000 in cash!

I look forward to seeing you at the Savings Seminar on 23/10/00.

Yours sincerely

Charles Seth
INVESTMENTS MANAGER

Enc

Letters also to:

	Category	Date
Mr Michael O'Connagh	Investment	10/09/00
Mrs Jane Prior	Pensions	10/12/00
Miss Anna Muller	Pensions	28/10/00

Unit 13
Exercise 13E – Merged letter

OFFTEC CORPORATE SERVICES
197 Highbury Road
WAKEFIELD WF3 2AS

Tel no: 01924 349211 e-mail: info@offtec.co.uk

Our Ref: OIS/CS

Date of typing

Miss Wendy Dyer
291 Thornfield Park
Wellsdean
WAKEFIELD
WF14 5GN

Dear Miss Dyer

Introductory Seminar on Savings

Thank you for your interest in our Seminar. I hope that you found the information in our booklet of use to you. I am sure that when you attend the Seminar, you will be fascinated to hear what we can do to help you to secure your financial future.

When my assistant telephoned you, you confirmed that you would be able to attend the Seminar at the New Miller Inn on **23/10/00**. The Seminar will commence at 7.00 pm and light refreshments will be served. Please bring along a friend or colleague if you wish. Simply return the enclosed reply card to confirm your attendance and add the name of the person who will accompany you.

Everyone who comes along to the Seminar will have free entry to our £2,000 Prize Draw. You may win a Mediterranean Cruise for two or £2,000 in cash!

I look forward to seeing you at the Savings Seminar on 23/10/00.

Yours sincerely

Charles Seth
INVESTMENTS MANAGER

Enc

Letter also to:
Mrs Mandy Sands

Unit 13
Exercise 13F – Merged letter

OFFTEC CORPORATE SERVICES
197 Highbury Road
WAKEFIELD WF3 2AS

Tel no: 01924 349211 e-mail: info@offtec.co.uk

Our Ref: OIS/CS

Date of typing

Mrs Jane Prior
67 Ascot Lane
Moordene
WAKEFIELD
WF7 7MV

Dear Mrs Prior

Introductory Seminar on Pensions

Thank you for your interest in our Seminar. I hope that you found the information in our booklet of use to you. I am sure that when you attend the Seminar, you will be fascinated to hear what we can do to help you to secure your financial future.

When my assistant telephoned you, you confirmed that you would be able to attend the Seminar at the New Miller Inn on **10/12/00**. The Seminar will commence at 7.00 pm and light refreshments will be served. Please bring along a friend or colleague if you wish. Simply return the enclosed reply card to confirm your attendance and add the name of the person who will accompany you.

Everyone who comes along to the Seminar will have free entry to our £2,000 Prize Draw. You may win a Mediterranean Cruise for two or £2,000 in cash!

I look forward to seeing you at the Pensions Seminar on 10/12/00.

Yours sincerely

Charles Seth
INVESTMENTS MANAGER

Enc

Letter also to:
Miss Anna Muller

Unit 13
Exercise 13G – UNIT13DATA3

FirstName	LastName	Address1	Address2	City	PostalCode	Seminardate
Wendy	Dyer	291 Thornfield Park	Wellsdean	WAKEFIELD	WF14 5GN	23/10/00
Mandy	Sands	31 Hexham Grove	Uppertown	LEEDS	LS11 8AA	23/10/00
Michael	O'Connagh	The Manor House	Buckland	WAKEFIELD	WF23 4FD	10/09/00
Morag	Usquaebae	Flat 10A	Royal Avenue	HARROGATE	HG2 9AS	06/11/00
Jane	Prior	67 Ascot Lane	Moordene	WAKEFIELD	WF7 7MV	10/12/00
Anna	Muller	1 Rowan Rise	Alderton	WAKEFIELD	WF18 3DX	28/10/00

Unit 14
Exercise 14A

FirstName	LastName	Address1	Address2	City	PostalCode	Department
Sharon	Atkiinson	8 Windsmoor Grove	Holmehurst	ILKLEY	LS34 7DP	Customer Services
Shamsa	Jamil	17 Wheatwood Street	East Head	BRADFORD	BD8 9EH	Telesales
Clive	Leadbeater	20 Shaftesbury Drive	Park Lane Top	LEEDS	LS10 3LV	Technical
Duncan	MacLeod	28 Bourne Road	Holmehurst	ILKLEY	LS34 7DB	Design
Diane	Molyneux	25 Ashurst Avenue	Beech Heights	KEIGHLEY	BD22 2GE	Design
Asma	Pazeerah	Belle Vue House	Craven Hill	BRADFORD	BD18 4OE	Customer Services
Colin	Stanley	16 Fountain Park Road	Woodbottom	SHIPLEY	BD17 5NT	Telesales
Allan	Tomlinson	21 Devonshire Lane	Gloveley	KEIGHLEY	BD21 4DA	Payroll
Pauline	Inman	24a Jackson Cross	Cross Lanes	SHIPLEY	BD24 9MV	Payroll
Norman	Forster	16 Tennyson Street	High Close	LEEDS	LS24 3SE	Technical

Unit 14
Exercise 14B – Main Document

OFFTEC CORPORATE SERVICES

MEMORANDUM

To: «FirstName» «LastName», «Department» Department
From: Barry Davidson, Training Officer
Date: Date of typing

Staff Focus Group

Thank you for returning the tear-off slip from the latest Staff Bulletin and, more importantly, for volunteering to join the newly-formed Staff Focus Group.

The aim of the Group is to ensure that we work towards achieving a reputation, based on real improvements, as a forward-thinking and caring employer. Your contribution as a representative of your department is very valuable.

Our first meeting will be held at 4.00 pm on Thursday 20 October in the Training Room on Floor 5. I look forward to seeing you and working with you.

Unit 14
Exercise 14B – Merged letters

OFFTEC CORPORATE SERVICES

MEMORANDUM

To: Clive Leadbeater, Technical Department
From: Barry Davidson, Training Officer
Date: Date of typing

Staff Focus Group

Thank you for returning the tear-off slip from the latest Staff Bulletin and, more importantly, for volunteering to join the newly-formed Staff Focus Group.

The aim of the Group is to ensure that we work towards achieving a reputation, based on real improvements, as a forward-thinking and caring employer. Your contribution as a representative of your department is very valuable.

Our first meeting will be held at 4.00 pm on Thursday 20 October in the Training Room on Floor 5. I look forward to seeing you and working with you.

Memo also to:
Norman Forster,
Technical Department

Unit 14
Exercise 14C

FirstName	LastName	Address1	Address2	City	PostalCod e	Departme nt	Supervisor	Startdat e	Scale
Sarah	Arnold	10 Aire View	East Head	BRADFO RD	BD8 7HN	Customer Services	S Smith	08/96	A3
Sharon	Atkinson	8 Windsmoo r Close	Holmehurs t	ILKLEY	LS34 7DP	Customer Services	S Smith	07/99	A3
Christopher	Day	18 Barr Road	Halton	SHIPLEY	BD24 5SA	Payroll	J Porter	12/97	A4
Michael	Dowgill	82 Trinity Hill	Easton	LEEDS	LS14 6HY	Telesales	M Fosse	12/98	A3
Siobhan	Doyle	28 Longcross Place	High Close	LEEDS	LS24 4MJ	Technical	I Jones	06/99	T2
Martin	Ford	Glen House	Gloveley	KEIGHLE Y	BD21 6DH	Telesales	M Fosse	07/97	A3
Norman	Foster	16 Tennyson Street	High Close	LEEDS	LS24 3SE	Technical	P Pieterson	01/99	T2
Lucy	Hall-Woods	42 Radfield Way	Halton	SHIPLEY	BD24 4JS	Design	K Joy	04/96	T2
Louise	Hare	54 Derwent Street	Parkway	BRADFO RD	BD16 3WR	Technical	I Jones	02/96	T2
Jeff	Harvey	37 Ingfield	Ings Dale	KEIGHLE Y	BD19 7PC	Telesales	V Barrett	01/99	A2
Pauline	Inman	24a Jackson Cross	Cross Lanes	SHIPLEY	BD24 9MV	Payroll	J Porter	10/98	A3
Karen	Jacques	Dean Cottage	Dean Bank	SHIPLEY	BD24 8LU	Design	M Mohan	11/97	T4
Shamsa	Jamil	17 Wheatwoo d Street	East Head	BRADFO RD	BD8 9EH	Telesales	M Fosse	06/98	A4
Callum	Leadbeater	20 Shaftesbur y Drive	Park Lane Top	LEEDS	LS10 3LV	Technical	L Hoban	09/99	T2
Duncan	MacLeod	28 Bourne Road	Holmehurs t	ILKLEY	LS34 7DB	Design	K Joy	04/97	T4
Nicky	Marcou	10 Queens Drive	High Close	LEEDS	LS24 6PT	Telesales	V Barrett	06/98	A3
Penny	Marr	1 Rosslyn View	Craven Hill	BRADFO RD	BD18 9LL	Customer Services	A Burns	04/97	A3
Diane	Molyneux	23 Ashurst Avenue	Beech Heights	KEIGHLE Y	BD22 2GE	Design	M Mohan	01/97	T3
Anna	Nesovic	126 Manor Street	Cross Lanes	SHIPLEY	BD24 5SH	Technical	P Pieterson	10/96	T4
Jenny	Payne	1 Seed Hill	Wheatburn	LEEDS	LS18 3JJ	Design	K Joy	03/96	T3
Asma	Pazeerah	Belle Vue House	Craven Hill	BRADFO RD	BD18 4OE	Customer Services	A Burns	08/96	A4
Claire	Smalley	60 Colne Road	Gloveley	KEIGHLE Y	BD21 7NL	Payroll	J Porter	06/98	A5
Katie	Stubbs	81 Delph Close	Holmehurs t	ILKLEY	LS34 4HT	Customer Services	S Smith	10/99	A5
Robert	Sugden	Heather Glen	Dean Bank	SHIPLEY	BD24 3SS	Customer Services	A Burns	05/99	A5
Audrey	Thornton	3 Walker Park	Parkway	BRADFO RD	BD16 1FW	Technical	I Jones	04/95	T3
Keith	Thorpe	14 Pasture Lane	Beech Heights	KEIGHLE Y	BD22 1HC	Customer Services	A Burns	07/98	A2

Unit 14
Exercise 14C Continued

FirstName	LastName	Address1	Address2	City	PostalCode	Department	Supervisor	Startdate	Scale
Allan	Tomlinson	21 Devonshire Lane	Gloveley	KEIGHLEY	BD21 4DA	Payroll	J Porter	11/98	A2
Li	Yeung	106 Bradford Road	Easton	LEEDS	LS14 2MQ	Design	M Mohan	05/96	T2
Safina	Zafar	51 Holly Street	Lane Side	BRADFORD	BD10 4CT	Technical	P Pieterson	10/98	T2

Unit 14
Exercise 14D – Main Document

OFFTEC CORPORATE SERVICES
197 Highbury Road
WAKEFIELD WF3 2AS

Tel no: 01924 349211 e-mail: info@offtec.co.uk

Our Ref: PSU/LK/Review/PREF «Startdate»

Date of typing

«FirstName» «LastName»
«Address1»
«Address2»
«City»
«PostalCode»

Dear «FirstName»

«Department» Department - Review of Salary Scales

The annual review of staffing and salary scales is now complete. All managers, supervisors and other staff have been involved in the appraisal procedure. I hope that you found your own appraisal helpful and stimulating.

I am writing to inform you that, at the request of your supervisor, «Supervisor», your post will be upgraded. As from the end of next month, your **Scale «Scale»** post will be upgraded by one scale point. Your increased salary will be paid at the end of the following month as pay is one month in arrears.

Your supervisor and manager will discuss the responsibilities of your post with you in the next two weeks. If you have any matters which you wish to discuss, please do so at this time.

Yours sincerely

Leanne Kindersley
Personnel Unit Assistant

Copy: «Supervisor»
«Department»

Unit 14
Exercise 14D – Merged document

OFFTEC CORPORATE SERVICES
197 Highbury Road
WAKEFIELD WF3 2AS

Tel no: 01924 349211 E-mail: info@offtec.co.uk

Our Ref: PSU/LK/Review/PREF 08/96

Date of typing

Sarah Arnold
10 Aire View
East Head
BRADFORD
BD8 7HN

Dear Sarah

Customer Services Department - Review of Salary Scales

The annual review of staffing and salary scales is now complete. All managers, supervisors and other staff have been involved in the appraisal procedure. I hope that you found your own appraisal helpful and stimulating.

I am writing to inform you that, at the request of your supervisor, S Smith, your post will be upgraded. As from the end of next month, your **Scale A3** post will be upgraded by one scale point. Your increased salary will be paid at the end of the following month as pay is one month in arrears.

Your supervisor and manager will discuss the responsibilities of your post with you in the next two weeks. If you have any matters which you wish to discuss, please do so at this time.

Yours sincerely

Leanne Kindersley
Personnel Unit Assistant

Copy: S Smith
Customer Services

Letters also to:
Sharon Atkinson
Penny Marr

Unit 14
Exercise 14D – Merged document

OFFTEC CORPORATE SERVICES
197 Highbury Road
WAKEFIELD WF3 2AS

Tel no: 01924 349211 e-mail: info@offtec.co.uk

Our Ref: PSU/LK/Review/PREF 06/98

Date of typing

Shamsa Jamil
17 Wheatwood Street
East Head
BRADFORD
BD8 9EH

Dear Shamsa

Telesales Department - Review of Salary Scales

The annual review of staffing and salary scales is now complete. All managers, supervisors and other staff have been involved in the appraisal procedure. I hope that you found your own appraisal helpful and stimulating.

I am writing to inform you that, at the request of your supervisor, M Fosse, your post will be upgraded. As from the end of next month, your **Scale A4** post will be upgraded by one scale point. Your increased salary will be paid at the end of the following month as pay is one month in arrears.

Your supervisor and manager will discuss the responsibilities of your post with you in the next two weeks. If you have any matters which you wish to discuss, please do so at this time.

Yours sincerely

Leanne Kindersley
Personnel Unit Assistant

Copy: M Fosse
Telesales

Letters also to:
Nicky Marcou

Unit 14
Exercise 14D – Merged document

OFFTEC CORPORATE SERVICES
197 Highbury Road
WAKEFIELD WF3 2AS

Tel no: 01924 349211   e-mail: info@offtec.co.uk

Our Ref: PSU/LK/Review/PREF 12/98

Date of typing

Michael Dowgill
82 Trinity Hill
Easton
LEEDS
LS14 6HY

Dear Michael

Telesales Department - Review of Salary Scales

The annual review of staffing and salary scales is now complete. All managers, supervisors and other staff have been involved in the appraisal procedure. I hope that you found your own appraisal helpful and stimulating.

I am writing to inform you that, at the request of your supervisor, M Fosse, your post will be upgraded. As from the end of next month, your **Scale A3** post will be upgraded by one scale point. Your increased salary will be paid at the end of the following month as pay is one month in arrears.

Your supervisor and manager will discuss the responsibilities of your post with you in the next two weeks. If you have any matters which you wish to discuss, please do so at this time.

Yours sincerely

Leanne Kindersley
Personnel Unit Assistant

Copy: M Fosse
Telesales

Letter also to:
Martin Ford

Unit 15
Document 1 – UNIT15DATA1

FirstName	LastName	Address1	Address2	City	PostalCode	Department	Supervisor	Startdate	Scale	Leave Days
Emile	Amiens	16 Ringway	Wheatburn	LEEDS	LS18 8ST	Customer Services	A Burns	10/96	A4	29
Sara	Arnold	10 Aire View	East Head	BRADFORD	BD8 7HN	Customer Services	S Smith	08/96	A3	29
Sharon	Atkinson	8 Windsmoor Close	Holmehurst	ILKLEY	LS34 7DP	Customer Services	S Smith	07/99	A3	25
Anser	Azam	252 Lee Park	Parkway	BRADFORD	BD16 8RT	Technical	I Jones	10/97	T3	23
Claire	Bacon	60 Colne Road	Gloveley	KEIGHLEY	BD21 7NL	Payroll	J Porter	06/98	A5	25
Suraya	Begum	84 Dalton Road	Lane Side	BRADFORD	BD10 6TW	Technical	L Hoban	08/98	T3	24
Michael	Bourne	20 Conrad Street	Holmehurst	ILKLEY	LS34 6KL	Telesales	V Barrett	04/98	A3	24
Janet	Browning	12 Hamlet Close	Cross Lanes	SHIPLEY	BD24 8TD	Payroll	J Porter	06/96	A4	29
Christopher	Day	18 Barr Road	Halton	SHIPLEY	BD24 5SA	Payroll	J Porter	12/97	A4	22
Michael	Dowgill	82 Trinity Hill	Easton	LEEDS	LS14 6HY	Payroll	M Fosse	12/98	A4	24
Laura	Downes	49 Chandler Street	Ings Dale	KEIGHLEY	BD19 4MJ	Customer Services	J Porter	09/98	A4	25
Siobhan	Doyle	28 Longcross Place	High Close	LEEDS	LS24 4MJ	Technical	I Jones	06/99	T2	25
Howard	Endsley	Moor House	Beech Heights	KEIGHLEY	BD22 5CH	Design	M Mohan	12/97	T2	26
Martin	Ford	Glen House	Gloveley	KEIGHLEY	BD21 6DH	Telesales	M Fosse	07/97	A3	22
Norman	Foster	16 Tennyson Street	High Close	LEEDS	LS24 3SE	Technical	P Pieterson	01/99	T2	25
Lucy	Hall-Woods	42 Radfield Way	Halton	SHIPLEY	BD24 4JS	Design	K Joy	04/96	T2	29
Louise	Hare	54 Derwent Street	Parkway	BRADFORD	BD16 3WR	Technical	I Jones	02/96	T3	29
Geoff	Harvey	20 Green Lane	Ings Dale	KEIGHLEY	BD19 4LV	Telesales	V Barrett	01/99	A2	25
Pauline	Inman	24a Jackson Cross	Cross Lanes	SHIPLEY	BD24 9MV	Payroll	J Porter	10/98	A3	24
Shamsa	Jamil	17 Wheatwood Street	East Head	BRADFORD	BD8 9EH	Telesales	M Fosse	06/98	A4	25
Hassan	Lazar	72 Aireway	East Head	BRADFORD	BD8 6NQ	Telesales	M Fosse	05/97	A2	26
Callum	Leadbeater	20 Shaftesbury Drive	Park Lane Top	LEEDS	LS10 3LV	Technical	L Hoban	09/99	T2	25
Donna	Leyburn	6 High Place	High Close	LEEDS	LS24 3TU	Customer Services	S Smith	07/96	A2	27
Jeanne	Lund	14 Meadow	Craven Hill	BRADFORD	BD18 7PP	Customer Services	A Burns	02/97	A3	23

Unit 15
Document 1 – UNIT15DATA1 continued

FirstName	LastName	Address1	Address2	City	PostalCode	Department	Supervisor	Startdate	Scale	Leave Days
		Road								
Duncan	MacLeod	28 Bourne Road	Holmehurst	ILKLEY	LS34 7DB	Design	K Joy	04/97	T4	22
Nicky	Marcou	10 Queens Drive	High Close	LEEDS	LS24 6PT	Telesales	V Barrett	06/98	A4	26
Penny	Marr	1 Rosslyn View	Craven Hill	BRADFORD	BD18 9LL	Customer Services	A Burns	04/97	A3	22
Pauline	McIver	1 Rose View	Easton	LEEDS	LS14 1GP	Technical	L Hoban	10/97	T3	23
Diane	Molyneux	23 Ashurst Avenue	Beech Heights	KEIGHLEY	BD22 2GE	Design	M Mohan	01/97	T3	22
Anna	Nesovic	126 Manor Street	Cross Lanes	SHIPLEY	BD24 5SH	Technical	P Pieterson	10/96	T4	29
Deborah	Palak	63 Pike Close	Gloveley	KEIGHLEY	BD21 7DW	Design	K Joy	01/99	T2	22
Maria	Paulo	Elm Cottage	Dean Bank	SHIPLEY	BD24 4JH	Telesales	M Fosse	01/99	A2	25
Jennie	Payne	1 Seed Hill	Wheatburn	LEEDS	LS18 3JJ	Design	K Joy	03/96	T3	29
Asma	Pazeerah	Belle Vue House	Craven Hill	BRADFORD	BD18 4OE	Customer Services	A Burns	08/96	A4	29
Margaret	Smythe	180 Solar Road	Halton	SHIPLEY	BD24 7AS	Design	M Mohan	11/98	T2	24
Katie	Stubbs	81 Delph Close	Holmehurst	ILKLEY	LS34 4HT	Customer Services	S Smith	10/99	A5	29
Robert	Sugden	Heather Glen	Dean Bank	SHIPLEY	BD24 3SS	Customer Services	A Burns	05/99	A5	29
Keith	Thorpe	14 Pasture Lane	Beech Heights	KEIGHLEY	BD22 1HC	Customer Services	A Burns	07/98	A2	25
Allan	Tomlinson	21 Devonshire Lane	Gloveley	KEIGHLEY	BD21 4DA	Payroll	J Porter	11/98	A2	25
Jacqui	Willson	64 Easton Lane	Cross Lanes	SHIPLEY	BD24 6DW	Telesales	V Barrett	04/98	A2	25
Li	Yeung	106 Bradford Road	Easton	LEEDS	LS14 2MQ	Design	M Mohan	05/96	T3	28
Safina	Zafar	51 Holly Street	Lane Side	BRADFORD	BD10 4CT	Technical	P Pieterson	10/98	T2	24

Unit 15
Document 2 – DATA

Title	FirstName	LastName	Address1	City	PostalCode	Answer
Ms	A	Farooq	36 Overdale Mount	BARROWCROFT	BA4 7RQ	Macbeth
Mr	E S	Jowett	89 Leyden Avenue	BURNCHESTER	BR9 4HC	Hamlet
Miss	M T	Salmon	1 Denwick Lane	FORDWICKTON	FN6 6KW	King Lear
Mr	J C	Stanley	Croft Edge	BARROWCROFT	BA4 8RS	Macbeth
Mrs	R	Qureshi	Pendle View	BURNCHESTER	BR10 7MP	Coriolanus
Miss	K	Kirkbright	10 Fielden Road	FORDWICKTON	FN6 8EN	Macbeth
Mr	L W	Gregory	High Ridge Barn	BARROWCROFT	BA5 8GE	Much Ado about Nothing
Ms	J	Dalby	254 Barrowcroft Road	BURNCHESTER	BR10 8TY	Romeo and Juliet
Mr	S	Brandt	55 Stones Park Grove	BARROWCROFT	BA4 6NB	Macbeth
Mrs	A	Ackroyd	72 Hill Top Road	BARROWCROFT	BA5 7LO	Macbeth

Unit 15
Document 3 – Main document

OFFTEC CORPORATE SERVICES

MEMORANDUM

To: «FirstName» «LastName»

From: «Supervisor»

Ref: «Department»/Leave

Date:

ANNUAL LEAVE

Your new Contract of Employment sets out a formula for calculating the total number of days of annual leave which are allocated to employees according to their scale and length of service.

According to our records, the month in which your employment commenced was «Startdate» and you are remunerated on Scale «Scale». Your annual leave is «LeaveDays» days.

Please complete the enclosed annual leave planner to indicate your preferred allocation of your leave days and let me have it before the end of next month, *(date inserted)*. After considering all employee requests and, of course, taking into account the need to maintain staffing levels at all times, I will produce an annual leave plan for the department.

Whilst I will do my best to meet your leave requests, I know that you will understand that this may not be possible in all cases. Leave planners which are returned after the date given above may not be accommodated.

Thank you.

Enc

Unit 15
Document 3 – Merged document

OFFTEC CORPORATE SERVICES

MEMORANDUM

To: Christopher Day

From: J Porter

Ref: Payroll/Leave

Date: Date of typing

ANNUAL LEAVE

Your new Contract of Employment sets out a formula for calculating the total number of days of annual leave which are allocated to employees according to their scale and length of service.

According to our records, the month in which your employment commenced was 12/97 and you are remunerated on Scale A4. Your annual leave is 22 days.

Please complete the enclosed annual leave planner to indicate your preferred allocation of your leave days and let me have it before the end of next month, *(date inserted)*. After considering all employee requests and, of course, taking into account the need to maintain staffing levels at all times, I will produce an annual leave plan for the department.

Whilst I will do my best to meet your leave requests, I know that you will understand that this may not be possible in all cases. Leave planners which are returned after the date given above may not be accommodated.

Thank you.

Enc

Memos also to:
Michael Dowgill
Pauline Inman
Claire Bacon
Allan Tomlinson
Janet Browning

Unit 15
Document 4 – Main document

OFFTEC CORPORATE SERVICES
197 Highbury Road
WAKEFIELD WF3 2AS

Tel no: 01924 349211 e-mail: info@offtec.co.uk

Ref: AL/BGT/Comp/«Answer»

Date of typing

«Title» «FirstName» «LastName»
«Address1»
«City»
«PostalCode»

Dear «Title» «LastName»

SHAKESPEARE COMPETITION

Thank you for returning the completed employee satisfaction questionnaire. Your responses, together with those of all employees who also returned the questionnaire, will be forwarded to the management team. It is hoped that an employee focus group will be formed in the near future and you will be invited to become a member of this group.

However, the main purpose of this letter is to let you know that you have been successful in the Shakespeare competition which was linked to the questionnaire. Your answer was correct: the quote was taken from Shakespeare's play «Answer».

The Northern Theatre Group is to perform this play at the «City» GRAND THEATRE and you have won 2 tickets in the Dress Circle for the performance on Saturday 27 November at 8.00 pm. You will also receive a 2-course dinner with wine in the Forum Restaurant at the theatre before the performance. We have made restaurant bookings and reserved theatre tickets for other employees who were also successful in the competition.

Our company has established links with the Grand Theatre through sponsorship and corporate entertainment. I am sure that you will thoroughly enjoy your evening. Please call in to the Marketing Unit to collect your tickets within the next few days.

Yours sincerely

Alyson Lindley
Marketing Assistant

Unit 15
Document 4 – Merged document

OFFTEC CORPORATE SERVICES
197 Highbury Road
WAKEFIELD WF3 2AS

Tel no: 01924 349211 e-mail: info@offtec.co.uk

Ref: AL/BGT/Comp/Macbeth

Date of typing

Ms A Farooq
36 Overdale Mount
BARROWCROFT
BA4 7RQ

Dear Ms Farooq

SHAKESPEARE COMPETITION

Thank you for returning the completed employee satisfaction questionnaire. Your responses, together with those of all employees who also returned the questionnaire, will be forwarded to the management team. It is hoped that an employee focus group will be formed in the near future and you will be invited to become a member of this group.

However, the main purpose of this letter is to let you know that you have been successful in the Shakespeare competition which was linked to the questionnaire. Your answer was correct: the quote was taken from Shakespeare's play Macbeth.

The Northern Theatre Group is to perform this play at the BARROWCROFT GRAND THEATRE and you have won 2 tickets in the Dress Circle for the performance on Saturday 27 November at 8.00 pm. You will also receive a 2-course dinner with wine in the Forum Restaurant at the theatre before the performance. We have made restaurant bookings and reserved theatre tickets for other employees who were also successful in the competition.

Our company has established links with the Grand Theatre through sponsorship and corporate entertainment. I am sure that you will thoroughly enjoy your evening. Please call in to the Marketing Unit to collect your tickets within the next few days.

Yours sincerely

Alyson Lindley
Marketing Assistant

Letters also to:
Mr J C Stanley
Mr S Brandt
Mrs A Ackroyd